An Introduction to Hedge Funds

An Introduction to Hedge Funds

Mark Berman

Risk*books*

Published by Risk Books, a Division of Incisive Financial Publishing Ltd

Haymarket House
28–29 Haymarket
London SW1Y 4RX
Tel: + 44 (0)207 484 9700
Fax: + 44 (0)207 484 9800
E-mail: books@incisivemedia.com
Sites: www.riskbooks.com
www.incisivemedia.com

ISBN 978 1 904339 91 5

British Library Cataloguing in Publication Data
A catalogue record for this book is available from the British Library

Publisher: Clare Beesley
Commissioning Editor: Laurie Donaldson
Copy Editor: Andrew Armitage
Designer: Rebecca Bramwell

Typeset by Mark Heslington Ltd, Scarborough, North Yorkshire

Printed and bound in the UK by Cambridge University Press, Cambridge Printing Services Ltd

Contents

About the Author

Mark Berman, the founder and a principal of CompliGlobe Ltd, advises and conducts training programmes for hedge funds, investment managers, multi-national banks, investment firms and regulators on SEC practice, cross-border regulatory, compliance and AML matters. Mark was a senior lawyer with the Division of Corporation Finance and the Division of Market Regulation of the US Securities and Exchange Commission, where he worked on disclosure and trading practices issues, respectively. He was a senior lawyer with the London Stock Exchange where he advised on market supervision, surveillance, regulatory matters and drafted the 1994 re-write of the trading rules. In nearly 15 years of industry experience and apart from his time as a regulator, he held positions as head of legal and compliance, compliance officer, MLRO and assistant company secretary, and chaired and served on new product committees. Mark is the editor of and a contributor to *Hedge Funds and Prime Brokers* (Oct 2006, Risk Books) and *SEC Regulation Outside the United States* (6th ed. Q4 2007, Risk Books), and wrote *An Introduction to Hedge Funds* (2007, Risk Books). He founded and chairs the annual conference, "SEC Regulation Outside the United States", and the workshops, "SEC Basics" and "SEC Inspections and CCOs", given annually in London, Hong Kong and other locations in Europe and Asia. He is a Trustee of the SEC Historical Society and a member of the BSF Hall of Fame.

Introduction

Turning and turning in the widening gyre
The falcon cannot hear the falconer;

"The Second Coming", WB Yeats[1]

However beautiful the strategy, you should occasionally look at the results.

Winston Churchill

EVERY STORY HAS A BEGINNING

In writing this Introduction, I was reminded of a story that I was told early in my legal career while helping one of the lawyers who mentored me write a speech for our general counsel. "Young man", he told me, "when on a Friday afternoon a senior partner in a law firm asks a junior associate whether he knows anything about Swiss cheese futures, there are only two answers: 'no, but I've always wanted to learn about them'; or, 'yes, how can I help you'?"

I have always enjoyed and thrived on being the learner, in securities law, banking law, the laws of England and Wales, the "buy side" versus the "sell side" and EU law. Now: hedge funds.

My introduction to hedge funds came a few weeks before my team and I left for New Zealand and the I.S.F. World Championships. The call to me was: "what do you know about hedge funds? Can you launch, manage and advise them and their directors"? Without hesitation, my answer was: "When can I start?" It was thus that my career in financial services regulation and compliance led me to hedge funds.

In that time I have learned, and unlearned, more than I can imagine. I now know what hedge funds are and how they are structured and work. I realise that hedge funds are not just an "alternative investment", but a critical part of our integrated, single global world market – "globalisation" having long ago been achieved. Hedge funds are estimated to account for 1.5% of global assets, 40% of equity trading and 80% of distressed debt trading.[2] Hedge funds are providers of liquidity, stability and innovation in product development and trading strategy. They attract some of the world's best known and brightest players, as well as novices like me. They are not "unregulated" – the nearly 8,000 hedge funds incorporated in the Cayman Islands file original and amended prospectuses, satisfy continuing obligation requirements to maintain their registration and file interim and year-end audited financial statements. They have directors that must comply with legal requirements that impose duties on them. Their investment managers, prime brokers, administrators and other service providers are regulated. What is *not* known about them is who their investors are and their positions (under applicable large position reporting thresholds).

Having launched, advised and restructured hedge funds, negotiated service provider agreements (including prime broker agreements), advised investment managers and conducted mock exams, I have come to the conclusion that we need to concentrate our efforts not on regulating hedge funds, but on ensuring that those that govern and oversee hedge funds – directors, general partners and trustees – and those that operate them – investment managers, prime brokers and administrators – comply applicable legal and regulatory requirements, treat investors fairly and equally, trade to avoid market abuse and continue to contribute positively to the world's markets.

WE LIVE IN INTERESTING TIMES

A few years ago, the Gramm–Leach–Bliley Act rescinded the Glass–Steagall Act and let banks back into the securities business. Since then, levels of repo and commercial paper programmes reached new heights. More funds poured into hedge funds and private equity vehicles. More hedge funds were launched and increasingly sophisticated strategies became commonplace. The amounts of securities sold that represented packaged and repackaged assets, including mortgages, has reached new heights. More types of securities and investments have started to be used as collateral. The world's stock market indexes have reached new levels. Interest rates dropped, on the basis that "inflation was under control". Hedge funds played their part in all of this, as one of the only "true" players in the market. Because they can buy long and sell short and engage in relatively sophisticated trading strategies, hedge funds became the glue in the markets that bound equity investors and traditional long-only funds, on the one hand, and private equity and the derivatives markets, on the other, to create efficient markets. There were instances of market abuse and inside trading (these anomalies are unfortunately also found in the long-only markets), but overall hedge funds provided more good than bad.

A few months ago, 20 years after the "market break" and 40 years after the "Summer of Love", it began to unravel. Interest rates rose to curb inflation, touching off the sub-prime/credit crisis. Collateral held by prime brokers, once comprised of easy to price liquid assets but now including ever-increasing amounts of hard to price illiquid assets (cardboard collateral) had to be marked down. Banks could not unload large tranches of unsellable packaged debt. Investors began to redeem shares in ever-increasing amounts. The sterling-dollar exchange rate topped US$2. Unseen since Victorian times, there was a run on a British bank. The story, as they say, is well known. What is not appreciated is *what* the sub-prime/credit crisis portends. Our markets are, in a sense, the falcon described in Yeats' poem. We, the investors, regulators, central banks and others, are the falconers calling for our treasured asset to come home to prevent the revelation, described by Yeats in his poem as the beast slouching toward Bethlehem, from arriving. That revelation is the next 1929, brought about by significant losses on the balance sheets of some of the world's large banks and prime brokers and hedge funds, the write-off of collateral, a continuing weak dollar, the collapse of global market players and the failure of market participants to pull together to prevent this from happening. We will achieve the brink early next year when annual audited financial statements are published. Will the falcon not return and will we fall? I do not believe so, and am hoping for the best.

One must take a risk to make a profit. Hedge funds do this because this is their role in the markets. They do not, however, trade blindly in the face of risk. They trade based on sound research and quant teams and programmes that are dedicated to achieving a return regardless of market conditions – absolute return. They occasionally get it wrong, as was the case in Long-Term Capital Management and Amaranth. More often, they get it right. They do this by using carefully designed strategies and keeping their eye on the prize. Strategy is as important as result.

When I was commissioned to write this book, I was told to keep it "short and sweet". It is an introduction, I was told, not a treatise. The original manuscript was significantly longer than what appears between these covers. Topics are identified and surveyed, not treated in depth. In time, I hope to publish a version of this book that treats this fascinating and important subject in detail.

In closing, I am reminded that, when I launched my first hedge fund, I learned many important things. One of the Directors, Michael Austin, showed me what it means to be a hedge fund director. Paul Findley, also a fund manager, helped me understand that the lifeblood of every hedge fund is its investors. I am grateful to them and many others. I owe much to my mentors, Steve Hammerman, the late Jay Manning, Marty Portnoy and John Sprung.

This book would not have been possible without the review by and the guidance of Peter Cockhill and Denise Gower of Ogier, to whom I am indebted and grateful. Thank you to my publisher and editor, Laurie

Donaldson. And to you, readers of this book, many thanks for your patience as I continue to learn about hedge funds.

This book is for my wife.

1 With the permission of A.P. Watt Ltd on behalf of Gráinne Yeats.

2 "Ten key operational risks for hedge funds", 28 August 2007, Standard & Poor's. URL: www.financeasia.com/print.aspx?CIID=90122.

(London, November 2007)

1

Hedge Funds: What Are They?

Today, there are 10,000 hedge funds worldwide. At June 2007, this segment of the "alternative investment" community was continuing to attract figures in record numbers. Inflows into US hedge funds amounted to US$58.6 billion in Q2 2007[1] and assets under management were estimated to be US$1.67 trillion.[2] The first wave of the sub-prime/credit crisis slowed inflows: according to Hedge Fund Research, inflows into US hedge funds in Q3 2007 amounted to US$45.2 billion, bringing the figure of assets under management to US$1.8 billion.[3] Hedge funds hold in their portfolios nearly every conceivable type of investment, from equity securities and cash to the most sophisticated derivatives and special purpose vehicles. They employ a variety of strategies to achieve "absolute return".[4] Directly or indirectly (through funds of hedge funds or managed accounts), investors – from the largest institutions, endowments and pension funds to individuals – invest in hedge funds. Hedge funds, despite the fact that they are "not regulated", are a global market player. They make, and lose, significant amounts of money for themselves and their investors.

The first hedge fund traded in 1949.[5] From humble foundations, they have risen to play a leading role in the world's markets. They help shape the markets in terms of product development and corporate activism. This is remarkable, given the fact that hedge funds do not control their own activities and do not have executive officers or employees. They rely on others – directors/general partners/trustees, investment managers, administrators, accountants, lawyers, executing brokers, prime brokers and custodians – to provide them with the services that they require to operate.

Where does the money come from? According to research published in June 2007 by Greenwich Associates, institutional investors continue to increase in importance as an asset source for the world's largest hedge funds (more than US$1 billion under management).[6] Investments by funds of hedge funds accounted for 25% of the assets of such funds and another 25% came from endowments, foundations and pension funds (public and corporate).[7] High net worth individuals (HNWIs)[8] and "family offices" accounted for 21% of the investments in such funds.[9]

Where does the money go? The proceeds from subscriptions are used not only for investments, but also pay the fees of service providers. The figures as regards prime brokers, the primary source of funding for hedge funds, are striking. At year-end 2006:

- three firms, Morgan Stanley, Goldman Sachs and Bear Stearns, accounted for 75% of the US prime brokerage market;
- globally, prime brokers earned more than US$8 billion annually;[10]
- hedge funds controlled half the trading volume on the New York Stock Exchange (NYSE) and the London Stock Exchange (LSE), and 70% of the trading in convertible arbitrage.[11]

It was reported that hedge funds account for up to 35% of the commissions earned by Wall Street firms from trading equity securities.[12]

Historically, London and New York were the dominant centres of hedge fund investment and decision making for all markets, including Asia. More recently, Hong Kong, Singapore, Tokyo and Sydney have staked their claims as key decision centres. Increasingly, they are dictating the shape of this industry. European centres, such as Switzerland, also wield influence.

There are many books and academic papers discussing hedge funds and how they trade. Several are for the trader or the quants desk and explain the dynamics of trading and hedging strategies, managing hedge fund portfolios using options or derivatives or managing hedge fund "risk". A good alternative title for this book would be "Hedge Fund Basics".

This book is devoted to introducing and explaining hedge funds. It is meant for the individual who has been asked to be a director of a hedge fund for the first time, or for the new hire who is going to work for a hedge fund administrator or a prime broker. It is for the new sales assistant who has worked only on a "long-only" desk and who will join a "long-short" team. It is for the newly hired assistant vice president at a global bank who is joining the stock borrowing desk and will be in charge of lending equities and convertible debt to hedge funds.

This book will explain what hedge funds are, how they work and who invests in them. It surveys the role of hedge fund service providers and, along the way, touches on matters such as what documents are needed to launch and operate a hedge fund, who oversees hedge funds and aspects of hedge fund trading (but it is not devoted to this topic). It explains hedge structures, discusses what is included in offering materials and surveys what is involved in marketing the securities of hedge funds. Finally, it touches on what happens to a hedge fund when something goes wrong. Materials in the Appendix are designed to supplement the discussion contained in this book.

WHAT IS A HEDGE FUND?

What is the difference between a hedge fund and a long-only fund?

A hedge fund and a long-only fund[13] have much in common. Both are pooled investment vehicles that solicit funds from investors and invest the proceeds in a portfolio of securities. Both have assets under management (AUM) and strike a net asset value (NAV) per share for each class of shares (NAV per share). Hedge funds and long-only funds may be listed and, as such, must comply with requirements imposed by the listing authority. Both rely on third-party service providers.

There are features that distinguish a hedge fund from a long-only fund. A hedge fund is an investment primarily for institutional investors and HNWIs, whereas long-only funds are designed for retail investors. (Retail investors also invest in hedge funds via funds of hedge funds.)

Hedge funds are incorporated primarily in "offshore" jurisdictions.[14] On occasion, they seek a listing through which they achieve "light touch" regulation (as discussed below). However, certain hedge fund structures, in particular, side-by-side funds or master feeder structures, will have a Delaware limited liability company or limited partnership (LP), so the hedge fund (as a combination of the feeder funds and master fund or an aggregation of side-by-side funds) is both offshore and onshore. This is the predominant model for US-managed hedge funds.

Hedge funds typically do not have to pay tax by virtue of the tax laws of the countries where they are incorporated. Through listing, they become "liquid investments" and attract institution and pension money (they must observe caps on the amount of funds they may invest in illiquid instruments). This is the case, for example, with hedge funds that are registered in the Cayman Islands with the Cayman Islands Monetary Authority (CIMA) and are listed on the Cayman Islands Stock Exchange (CSX) or the Irish Stock Exchange (ISE). In other instances, hedge funds are not so registered or listed and are not regulated. By contrast, long-only funds require formal registration/authorisation, are listed and are subject to stringent regulation.

Investors in long-only funds pay a fee based on assets under management. Investors in hedge funds pay a performance (or incentive) fee and a fee based on funds under management.

Traditional mutual funds/authorised collective investment schemes strike a NAV per share on a daily basis, usually at the close of trading on the market where they are listed. Hedge funds strike a NAV per share monthly or quarterly.

There usually are no minimum investment amounts for long-only funds, while hedge funds require stated minimum investments, often set at US$250,000 or higher.

Shares of long-only funds are generally not subject to "lock-up" provisions. Long-only funds must, by law, comply with redemption requests when they are received, in full and without delay. Typically, hedge funds redeem shares on a monthly or quarterly cycle, according to the governing terms of their Articles of Association (Articles) (see Chapter 3). Shares of hedge funds might be subject to "lock-up" provisions whereby they cannot be redeemed for a fixed period of time (possibly as long as 36 months from subscription) and may be redeemed only upon the payment of a redemption fee. Hedge funds have and employ, "gate provisions" by which they can place restrictions on the timing and amount of redemptions, or even suspend redemptions. Hedge funds use these gate provisions when faced with requests from many investors or in large amounts, particularly in times of market stress. The implications of using gate provisions are discussed in Chapters 6 and 10.

The investment objective, policies and restrictions that are imposed on hedge funds come from the hedge fund's Articles, local requirements, offering memoranda and, if applicable, listing rules. Long-only funds must satisfy numerous requirements in order to achieve and retain authorisation and listing, and must, with the exception of UCITS III funds and certain listed funds called "130/30s", invest within defined parameters that forbid short selling and margin trading (borrowing to buy).

Ultimately, what distinguishes a hedge fund from a long-only fund is leverage. Leverage, as used in this book, includes selling short, borrowing to purchase or finance securities and other instruments and using derivatives to generate or enhance returns.

ALTERNATIVE INVESTMENTS

Hedge fund managers, in an effort to achieve absolute return, generate profits for themselves and their investors, keep portfolios at acceptable levels of capacity and prevent the worst-case scenario for any hedge fund manager – large-scale redemptions that hurt the fund or even force it to consider liquidation. They use a variety of investments. They lay off their risk through dynamic hedging and the use of portfolio insurance – credit default swaps that hedge against the risk of default, particularly in the case of buyout or M&A debt. The process of investing and hedging works as long as market conditions remain stable, there are buyers and sellers of instruments and the value of the assets underlying the hedges remains constant. It works if hedge funds can continue to obtain credit from prime brokers (and others) at, for them, affordable prices, and if the ability to borrow is not curtailed. It works if there are no issues with collateral that comprises not just liquid instruments for which there is a price and market, but increasingly illiquid instruments such as leveraged loan participations, contracts for differences (CFDs), swaps or other derivatives. If these factors change, liquidity dries up, investors begin to demand redemption in increasing numbers, prime brokers devalue collateral and returns diminish, as they are doing in the sub-prime/credit crisis – hedge funds face the prospect not just of losses, but of closure.

The term alternative investments includes many vehicles that are used to achieve absolute returns, returns that outperform a benchmark or other forms of non-mainstream investments. Given the numbers of private equity vehicles that are listing and the role played by hedge funds, one wonders whether this term is redundant.

PRIVATE EQUITY

Private equity may be broadly defined to include any form of investment that is made on an equity (ownership) basis, that is for a fixed term and that usually is not public. In recent months several equity vehicles have achieved or sought listings.[15] Private equity vehicles commonly take many forms, the most prominent of which are funds for venture and growth capital investments, buyout funds and mezzanine capital.

Private equity funds differ from hedge funds

Private equity funds are closed-end funds that require a fixed-term investment, often for a period of three to five years (possibly longer) and with no real provision for selling the investment. Hedge funds as open-end funds permit investors to redeem their shares or interests subject to the employment of lock-up and/or gate provisions and fees for redemptions, generally in the first two six-month periods (often, Articles permit the directors to waive these "for good reason").

Private equity funds have an investment purpose predicated upon specific investment opportunities, such as investing in a buyout or in an M&A transaction, on a long-term basis. Hedge funds, by contrast, make multiple investments in securities on a short-term basis.

Private equity vehicles operate with a fee structure that is based on a percentage of the capital commitments or size of the fund and, in some instances, a percentage of the invested capital after the stated investment period ends. Private equity funds may have a performance allocation payable to the general partner (equivalent to the incentive fee received by the hedge fund investment manager). Hedge funds have a dual charging structure, comprising a management fee and a performance fee (1% to 2% for management fees and 10% to 20% for performance fees).

Whereas hedge funds make continuous investments, private equity funds invest at the start of the investment term/project and after due diligence exercises.

Investors in private equity vehicles engage in extensive negotiations of documentation prior to close. Hedge funds experience continuous periods of subscription and redemptions and, save for side letters (if they are issued), do not negotiate documents.

Hedge funds commonly do not have provisions in their Memorandum of Association (Memorandum) or Articles that limit their life. Private equity funds are constituted for a fixed period of time.

As they attempt to satisfy investor needs and generate higher returns, hedge funds:

- take stakes in listed companies and force or attempt to force changes in activities, structure or management, or even to force the entity to engage in transactions, to forego a transaction or to "break itself up";
- build a stake in a company that is to be taken over, or made private in leveraged buyouts (LBOs); and
- invest in distressed debt, loans or loan participations, in leveraged loan participations or packaged products, to take advantage of restructurings.

It has been estimated that, in Europe, a large number of hedge funds have purchased nearly a quarter of the debt used to finance LBOs.[16] This debt is sold to hedge funds by investment firms and commercial banks. The selling institutions do this to lay off the credit risk that they have taken on to finance the deal. The packaging, placing and reselling of debt, not just LBO financing but also distressed debt, commercial and residential mortgages and other forms of lending, might, depending on market conditions, have a serious knock-on effect in the markets for these and other securities and tradable investments and on the balance sheets of industrial companies, lenders and other financial services industry participants (one of the causes of the sub-prime/credit crisis).

Hedge funds and private equity vehicles are starting to move toward each other and, on occasion, join forces to achieve desired results.[17]

Hedge funds are active investors in acquisitions[18] and, increasingly, join forces with other hedge funds or private equity vehicles as bidders or to force corporate changes. Among the most prominent of these are:

- the February 2006 joint unsolicited offer by Soros Fund Management, LLC, Atticus Capital LP (Atticus) and Almeida Oil Co, Inc for the reorganisation of Star Gas Partners LP;[19]
- the May 2005 efforts of the Children's Investment Fund (TCI), Atticus and others to object to the Deutsche Börse bid for the London Stock Exchange and the subsequent resignation of Deutsche Börse chairman Rolff Breuer;[20]
- efforts by Centaurus Capital Ltd (Centaurus) and Paulson & Co, Inc (Paulson) to break up the Dutch company Stork NV (the two hedge funds were reported as being committed to supporting the offer by Candover Investments);[21]
- the June 2006 acquisition of BAA by Grupo Ferrovial SA, in which hedge funds holding 30% of the target company combined their positions with a block of the shares of the bidder to secure the acquisition – after which

Ferrovial refinanced the acquisition with £9 billion of debt, a tranche of which included second-lien financing from hedge funds;
- the "encouragement" by Paulson and Centarus to Royal Ahold for it to sell certain of its US businesses, and the subsequent sale of portions of its business and return of cash to investors;[22]
- the proxy contest waged by Harbinger Capital Partners to elect directors of Ryerson Inc;[23] and
- the bidding war that broke out over Dutch bank ABN AMRO, facilitated in the first instance by TCI serving a letter on ABN AMRO's directors encouraging it to break up the group through spin-offs of certain divisions and returning proceeds to shareholders or by selling the entire entity.[24]

Also, and as a function of the coming together of hedge funds and private equity vehicles, "hybrid" funds have emerged. These offer in a single package investment "opportunities" in both hedge funds and private equity vehicles, but with separate fees for the hedge fund and the private equity sides of the hybrid.

It is not all rosy: some believe that, as hedge funds work more closely with (or look like) private equity and wield more and more influence in M&A activity, corporate governance, LBOs and contested battles for corporate control, they are inviting disputes with their investors.

Some of these strategies bear the hallmarks of 1980s corporate raiders or aggressive private equity investments. Whatever the motivation, the name of the game is to generate absolute return at a level that demonstrates to investors that, regardless of the circumstances, hedge funds will make them money.

TYPES OF HEDGE FUNDS

Hedge funds are structured as limited partnerships, companies, limited liability companies (LLCs) or unit trusts. The structure is largely a function of investor demand; for example, Japanese investors typically require hedge funds to be structured as unit trusts.

Hedge funds are governed according to their structure. Limited partnership hedge funds are governed by the general partner, an entity that performs multiple roles – operator, investment manager and administrator. It offers ease of organisation but is the structure that involves the most conflicts of interest. The limited partnership model is used primarily in the US. In this model, investors become limited partners, not shareholders.

Establishing a hedge fund as a company is the form that is used primarily outside the US. Company and LLC hedge funds are governed by boards of directors. In this model, investors purchase shares in the hedge fund directly or, if the hedge fund is established as a master feeder structure, in a feeder fund. Returns are realised when shares are redeemed. Dividends in any form are rarely declared or paid. The directors are accountable to the shareholders.

Hedge funds are single entities or master feeder structures. The choice is due to the types of investors involved and the tax implications of their investments.

Single entity hedge funds

In a single entity fund (see Figures 1.1 and 1.2), investors invest directly in the fund. The proceeds go directly in the portfolio which will, upon investment, include securities, derivatives, cash and other instruments. The hedge fund contracts directly with the investment manager, the administrator, the prime broker and other service providers. The general partner, trustee or directors are responsible for all aspects of governance, operation and oversight, and delegate under strict contractual provisions aspects of operations to the service providers.

Single entity hedge funds attract investments from non-US persons and US persons, taxpaying and tax-exempt. Single entity hedge funds provide a simple structure within which to work, but this may lead to complications for the investors involved – primarily US taxpaying investors. US taxpaying investors in non-US corporate funds may find that they have invested in a passive foreign investment company (PFIC). US taxpayers investing in a PFIC are taxed (and may also have to pay interest charges) on any gain derived from the sale of an investment or an excess distribution from the PFIC. They are taxed on their share of the PFIC's undistrib-

Figure 1.1 Single entity hedge fund, corporate structure

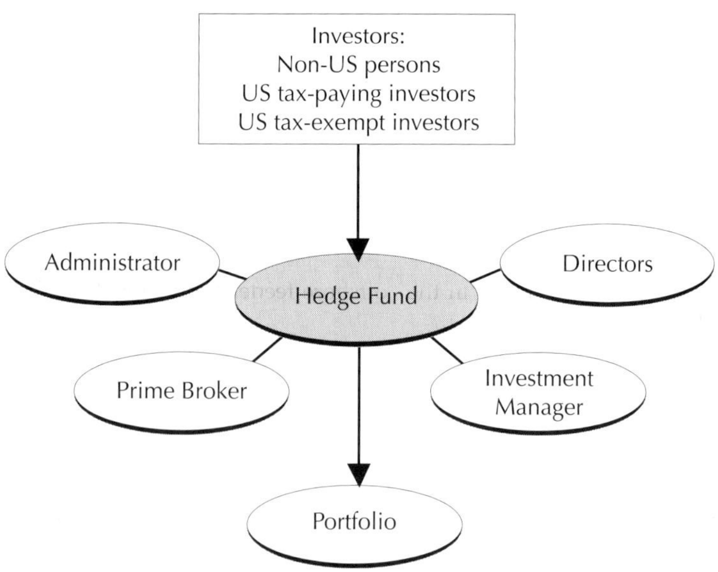

Figure 1.2 Single entity hedge fund, limited partnership structure

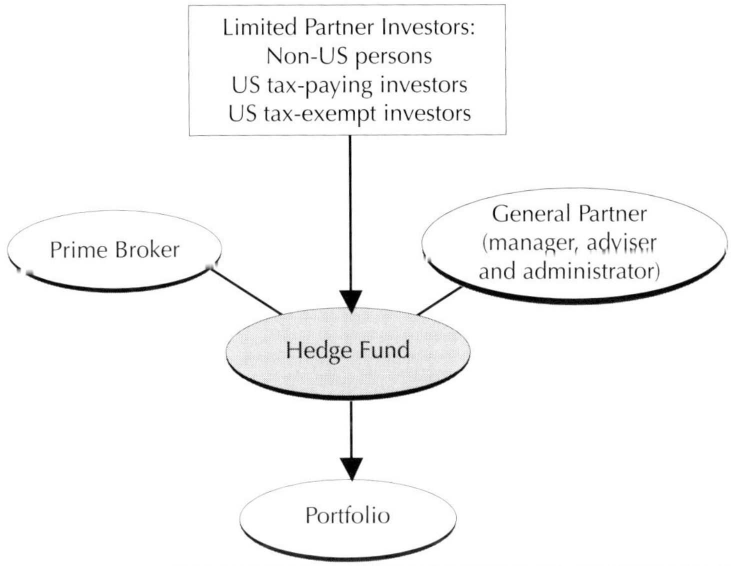

uted earnings unless they make the "qualified fund election" (QEF) to defer the tax. This is made by the shareholder, not the hedge fund, but the hedge fund must agree to provide certain information about its ownership and earnings. Another factor in opting for a master feeder structure is to help US tax-exempt investors avoid unrelated business-tax income (UBTI). UBTI is not an issue for US tax-exempt investors that invest in a single entity hedge fund, but it is in the master feeder structure if the US tax-exempt investors hold membership interests (Interests) in the onshore feeder fund.

Master feeder structures

The master feeder structure provides a means to address the PFIC and UBTI issues for US investors. US tax-exempt investors and non-US investors purchase shares in the "offshore feeder fund". Offshore feeder funds are companies or partnerships that are incorporated or organised, respectively, in "offshore jurisdictions" such as the Cayman Islands, Jersey, BVI and Bermuda. US taxpaying investors purchase Interests in the "onshore feeder fund" or, in certain models, invest directly the master fund. Onshore feeder funds are usually Delaware LLCs or LPs. Each feeder fund invests all or substantially all of its assets in the "master fund" which, in turn, holds the portfolio. Examples of feeder funds are illustrated in Figures 1.3 and 1.4.

Master feeders are structures that are more complicated than single

Figure 1.3 Master feeder structure, two feeder funds corporate structure

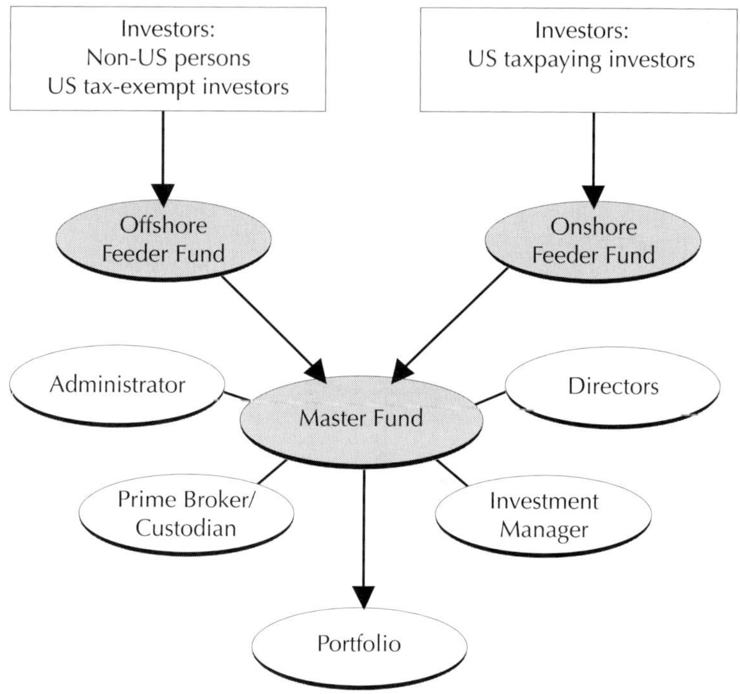

entity funds. There are multiple companies to manage, multiple boards of directors or general partners, additional and more complex agreements to have in place, a need to coordinate subscriptions, redemptions and exchanges to ensure the correct proportion of investment per class (and sub-class, if present) in the feeder funds and in the master fund and multiple layers of monitoring, oversight and control. There are tax issues, as well. Master feeder structures were established primarily to suit the requirements of US investors. The master feeder structure permits US taxpaying investors to invest without PFIC issues. It helps US tax-exempt investors, if they invest in the offshore feeder fund, avoid UBTI. It does require that any onshore feeder fund and the master fund elect to be treated as a partnership for US tax purposes in order to be able to pass through the tax benefits to US taxpaying investors.

Another benefit of master funds is that they permit an investment manager to manage a single, large portfolio compared with side-by-side funds, enabling them to achieve lower overall fees (eg, brokerage commissions).

Figure 1.4 Master feeder structure, one feeder fund corporate structure

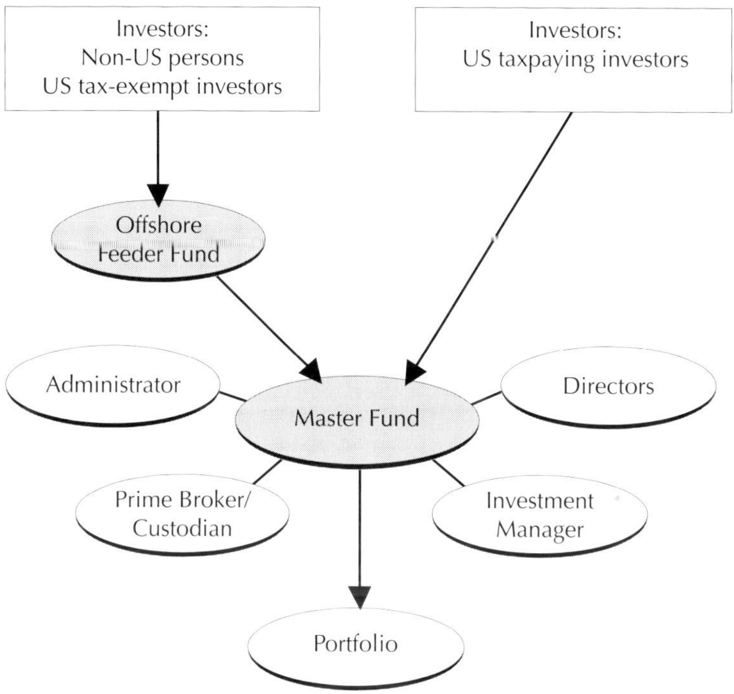

HEDGE FUNDS GLOBALLY

Hedge funds are established as single entities or as master feeder structures. However, the model differs from one region of the world to another.

European model

The European model often involves Cayman Islands companies as well as partnerships (with a preference towards the corporate model), organised as single funds or master feeder structures. In the single entity corporate structure, there will be a fund with a board of directors and key service providers, including an investment manager, an administrator and one or more prime brokers (and, depending on the scope of trading, additional custodians or sub-custodians who may or may not be affiliated with the prime broker). Master feeder structures feature three (or four) companies, including the two feeder funds and the master fund (or one feeder fund and the master fund), as well as a corporate director for the Delaware onshore feeder fund. There will be an investment manager, an administrator and one or more prime brokers and custodians. A key difference between single entity and master feeder structures is that, in the latter, the investment manager contracts directly with the master fund and not the onshore feeder fund. This is done to help ensure that the master fund does not have any US investors to avoid the registration requirements of the Advisers Act.[25] In pursuing this structure, a non-US, non-SEC registered adviser would wish to ensure that there was a separate onshore feeder fund in which US taxpaying investors would invest, rather than allowing such investors to invest directly into the master fund; not having this feeder fund would mean that the master fund had US investors, forcing the manager to start counting US investors towards the s.203 Cap.[26]

In single entity hedge funds, directors exercise control over the affairs of the hedge fund. In master feeder structures with two feeder funds, the feeder funds and the master fund have boards of directors. Adding to the structure the board of directors of the corporate director of the onshore feeder fund, there will be four boards. Many master feeder structures have between three and seven individuals serve as directors, and these individuals often conduct directors meetings for all companies in parallel.

Ireland features onshore hedge funds and funds of hedge funds where the registered funds are established as a unit trust. The trustee receives investor funds and safeguards them, although they are on deposit with the trustee if it is a custodian or, if not, a third-party custodian. The unit trust contracts with an onshore (Irish) investment manager, which, in turn, contracts with an administrator. The Irish model is closer to the European model (which features independence among the service providers), but is a unit trust and not a company.

Asian model

The Asian model usually features a company, but may be established as a partnership. In Japan, and for local investment and tax considerations, hedge funds are structured as unit trusts. There are single entity and master feeder structures. Within the Asian model there are variations.

In Hong Kong, and for tax considerations, the model includes an onshore investment manager and an offshore adviser, rather than a single manager. The offshore adviser identifies investment opportunities and is the "stock picker". It sends its recommendations to the onshore investment manager which "confirms" the investments and places orders with executing brokers. Most of the key responsibilities are "offshore" and these include daily investment management, service provider relationships and so on. The relationship is governed by an investment advisory agreement. This "split" in responsibilities helps the offshore adviser avoid licensing and regulation. This arrangement has tax advantages (fees generally are received and retained offshore), and reflects the realities of the Asian markets where there are offshore advisers to a single fund or master feeder structure in different locations. In Singapore, the model resembles that employed in Europe.

In terms of local licensing requirements, in the Hong Kong model the onshore investment managers are regulated, but the offshore advisers are not. In Singapore, hedge fund advisers may be required to register with the Monetary Authority of Singapore (MAS) but qualify for exempt fund manager status if they engage in asset management activities for not more than 30 "qualified investors". (Qualified investors are individuals with net personal assets of more than S$4 million and companies with net assets greater than S$10 million.) Such exempt status does not excuse exempt fund managers from other local requirements.[27]

United States

In the US model, and to accommodate tax, legal and regulatory requirements, hedge funds are structured as limited partnerships with the general partner performing multiple roles. Occasionally, hedge funds are established as LLCs or business trusts.[28]

Unlike in the European model, which features service providers that are independent and perform separate roles, the general partner in the US model performing multiple roles may not provide adequate safeguards to address or to prevent conflicts of interest or avoid attendant problems – such as problems with pricing and valuations. This was the case in *SEC v Beacon Hill*,[29] which involved, *inter alia*, the investment manager/sponsor, Beacon Hill Asset Management, LLC (Beacon Hill), misrepresenting the method used to value investments in the master fund's portfolio and manipulating the manner in which the AUMs of the funds that it managed were calculated.

SERVICE PROVIDERS

Apart from necessary governance activities by the directors, trustee or general partner, hedge funds rely on service providers for their activities (see Figure 1.5). The key service providers are the administrator, investment manager and prime broker(s). (Often, prime brokers also serve as custodian or arrange the custodial relationship.) Other service providers are the distributor, listing sponsor (if the fund or the offshore feeder fund is listed), legal counsel, company secretary, money laundering reporting officer (MLRO) if the administrator does not perform this role, auditors, executing brokers, trading counterparties, hardware and software providers, risk managers and transfer agents. (Occasionally, and in a manner that would not raise tax or corporate governance issues, the company secretarial and MLRO role may be performed by a service provider other than the administrator.) All operate under the oversight of the directors, the general partner or the trustee. Other parties that are involved include the investors, regulators, any exchange where the hedge fund is listed and tax and governmental authorities. The roles of service providers are discussed in Chapter 4.

Figure 1.5 Service providers and third parties

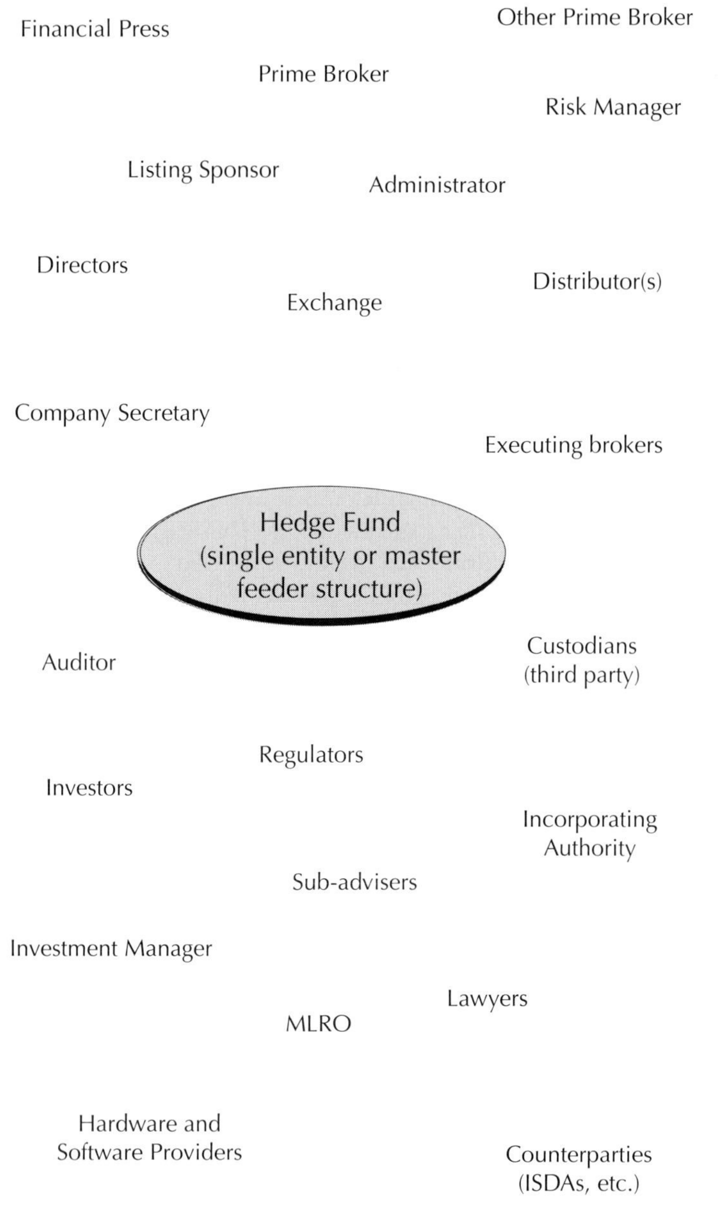

The investment manager contracts directly with the fund and/or the master fund in a master feeder structure. (The general partner performs this rule in the limited partnership structure.) It manages the portfolio on a discretionary basis in compliance with the investment management agreement between it and the hedge fund/master fund, its own regulatory requirements, the hedge fund's offering materials[30] and exchange requirements, if the hedge fund is listed. This includes managing the portfolio, instructing executing brokers to effect transactions, liaising with investors when queries arise about aspects of the portfolio, attending meetings of the directors, the trustee or the general partner and answering queries on reports and other matters expressly stated in the investment management agreement by which it was retained. Investment managers do not, and should not, price individual positions or portfolios (but they may provide information to the administrator to help it perform this function), do not select, add, subtract or replace service providers (but may provide advice), do not make recommendations or take decisions for directors, the trustee or the general partner (in order to avoid having the hedge fund taxed in the jurisdiction where the investment manager is located, eg, the UK), do not accept or reject investors and do not exercise oversight over the other service providers (this is a role that is to be performed by the directors, the trustee or the general partner).

The administrator values positions, handles subscriptions, redemptions and exchanges, serves as transfer agent, calculates the AUM and the NAV per share, handles the anti-money laundering (AML) requirements (if no one else does this), corresponds with investors, manages aspects of the annual audit and provides monitoring services. It signs an administration agreement with the hedge fund or the feeder funds and the master fund in a master feeder structure.

The prime brokerage agreement, annexes of or other documents related to this document and the disclosures in the Offering Materials establish, define and govern the relationship between hedge fund and prime broker(s). In a single entity structure, the prime broker contracts with the hedge fund. In a master feeder structure, only the master fund contracts with the prime broker.

SHOULD HEDGE FUNDS BE DEFINED AND REGULATED?

Hedge funds are sold to investors in dozens of jurisdictions. The 10,000 hedge funds that are operating today (this figure excludes now closed hedge funds) account for significant trading volume in exchange-traded securities and are major players in the over-the-counter (OTC) market, figures that have increased almost exponentially in the last few years. They generate vast sums of commission for the brokers with whom they effect transactions. They provide significant profits for prime brokers, the entities on whom hedge funds rely for their funding.

The issue that has drawn considerable attention in the last 15 years is whether it is necessary to regulate hedge funds. A separate issue is how one defines a hedge fund. Many attempt to resolve both of these at the same time, saying that a hedge fund can be regulated after, or only if, it is defined. Others maintain that it is necessary or in the public interest to regulate hedge funds but that a definition may not be necessary. Many devote time, attention and resources to regulating "aspects" of hedge fund operations, such as valuations, disclosures of side letters and large positions, risk management and the prevention of market abuse and insider trading

Can the term "hedge funds" be defined?

Are hedge funds "notoriously difficult to define"?[31]

In its November 2006 report, "The Regulatory Environment for Hedge Funds: A Survey and Comparison",[32] the International Organization of Securities Commissions (IOSCO) surveyed the current state of hedge fund regulation on a global basis. The IOSCO report also reviewed the regulatory requirements imposed on the sale of shares and interests in hedge funds in several jurisdictions and the requirements imposed on the investment managers that advise hedge funds. The IOSCO report came to four major conclusions, the first of which was that not one of the IOSCO members that participated in the survey underlying the study "has a comprehensive, legal definition of the term 'hedge fund'."

This does not mean that those regulators do not have valid opinions on what hedge funds are. They do. How those views change and mature – given market and other conditions – and perhaps converge might lead to some form of regulation of hedge funds in certain jurisdictions. Regulators work closely on issues germane to hedge funds and their service providers such as discussions with hedge funds and prime brokers concerning sources of funding and liquidity issues, risk management and stress testing and investigations into whether prime brokers and other market participants may have been passing information to hedge funds on which they traded.[33]

Johnson & Birnbaum in the *Washington Post* noted that "under certain scenarios, an over-leveraged fund could set off a string of events that could bring a large investment bank to its knees, touching off a dangerous chain reaction".[34] Would such a string of events be started by, or include, increasing interest rates, defaults in sub-prime mortgages, deterioration in collateral underlying packaged debt, the inability to package and sell such debt, large-scale redemption requests, declines in the equity markets, downward valuation of collateral,[35] prime broker margin calls on hedge funds, the employment of gate provisions to slow or cease redemptions, precipitous declines in hedge fund AUMs, the triggering of AUM decline, additional termination events and hedge fund insolvencies – being topped off with prime brokers investing billions in related hedge funds to keep them from going under? As White and Grant noted (see endnote 35), hedge funds use illiquid instruments as collateral to reduce their margin requirements – we call this "cardboard collateral". In a market dislocation, hedge funds might be unable to sell such securities. In this event, hedge funds would be subject to margin calls, which, if not met, would result in the liquidation of portfolio investments or possibly even an event of default.

Some regulators have attempted to define this type of alternative investment. In the SEC Hedge Fund Study and in its 2004 release[36] adopting Rule 203(b)(3)-2 and amending other rules under the Advisers Act, the SEC defined "hedge fund" as any pooled investment vehicle that is privately organised, administered by professional investment managers and not widely available to the public.[37] The UK Financial Services Authority (FSA) in consultation papers said that "[n]either 'hedge fund' nor 'hedge fund manager' are legally defined terms in the UK regulatory regime", but that there "appears ... to be general agreement on some key characteristics that can be associated with the hedge fund industry, both in terms of the investment management techniques employed and common structures used".[38] Many other regulators have issued consultation papers not just on the structure of hedge funds, but on the role that they play and on the risks that they pose.

Hedge funds have drawn scrutiny in hearings before the US Congress and other legislative bodies worldwide. In testimony before the US Congress, SEC Chairman Christopher Cox said that hedge funds provide "tangible benefits" and "contribute substantially to capital formation, market efficiency, price discovery, and liquidity", but that there is "[t]he potential for retail investors to be harmed by hedge fund risk" and that "there is a "lack of ... basic data" about hedge funds.[39]

A report published by the Autoriteit Financiële Markten, the Dutch regulator, stated that a lack of transparency was a concern and that it was not clear whether managers had a sufficient understanding of their hedge funds' investment policies and risk profiles, but that hedge funds did contribute to the markets by providing liquidity.[40]

For the purposes of this book, we will define a hedge fund as an unregulated collective investment vehicle that receives funds from its investors (institutions, pension funds, HNWIs and others) from private placements of securities and, via its investment manager, invests those monies using one or more strategies and trading techniques, with or without leverage, in order to achieve a profit or absolute return regardless of market conditions.

Should hedge funds be regulated?

Certain jurisdictions plan to regulate hedge funds. South Africa, for example, intends to achieve hedge fund regulation to increase investor protection.[41] In India, hedge funds will be able to register directly as foreign institutional investors, enabling them to participate in the Indian equity market directly rather than indirectly (through participatory notes or derivatives).

In certain instances, decisions have been taken not to regulate hedge funds. This has been the case at the country and regional levels – witness the statement of the 27 EU finance ministers saying that hedge funds contribute to the efficiency of the financial system, that hedge funds do pose risks but that the present system of supervision was adequate.[42]

By regulation, we mean substantive requirements imposed directly on the hedge fund, as is the case with authorised long-only funds.

Whether or not a definition is required or is achievable, the fundamental question is whether, to achieve investor protection and ensure orderly markets, hedge funds must be regulated as if they were authorised and regulated mutual funds (in the US) or authorised collective investment schemes (in the EU), and, if so, how. In order to resolve this issue, it is necessary in the first instance to confirm that there is a level of regulation imposed on the service providers of and key players involved with a hedge fund (directors/trustee/general partner, administrator, prime broker, investment manager and executing broker), ensure that key information about the hedge fund is available (how it trades and its positions) and ensure that trading is free from market abuse. Properly in place, this should be sufficient to protect investors and ensure orderly markets.

Regarding hedge funds, what is at the heart of investor protection and orderly markets is the need to generate, provide and analyse trading and position data (and report large positions), help ensure proper risk management and stress testing, provide for independent valuations, ensure assets (cash and securities) are properly held, protected and accounted for, engage in proper disclosure when selling shares and interests in hedge funds, ensure full and fair (and correct) disclosures and communications with investors (and, when necessary, third parties) to avoid material misstatements and omissions and protect against market abuse.

Would imposing such requirements directly on hedge funds tip the balance against the benefits that these entities provide to investors and the markets? Might regulation stifle innovation?

Would a voluntary code of conduct work? The Bank of England proposed that hedge funds adopt a "light touch" to regulation through a voluntarily, industry-sponsored code of conduct. On 1 October 2007, the UK-based Hedge Fund Working Group (HFWG) published "Hedge Funds Standards: Consultation Paper", a document that would propose "best standards for hedge funds" (Standards Paper). The Standards Paper contains a series of proposals, specific and aspirational, addressing points such as valuations, governance, activism, improved disclosure to investors, financial stability and other information that would, as indicated by Sir Andrew Large, chairman of the HFWG, give "real substance" as to how FSA authorised hedge fund investment managers would "comply with FSA principles".[43] The issues surrounding any code concern enforcement of guidelines, employing a multilevel layer of regulation – the UK is already regulated by the Financial Services and Markets Act 2000, administered by the FSA, and it is not certain where the FSA regime would end and the voluntary code would begin. Certainly, any code would need to be based on unambiguous, statutory regulation. The consultation process on the Standards Paper is underway. There are some issues that have been raised at the start of the consultation.

- Would small and medium-sized investment managers be able to observe the standards, in terms of actual compliance and cost implications?
- Would prospects "require" investment managers that opted not to implement the standards to adopt them or lose potential investments?
- Would failure to comply with the standards after adoption render an investment manager liable to regulatory action?
- Would investment managers in jurisdictions other than the UK be required to adopt the standards "by proxy"?

The proposals are welcome, but it remains to be seen how the standards are adopted, in part or in whole.

Despite not being defined or regulated directly, hedge funds play a significant, positive role in the world's securities and derivatives markets. This is not to say that regulation is not required. Regulation is needed, to protect investors and to ensure orderly markets, to prevent market abuse and insider trading (and tipping), to ensure that large positions are reported and to avoid issues such as "parking". It is needed to help ensure that market events or imbalances such as the effect that the sub-prime credit crisis is having on the markets do not result in systemic failures.

Hedge funds act through their service providers. It is preferable to imposed requirements on these entities, not hedge funds, to address and satisfy these, and other, critical points. If hedge funds are not regulated and it is ultimately decided to regulate them, any form of "regulation" should be disclosure-based and focus on relevant measurables such as transaction reporting, subject to the proper limits of the reach of regulation, legal precedents and protections and the nature of the clients, underlying investors in a hedge fund and markets and products involved.

DO HEDGE FUNDS POSE RISKS?

Some hedge funds are not listed on CIMA or otherwise approved and may operate under a cloak of invisibility, in an effort not only to avoid regulation but, possibly, to shelter positions and strategies from investors. The hedge funds that are listed or are held by pension plans and other institutional investors are managed by regulated investment managers, funded by authorised prime brokers and offer their securities in reliance on Offering Materials that state the investment objective, policies and restrictions (which may be changed by shareholder approval). These hedge funds are required to publish annual reports with information about positions and profits and, because they are listed, must comply with exchange-imposed positions disclosure. The prime brokers and administrators of such funds monitor positions and require disclosure to regulatory authorities of large positions – 3% in the UK and Germany and 5% in the US. It would not be true to say that all, or the majority, of hedge funds "remain secretive about their positions and strategies, even to their own investors".[44] If this was truly the case, legitimate money in hedge funds would soon disappear, prime brokers would contract only with authorised and listed hedge funds and investment managers would cease managing hedge fund portfolios.

Hedge funds trade to achieve absolute returns, aside from event-driven funds that take positions to become catalysts for change. Investment managers must achieve profits sufficient to cover not only their management fee and performance fee, but to provide a return to investors.

Poor performance translates into redemptions. Small portfolios generate lower returns and require more concerted efforts and increased leverage to extract profit. This may strain investment and hedging strategies and lead to trading on the edge, or in violation, of investment objectives and policies. Redemptions may also lead to more redemptions and a cascade effect that, if precipitous and in the presence of AUM triggers as additional termination events in ISDAs, might result in the liquidation of positions and, possibly, cross defaults, bringing a prime brokerage agreement into default and possibly closing the hedge fund.

Leverage permits a hedge fund to achieve returns greater than by trading merely to outperform standard benchmarks or to invest directly in instruments. Leverage, to a hedge fund, is not just selling short or borrowing, but utilising complex and sometimes interlocking trading strategies over combinations of purchases and sales of investments, simple and complex, liquid and illiquid, that generate enhanced return. The instruments that help to achieve this are loan participations, collateralised debt obligations (CDOs), CLOs, collateralised bond obligations (CBOs), repos, swaps, exchange-traded funds (ETFs), credit derivatives, credit default swaps (CDSs), contracts for differences (CFDs), OTC derivatives, futures, warrants, options, special purpose vehicles (SPVs), indexes and other instruments that exist or that are created to achieve a desired effect – individually or in combinations. Value needs to be derived not just from each strategy, but from each instrument in a portfolio. In a sudden market movement, to generate cash to handle large redemptions or in the event of a need to rebalance a portfolio it may become necessary to unwind parts of a strategy or hedge, buy increasing amounts of portfolio insurance or even sell core positions. It is not always possible to do this, particularly when markets move quickly and the instruments that form the collateral held by prime brokers rapidly devalue. In such circumstances, prime brokers may sell the assets that lie at the core of multiple trading, investment and hedging strategies, or even slow or stop securities lending and margin financing. This would force a hedge fund to engage in a fire sale of assets. The use of illiquid assets as collateral and trading tools to help generate leverage is leading to the risk of unsellable instruments or imbalanced portfolios. The more that cardboard collateral is relied on, the more likely it is that, in times of market stress, "the chickens will come home to roost".

Another risk is regulation. Regulators or tax authorities may change laws or regulations, resulting in changes to the treatment of positions and the need to alter requirements or portfolios. Trading to avoid regulation is another risk. Trading CFDs or swaps in the UK to avoid buying exchange-traded equities to avoid stamp duty or stamp duty reserve tax may, if done with incorrect documentation or in extraordinary volumes or complex transactions, draw regulatory scrutiny and result in the imposition of assessments, interest charges and penalties.

Leveraging returns involves elements of avoiding or hedging risk, achieving cash returns and realising enhanced returns. In an effort to generate increased returns and to find and profit from inconsistencies in the pricing of instruments, spreads or funding gaps – and to keep investors – managers look to extract value from nearly any source. Doing so shifts risk from one portfolio to another. Value can be derived from nearly any asset. So, too, can leverage, but spreads and leverage are small when liquid, exchange-traded securities are involved.

According to the SEC, hedge funds "assume risks by serving as ready counterparties to entities that wish to hedge risk".[45] One such risk is credit risk. In the last six years, the credit markets have grown exponentially. There are many factors involved with this, not the least of which was the M&A and LBO booms fuelled by inexpensive loans (often "covenant lite"), the dramatic growth in the sub-prime mortgage market and the repackaging of these loans by investment firms and commercial banks to be sold to hedge funds, the increasing use of derivative instruments as collateral and other factors.

Since the end of the "Internet bubble", trading volumes, prime broker financing and the growth of the credit markets, the explosion of packaged products and other market factors have changed the fundamentals of the world's markets to a point that the risk of a market implosion, however remote this is deemed by market participants, was likely. Until early 2007, inflation remained at a relatively constant low rate and interest rates stayed low. Credit was cheap and there was no dearth of opportunities to invest – or to force change and make money. Quietly, and during the growth of the credit markets:

- credit risk moved from the balance sheet of banks to hedge funds and private equity vehicles;
- the amount of repo funding skyrocketed;
- collateral, which for many years consisted of "hard securities" (equity securities, bonds and other relatively liquid instruments), began to include "soft securities" (derivatives, swaps and other semi-liquid or illiquid securities) – cardboard collateral;
- relaxed lending led to increasing amounts of loans to borrowers with credit difficulties, not just in context of mortgages;
- investment firms and commercial banks took on increasingly large amounts of loans to package and resell; and
- quant models used by hedge funds (and programmed trading by others) began to be based on assumptions that presumed only an "upmarket" – a factor, it was discovered, that was evident on Monday, 19 October 1987.

A change in one of these factors leads to market disruption. The sub-prime/credit crisis is evidence of this.

When the markets fall, when collateral is devalued or when loans are called, someone has to come up with the cash. A single industrial company going into insolvency may not cause hedge funds and/or prime brokers worldwide to fail – systemic risk. A slowdown in the credit market or another event that triggers defaults in lending (sub-prime lending) in tandem with or caused by rising interest rates may cause not just one large hedge fund that might not have readily available cash to have to liquidate part of a portfolio to cover redemptions and, possibly, margin calls. Such a slowdown might result in not just one commercial bank or an investment firm that packaged credit derivatives for sale, took on and resold loans and funded hedge fund purchases, to suffer losses. As has been seen, it is more than one prime broker and one large fund that are suffering during the credit crisis. Lowering interest rates is not necessarily the long-term solution. Such a cycle, one started, might be hard to control. There is no guarantee that the run on Northern Rock will be a "one off" event, or that the next run will not involve a global hedge fund or a prime broker.

WHAT TYPE OF HEDGE FUND WILL FEATURE IN THIS BOOK?

The model hedge fund that will form the basis for our discussions in our book will be the European model, which is a corporate master feeder structure that is incorporated in the Cayman Islands,[46] has a European-based investment manager, a European (or European-based subsidiary of a non-European bank) prime broker, a European (Dublin) administrator and is listed on the ISE.[47] When helpful, we will discuss aspects of the American, Asian and Irish models.

1 "US hedge funds see less Q3 money but demand remains", Herbst-Bayliss, Reuters, 23 October 2007, citing data released by Hedge Fund Research on Tuesday, 23 October 2007. URL: www.today.reuters.com/news/articleinvesting.aspx?type=fundsFundsNews&storyID=2007–10–23T200930Z_01_N23325484_RTRIDST_0_HEDGEFUNDS-FLOWS.XML.

2 "Hedge inflows $41 billion in second quarter", Seigel, InvestmentNews.com, 28 August 2007, citing a report by Lipper TASS Assets Flows report. See "Wall Street-on-Sea feels the chill amid talk of shake-out", Clark, *Guardian*, 28 August 2007, in which it was reported that hedge fund assets stood at the US$1.74 trillion figure. URL: www.investmentnews.com/apps/pbcs.dll/article?AID=/20070828/REG/ 70828018.

4 Hedge fund returns are not measured against a benchmark, such as an index. Hedge fund managers strive to make a profit, regardless of market conditions. This is absolute return.

5 The first hedge fund was established by Alfred Winslow Holmes in 1949. He sold short equity securities to hedge investments in other securities, used leverage and, a few years later, was the first to charge a performance fee. See "Implications of the Growth of Hedge Funds, Staff Report to the US Securities and Exchange Commission" (SEC), September 2003 (SEC Hedge Fund Report). See also "Hedge Funds", from *Wikipedia*, URL: www.en.wikipedia. org/wiki/Hedge_fund.

6 "Institutional Money Tops 25% of Large Hedge Funds", Greenwich Associates, June 2007 (Greenwich Report).

7 *Ibid.*

8 "HNWI" encompasses defined terms such as "accredited investor", "qualified purchaser" and "qualifying investor". For the purposes of this book, HNWI refers to individuals that, under the private placement laws of the jurisdictions where hedge funds are sold, are qualified to buy securities on a private placement basis – including the securities of hedge funds. For more information, see Chapter 7.

9 *Ibid.*

10 "Banks' Leases to Hedge Funds Questioned", Anderson, *New York Times*, 2 January 2007, URL: www.nytimes.com/2007/01/02/business/02hedge.html?ex=1325394000&en=9714b1d46a34a283&ei=5088&partner=rssnyt&emc=rss.

11 *Ibid.*

12 *Ibid*, quoting Brad Hintz of Sanford C. Bernstein & Company.

13 References to "long-only" funds means non-hedge fund open-end funds (continuous offering of shares and rights of redemption) and closed-end funds (fixed offerings of shares and no right of redemption), known as mutual funds, investment trusts, unit trusts, OEICs, UCITS, SICAVs and SICAFs, among others. The discussion in this book relates to hedge funds that are open-end funds.

14 The "offshore" jurisdictions are Bermuda, the British Virgin Islands (BVI), the Cayman Islands, Guernsey and Jersey and even Mauritius and Cyprus. Hedge funds may be incorporated in onshore jurisdictions, including Ireland (for Irish unit trusts) and Denmark.

15 See, eg, the Blackstone Group LP (SEC File No. 001–33551).

16 "Trends in private equity financing", *PLC*, March 2007. See URL: www.practicallaw.com.

17 See, eg, "The Challenges of Convergence", Debevoise & Plimpton Private Equity Report, Vol 5, No 3, Spring 2005.

18 See "Management in an Era of Shareholder Activism", report by Morgan Joseph & Co, 31 July 2006, available from Morgan Joseph & Co.

19 "Soros Fund Makes Bid for Star Gas", Gurufocus, 20 February 2006, URL: www. gurofocus.com.

20 "A Little Fund with Big Demands", *BusinessWeek Online*, 23 May 2005, URL: www.businessweek.com/managine.

21 "Stork may consider rival bid of at least 49.35 eur, says Candover offer memo", Thomson Financial, 10 August, 2007, URL: www.hemscott.com/news/latestnews/item.do?newsId=48500918266625. See "Recommended cash offer of EUR 47 per share for all of the issued and outstanding ordinary shares of Stork", Press Release, 10 August, 2007, URL: www.stork.com/Downloads/Corporate/CORP.%20GOVERNMENT/Candover/PB_Candover%20Offer-eng.pdf.

22 "Ahold succumbs to pressure from hedge funds", McCandless, Financial News, URL: www.financialnews-us.com/?page=ushome&contentid=1046636431.

23 "Harbinger hedge fund to run board slate at Ryerson", 2 January 2007, Reuters.com; URL: www.today.reuters.com/news/articleinvesting.aspx?view=CN&storyID-2007–01–02T. See also "Sides square off in Ryerson Inc. proxy battle", Miller, *Chicago Tribune*, 16 August 2007, URL: www.topix.net/content/trb/2007/08/sides-squaring-off-in-ryerson-inc-proxy-battle.

24 "ABN Amro vs TCI: The Bank Gets Ready to Build Its Defence", *Financial Times*, 2 March 2007. This was off the back of TCI's 1% shareholding in ABN Amro.

25 Under s.203 of the US Investment Advisers Act of 1940 (Advisers Act), an entity must register with the SEC if it holds itself out as being in the business of providing investment advice for compensation and, in a 12 month period, has more than 14 clients (s.203 Cap). Non-US managers count only US-person clients towards this threshold.

26 It will also be important to ensure that controls are put into place to monitor the levels of holdings of US investors – a non-US fund is required to "look through" and count any US investor that owns more than 10% of its voting securities towards the s.203 Cap.

27 See, eg, "Special Report: Regulatory aspects and tax considerations", Ho Han Ming, Hedge-Fund Intelligence, July 2007.

28 SEC Hedge Fund Report, p. 9, n. 27.

29 *SEC v Beacon Hill Asset Management, LLC et al*, Civil Action 02–8855(LAK), 15 June 2004 (*Beacon Hill Amended Complaint*).

30 "Offering Memorandum" means the document by which shares in a single entity hedge fund or the "offshore feeder fund" in a master feeder structure are sold. "Private Placement Memorandum" (or PPM) is the document by which Interests are sold to US taxpaying investors in an "onshore feeder fund". "Offering Materials" refers to both. In certain master feeder structures, a single document may be used to sell shares and interests.

31 *Goldstein v SEC*, No 04–1434 (DC Cir. 23 June, 2006) ("*Goldstein*"), p.2.

32 (*IOSCO Report*), URL: www.iosco.org/library/pubdocs/pdf/IOSCOPD226.pdf.

33 See "Hedge funds begin to show up on regulators' radar", *Washington Post*, 9 February, 2007, URL: www.washingtonpost.com/wp-dyn/content/article/2007/02/08/AR2007020801829.html (Johnson & Birnbaum).

34 *Ibid.*

35 See "Regulators see dangers in hedge fund collateral", White & Grant, FT.com, 30 January 2007, URL: www.ft.com/cms/s/cb0a9650-b006–11db-94ab-0000779e2340.html (White & Grant).

36 Advisers Act Release 2333, 69 FR 72054 (10 December 2004) (Release 2333).

37 SEC Hedge Fund Report p 3.

38 "Hedge Funds", A discussion of risk and regulatory engagement, Discussion Paper 05/4, June 2005 (FSA Hedge Fund Discussion Paper).

39 "Testimony Concerning the Regulation of Hedge Funds", SEC Chairman Christopher Cox, 25 July, 2006, URL: www.sec.gov/news/testimony/2006/ts072506cc.htm.

40 "Hedge Funds: An exploratory study of conduct-related issues", report by the Autoriteit Financiële Markten, 6 September 2005, URL: www.afm.nl/consumer/default.ashx?DocumentId=5249.

41 "Update 1 – S. Africa plans to regulate hedge funds", Reuters, 25 April 2007, URL: www.today.reuters.com/misc/PrinterFriendlyPopup.aspx?type=bondsNews&storyID.

42 Press Release, 2798th Council Meeting, Economic and Foreign Affairs, Brussels, 8 May 2007.

43 "Leading hedge fund managers advocate improved disclosure to investors", AIMA press release, 10 October 2007. URL: www.hfwg.co.uk/sites/10085/files/consultation_paper_press_release.pdf.

44 *Goldstein* p 4; SEC Hedge Fund Report pp 46, 47.

45 SEC Hedge Fund Report p 4.

46 The Cayman Islands will begin to experience competition when Jersey and other offshore jurisdictions implement similar regimes and industry participants become comfortable with the single-cell structure, implemented in Jersey and other jurisdictions.

47 In certain jurisdictions (eg, Ireland), hedge funds have obtained a listing. In other jurisdictions, funds of hedge funds are listed.

2

Types and Structures of Hedge Funds

Having introduced hedge funds, we now turn our attention to hedge fund structures. This will involve examining aspects of the corporate, unit trust and limited partnership arrangements, comparing single entity hedge funds and master feeder structures, identifying strategies and considering models across Asia, Europe and the US, with local variations. We will touch on variants such as segregated portfolio companies, multi-class funds and side-by-side funds, and outline the types of securities that hedge funds issue.

CORPORATE, LIMITED PARTNERSHIP AND UNIT TRUST MODELS

The choice of setting up a hedge fund as a company, limited partnership or unit trust is a matter of key factors: investor requirements; tax efficiency; limitations on liability; and local regulatory and market considerations. Hedge funds, like their investors, wish to pay minimal tax or be free from tax altogether, and the jurisdiction of incorporation and structure that is employed will dictate whether this will be possible. The limited partnership model is used primarily where the hedge fund manager is located in the US, whether or not the manager is registered with the SEC, and where the US investors, institutions or HNWIs are taxpayers. Hedge funds are established as companies in other jurisdictions. This is not to say that it is tax disadvantageous to establish a hedge fund as a company. Hedge funds are established as companies in jurisdictions such as the Cayman Islands, BVI and Bermuda in order to take advantage of limited disclosure, limited liability, minimal regulatory obligations and favourable tax treatment (subject to compliance with relevant conditions, the hedge fund would not be liable to taxation on its profits, a benefit that investors seek from investing in a hedge fund).

Limited partnerships

A limited partnership is a legal structure in which one or more general partners manage the business and affairs of the partnership for the benefit of one or more limited partner investors. The general partner is responsible for all activities of the limited partnership. The limited partners are passive investors who play no role in the daily operations of the vehicle.

The general partner assumes unlimited liability for the debts and obligations of the limited partnership. In contrast, the limited partners are liable only up to the amount of their actual contributions.

Limited partners receive partnership interests which are undivided interests in the property of the partnership. In order to sell their partnership interests, limited partners must in compliance with the partnership agreement receive the consent of the general partner.

In the partnership model, which is the predominant structure for hedge funds that are managed in the US, the general partner performs multiple roles. It is the manager of the hedge fund that exercises power over the partnership and its assets, as do the directors of a corporate vehicle. It also serves as administrator and investment manager. While tax and regulatory considerations dictate that the general partner performs multiple roles, combining these functions gives rise to conflicts of interest. As discussed elsewhere in this book, the combination of roles has, on occasion, led to problems such as wrongly pricing securities in the portfolio, publishing incorrect valuations and striking inaccurate NAVs – often materially different from what would have been struck had there been an independent administrator (as in the European and Asian models) receiving prices for illiquid or hard-to-value securities from independent sources.

There are benefits in the limited partnership structure in that it reduces the number of service providers involved and facilitates a simplified operating structure. The important factor in the limited partnership structure is whether sufficient checks and balances are in place to help identify and address conflicts of interest, primarily from the multiple roles played by the general partner. Where the general partner has opted to be regulated by, for example, the SEC, it will be obliged to identify and discuss conflicts of interest in its disclosure documents,[1] treat clients fairly and avoid materially misleading statements or omissions.[2]

Companies

The company structure is similar across the world. It includes directors that are responsible for the company. There are no officers or employees of a hedge fund, as there are in industrial companies.[3] The operative documents of a company are: the Memorandum, which sets forth the powers of the company; the Articles, which contains the operative requirements imposed on the company under the law of the jurisdiction where the company is incorporated and the rights of the shareholders; and the Offering Materials, by which the securities of the hedge fund are offered and sold.

A company has a legal personality, separate and apart from its shareholders. It can sue and be sued, issue securities in more than one class and in sub-classes, contract with third parties and, perhaps most importantly, provide for the limited liability of its shareholders.

The majority of hedge funds outside the US are companies.

Unit trusts

A unit trust is a structure in which, under the terms of a deed or indenture, investors subscribe for units of beneficial interest. Unit holders become beneficiaries of the trust. Units are fractional undivided interests in the property that comprises the trust. Under and according to the terms of the trust deed, the proceeds of the sale of units are received by the trustee who assumes fiduciary duties to the unit holders. Generally speaking, under relevant law and the trust deed, the trustee of a unit trust performs the management and oversight role for a unit trust in a manner similar to the directors of a company and the general partner of a limited partnership.

Unlike a company, a unit trust does not does not provide for a separate legal personality.

Generally, the trustee performs the role(s) of investment manager, administrator and custodian. The trustee will usually, depending on local legal considerations and provisions of the trust deed, delegate these roles to third parties.

One variation on this model is the authorised unit trust regime that operates in Ireland under the Irish Unit Trust Act. In this model, the unit trust is authorised by the Irish Financial Services Regulatory Authority (Financial Regulator) and is listed on the ISE. Under the trust deed, the Trustee is responsible for the custody of the fund's assets and, under this authority, appoints one or more prime brokers and custodians. The investment manager is responsible for the management and administration of the fund. In the discharge of its responsibilities, it manages the assets in the fund's portfolio and appoints an administrator to discharge the administrative tasks involved in operating the fund. The manager would appoint one or more distributors to market units and retain a sponsor to handle ISE listing matters.

OVERSIGHT

There are many questions that are asked by prospects that submit due diligence questionnaires (DDQs) or meet with promoters or investment managers of hedge funds prior to investing.[4] Of these, one assumes paramount importance: who is responsible for the hedge fund?

Responses to queries in DDQs and interviews state, correctly, that the fund is managed by the directors of the company, the trustee of the unit trust or the general partner of the limited partnership. However, these overlook the role of the investment manager in the Asian and European models (and American corporate models with no general partner) as "first among equals" among service providers and the powers granted to prime brokers in prime brokerage agreements.[5]

The directors, the trustee or the general partner assume the legal responsibility of the hedge fund. The investment manager and the prime broker "operate" the hedge fund. The investment manager manages the portfolio, is responsible for trading activity and, when directors are not available (and with director approval), is in discussions with the administrator over matters such as which investors to admit or redeem or how to price or value illiquid instruments. Also, it is often the case that the investment manager will assume the responsibility for assembling the board packs for the directors meetings, instructing lawyers to draft documents for matters such as negotiating ISDAs and trading or credit documents, managing the preparation of shareholder communications and assisting the auditors with the preparation of audited financial statements and annual reports. The prime broker is the primary source of credit (lending securities and providing loans to leverage/engage in margin transactions) and is empowered to place the hedge fund in default in many situations and liquidate the portfolio – effectively, shutting down the fund.

The directors, trustees and general partners sign agreements, consider matters and make decisions. They also consider important issues such as changes to the investment objective, policies and restrictions, handle difficult valuation and pricing queries, delegate activities to service providers (even add or change service providers) and, when required, review, approve and sign the audited financial statements. They review the activities of service providers.

In terms of answering the question, who is responsible for the hedge fund, operating does not confer the right to exercise oversight or assume legal responsibility.

Oversight – objectively supervising service providers and being legally responsible for a hedge fund on an independent and objective basis – belongs to the directors, trustee or limited partner. Often, the directors, trustees or general partners do not actively exercise oversight and leave it to the investment manager. On occasion, oversight is overlooked. This should not be the case. Directors, trustees and general partners must exercise oversight in a meaningful manner.

There are many issues involving hedge funds that are before regulators. These include side letters, valuations, insider trading, market abuse, the registration of investment managers, how to look through a hedge fund to protect investors and the "dark side" of collateral, credit, derivatives and highly leveraged investments, such as CDOs, CBOs and SPVs involving leveraged loan portfolios. It includes the issue whether hedge funds should be defined or regulated. Oversight is an issue that is finding its way onto the regulator's radar screen.

Oversight matters to investors in hedge funds because it helps ensure that no one service provider might control hedge fund activities to its benefit (whether or not intentionally), that the right amounts of fees are being paid and that investors are being protected. It also helps secure the role of directors, trustee or general partner as being the sole entity responsible for the hedge fund. Oversight means that the directors, the trustee or the general partner, or an independent entity appointed by them or it, is receiving all of the information that it requires, reviewing all activities of the hedge fund, including the service providers, comparing roles and contractual provisions and providing objective, verifiable and meaningful information to the directors to enable them to ensure a number of factors. These include transparency and consistency in operations and trading, proper and timely valuations, a legally permissible side letter policy, fees that are within acceptable market parameters, non-settled or failed trades (DK'd trades, as they are known) are caught and dealt with and that information provided to the directors, trustee and general partner by the service providers is reconciled and complete.

THE SECURITIES OF HEDGE FUNDS

Securities and legal entities

In the case of a single entity hedge fund, proceeds from the sale of securities will go into the portfolio to be used to purchase investments. For a master feeder structure, the proceeds will become assets of the feeder fund used to purchase shares or interests in the master fund. In the case of onshore feeder funds, which usually are Delaware LLCs or LPs, US investors (taxpayers) will purchase US dollar-denominated Interests. The rights and obligations of investors in LLC onshore feeder funds are governed by an operating agreement (Operating Agreement) between each holder of Interests and the corporate director of the LLC onshore feeder fund, and in LP onshore feeder funds by the limited partnership deed. All or substantially all of the assets in the onshore feeder fund (eg, the investments of holders of Interests) will be invested in the master fund.

Investors in a limited partnership hedge fund will purchase partnership interests in the hedge fund. The partnership agreement will define the rights and obligations of limited partners. The liability of limited partners in such an entity will generally be limited to the amount of their investment in the hedge fund.

Investors in a unit trust hedge fund receive units of beneficial interest. Units are undivided fractional interests in the property of the hedge fund. The trust deed (or declaration of trust) provides for the rights of the unit holders as beneficiaries, including the manner in which they may transfer or redeem their units.

A hedge fund that is a company will issue one or more classes of securities, with or without voting rights and with special rights attendant to them.[6] The rights of classes of securities are established by the Articles of the hedge fund and applicable law.

Classes of shares

Potentially, there is no limit to the number of classes of shares a corporate hedge fund may issue. Classes of shares usually are denominated by currency and voting rights. Beyond this, considerations such as enhanced rights and the impact of certain regulatory requirements (such as NASD Conduct Rule 2790) dictate multiple classes of shares. Depending upon local legal requirements, fractional shares may be issued.

Classes of securities are also used to distinguish certain rights, redemption features and other factors, to take into account the needs of certain investors.

A simple Cayman Islands single entity corporate hedge fund (or the offshore feeder fund in a master feeder structure) might have the following classes of shares:

❑ US$ voting shares
❑ US$ non-voting shares
❑ € voting shares
❑ € non-voting shares
❑ HK$ voting shares
❑ HK$ non-voting shares

The administrator of the fund would be required to strike a NAV for each class of shares. Thus, in our example, the fund or offshore feeder fund would strike and publish six NAVs per share.

In addition to establishing classes of shares, the Articles may provide for sub-classes of shares. The issuance of sub-classes of shares helps to address the need to respond to the considerations that might otherwise lead to having to create multiple share classes and strike several NAVs. Sub-classes are used, for example, to distinguish shares held by "Restricted Persons" under Rule 2790. A fund or offshore feeder fund with sub-classes might look like this:

❑ US$ voting shares (sub-classes Restricted and Non-Restricted)[7]
❑ US$ non-voting shares (sub-classes Restricted and Non-Restricted)
❑ € voting shares (sub-classes Restricted and Non-Restricted)
❑ € non-voting shares (sub-classes Restricted and Non-Restricted)
❑ HK$ voting shares (sub-classes Restricted and Non-Restricted)
❑ HK$ non-voting shares (sub-classes Restricted and Non-Restricted)

Administrators strike NAVs at the share class level (usually, they do not strike NAVs for sub-classes). They, would, however, allocate profits and losses from transactions in initial public offerings (IPOs) of securities caught by the provisions of rule 2790 to holders of the Non-Restricted sub-classes. Thus, if there were 67 holders of record of the euro voting shares, of which two were Restricted Persons and the remaining 65 were not, the profits resulting from any transaction caught by rule 2790 would go to the 65 Non-Restricted Persons. Entries would be made on the books of each class of shares at the sub-class level, showing the profits and losses (for holders of Non-Restricted shares), and no entries would appear (for holders of Restricted shares). Appropriate notations would be made when the NAVS per share were published, indicating that Rule 2790 allocations have been made at the sub-class level for Non-Restricted Persons holding shares, particularly close to the launch of the hedge fund and at a time when the hedge fund's AUM is not high.

Founders Shares

The Articles of Cayman Islands hedge funds may provide for the issue of Founders Shares. These are a special class of shares that are issued at the time the hedge fund is incorporated and before shares are offered at all. Founders Shares may be held by the investment manager or one of its affiliates, or the trustee in a unit trust. They may also be held by the directors of the fund (or, in the case of a master fund, by its directors or by the offshore feeder fund).

Unlike the shares offered to and held by investors, Founders Shares are not redeemable, are not entitled to a dividend and, in the event of a winding up, rank for the return of capital only after all other outstanding shares.

The Articles may confer special rights on the holders of Founders Shares:

- ❑ to vote to the exclusion of all other shareholders to wind up the fund or amend the Articles or the Memorandum – as long as this would not adversely affect the rights of shareholders;
- ❑ to issue new shares and create new classes of shares and to set the number, par value and denomination; and
- ❑ to create sub-classes of shares, subject to this not adversely affecting the rights of existing shareholders.

STRATEGIES AND WEIGHTING

Hedge funds do not engage in all types of trading activities – although it may seem that they do. When the decision is taken to launch a hedge fund, the promoters will agree a strategy that their hedge fund will follow. This strategy is intended to carry out the investment objective and policies, but is subject to the stated restrictions.

Strategies

Hedge funds are equity funds, fixed income or credit funds, derivative funds, emerging markets fund, currency funds or special situation or event-driven funds. Strategies are dictated by market conditions and opportunities, the use (or the non-use) of leverage, investing techniques, types of securities, geographic considerations, interest rates, credit structures and other factors. They are framed by the investment objective, policies and restrictions. They are followed, or changed, to help the investment manager trade and earn money in any market condition – absolute return. By "absolute return", we mean making money regardless of market conditions and not in comparison to a benchmark.

A hedge fund may be established as a long-short single country fund, where the investment manager is looking to buy and sell or short[8] equity securities of issuers in that jurisdiction and lock in a profit. Other hedge funds are more complex, such as credit funds that invest in portfolios comprising debt securities, convertible bonds, loan participations, CDSs, CDO participations and SPVs over leveraged loan participations.

There are many types of strategies, and variations on each.[9] One may even say that there are as many strategies as there are hedge funds. The following is a brief summary of some of the more widely recognised hedge fund strategies.

Arbitrage: The investment manager will buy or sell securities or other investments (or assets) that have in some way moved away or deviated from a benchmark or relationship. Arbitrage funds include convertible arbitrage (between convertible bonds and shares), debt, or fixed income (between bonds and other debt instruments), depositary receipts (between shares and depositary receipts), derivative (to exploit differences between a derivative and the underlying security), merger (buy and sell shares of the bidder and the target, or even the "white knight") and risk (where prices for shares or other securities appear to offer different probabilities for, or based on, an event).

Bias: The investment manager is seeking to capitalise on a certain security, class of investment or market. Examples of bias hedge funds include short bias (selling short primarily) and distressed securities (low rated high risk debt, distressed debt and other instruments of generally poor credit quality, or even the securities of issuers in or emerging from bankruptcy).

Convergence: The investment manager is looking for convergence in securities underlying derivatives, eg, shares and convertible securities, underlying futures and options, and so on.

Event driven: The investment manager is motivated to buy or sell based on an event – be it a merger or proposed merger, the idea that taking a stake in a company and pressing for corporate reforms may unlock potential in a company's balance sheet or for any idea based on research.

Long-short: In a long-short fund, the investment manager is investing in a directional manner, seeking to profit from simultaneously buying and selling securities.

Macro: In these funds, the investment manager is seeking to derive value from buying or selling securities that are or that may become mispriced relative to alternatives on a market, country, regional or global basis.

Market neutral: Here, the investment manager trades to maintain a balance or relationship between long and short positions in the same security.

These strategies generally involve individuals making investment decisions.

Quantitative: In quantitative (quant) funds, investment managers use sophisticated trading programmes with algorithms designed to spot patterns, opportunities, pricing discrepancies or economic factors (referred to as "statistical arbitrage"). Programmes in quant funds, not individual fund managers, generate orders to simultaneously buy and sell different securities and capture a return. Quant strategies generate returns, but, as discussed in Chapter 10, it is not always a one-way street to profits.

Not every hedge fund engages in all of these strategies. According to the Greenwich Report, 78% of hedge funds with assets of less than $100 million use a long-short strategy.[10] This same strategy was reported to be the "most popular investment strategy" for hedge funds with more than US$1 billion, with event-driven and volatility arbitrage increasing in 2007 from 2006.[11]

Weighting

Beyond this, there is the issue of weighting: what instruments or sectors, long or short, comprise what percent of the hedge fund's portfolio. Weighting reflects the strategy of the fund in relation to the direction of the markets in which the portfolio is invested. Weightings change to reflect or take advantage of market conditions. Changes in weightings do not just mean buying or selling securities, but may involve adding or dropping sectors or increasing numbers in one or more categories – within the investment objective, policies and restrictions.

In a long-short equity fund, the portfolio might largely comprise equity positions, long and short, convertible bonds, some derivatives and cash. In a fixed income fund, the portfolio would consist of debt, loan participations, derivatives, distressed debt and other instruments. In an event-driven fund, there would be equity securities (mostly long positions with some shorts) and possibly side pockets of investments in LBOs and stakes in listed companies.

The following Table shows an example of weighting by instruments.

Table 2.1 Weighting by instruments

Weighting by investment	January 2006	February 2006	March 2006
Major markets equity long	24	24	22
Emerging markets equity long	9	9	8
Major markets equity short	12	12	12
Emerging markets equity short	5	6	8
Convertible bonds	4	3	6
ETFs	10	10	8
Options	9	10	10
Futures	9	8	8
Other derivatives	12	14	15
Cash	6	4	3
Totals	100%	100%	100%

Weighting of investments in sectors might look as in this Table.

Table 2.2 Weighting of investments in sectors

Weighting by sector	June 2007	July 2007	August 2007
Energy	22	23	23
Banking	23	23	15
Healthcare	8	8	12
Financial services	17	18	15
Utilities	4	5	5
Technology	5	5	4
Derivatives	10	10	10
Cash	11	8	12
Totals	100%	100%	100%

A portfolio might be allocated across geographic regions as depicted in Figure 2.3.

Weightings change to reflect many factors, such as market developments, changes in investor appetite, economic factors and other developments.

Figure 2.3 A portfolio allocated over geographic regions

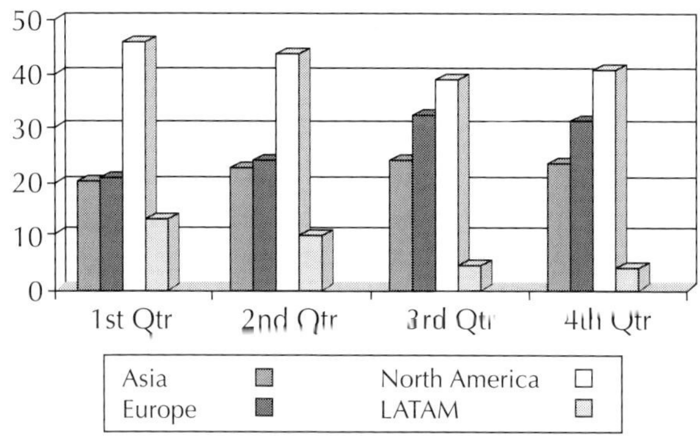

Within the category of weighting there is the factor of "drift". Drift represents a subtle change in investments, weighting or strategy that does not represent a material change. For example, in Table 2.1, the figures for major markets equity short positions remained unchanged in the three-month period. This is not to say that the actual figures remained the same: during this time, short positions were opened, closed and adjusted to take account of share price movements and other factors. The weighting of such short positions may have remained within one percentage point. Also, the short positions may have changed across geographic boundaries: if the hedge fund involved was a global fund with investments in the four areas shown above, the short positions may have increased in one market (say Germany) while decreasing in another (for example, Japan). Such changes represent drift.

RESTRICTIONS

The term "restrictions" refers to the parameters imposed on hedge funds within which the investment manager must remain. Common investment restrictions, or diversification benchmarks, may include the following:

- ❑ limits or prohibitions on investing in real estate or physically settled commodities;
- ❑ not investing more than 1% of the portfolio assets (or gross assets) in the securities of any one issuer, or a cap on illiquid investments;
- ❑ not making loans – but this may not prevent a hedge fund from buying loan participations;
- ❑ not taking control of an issuer;
- ❑ complying with stated "limitations";
- ❑ observing borrowing restrictions; and
- ❑ "cash" investments – by this, we mean restrictions on the amount of

cash invested in a particular type of money market instrument or even a prohibition on a money-market fund managed by the investment manager.

Borrowing restrictions may be expressed in several ways. These include the following:

- limits on the amounts that may be borrowed – this is leverage, and the limits are set as percentages, ranging from 100% to as high as 500% of the AUM (calculated, often, by dividing the market value of the long positions by the AUM; this may or may not exclude short positions, currency transactions to hedge the portfolio's currency exposure[12] or even the market exposure of derivatives); or
- caps on the market value of short positions – this may be stated as a firm figure or, possibly, as an expectation (creating the possibility of drift) that short will not exceed a stated percentage of the AUM.

Limitations may include: capital limits (no companies with a market capitalisation of less than or more than a given amount); position limits (longs vs shorts, expressed as a percentage of the NAV); and net exposure (long positions less short positions).

In summary, the return that a hedge fund generates is a product of many factors. This is not just a reflection of the investment objective, policy and restrictions, together with limits, strategies and weighting. It takes a skilled investment manager to spot investment opportunities in the context of sophisticated, ever-changing markets and increasing investor demands for alpha.

FUNDS OF HEDGE FUNDS

A fund of hedge funds (FoHF) is a pooled investment vehicle that offers one or more sub-funds under a parent company for investment. FoHFs are a type of umbrella fund, but are not segregated asset or portfolio companies (see below). The company and its sub-funds are deemed to be a single legal entity, and the creditor of one sub-fund may realise against the assets of another sub-fund if claims are not satisfied from the portfolio of the first sub-fund.

Each sub-fund of a FoHF will issue one or more classes of shares. In this regard, each sub-fund functions like a hedge fund. Each will have its own investment objective, policy and restrictions. The investment manager will invest the assets of each sub-fund in a portfolio of other hedge funds (single entities and offshore feeder funds in master feeder structures), according to the investment objective, policies and restrictions. The restrictions may reach through the sub-fund's investments (target fund) to their portfolios and include provisions such as no real property and no physically settled commodities transactions, or apply at the fund level and provide that the sub-fund many not invest in a target fund that is incorporated in a jurisdiction other than a country that complies with the AML requirements of the Financial Action Task Force (FATF). There may be other types of restrictions, common to hedge funds, such limits on investing the assets of the sub-fund itself. Such limits are usually percentage caps on a single fund or family of funds, non-UCITS compliance schemes, bank deposits or money market instruments or hedge funds managed by the investment manager of the sub-fund itself. Other limits may include caps on pledging assets, borrowing, short sales, lending or even criteria that relate to the investment manager of the prospective target fund.

The redemption cycles of FoHFs function like those of hedge funds, but with differences. Whereas single entity hedge funds or offshore feeder funds may be able to calculate their AUM and strike NAVs per share, FoHFs depend on funds that form the portfolio of the sub-fund striking NAVs. This being the case, the NAVs per share that FoHFs strike are, in some instances, based on NAVs per share of underlying funds that are more than one month old or possibly longer, depending on the cycle by which the underlying fund strikes a NAV per share, or may be based on estimates published by the hedge fund's administrator.

Sub-funds of FoHFs rely on the investment manager to invest its assets in the securities of hedge funds. FoHFs, like hedge funds, invest on the

Table 2.4 FoHF1

Strategy and allocations	**Q1**	**Q2**	**Q3**	**Q4**
Credit	35	36	36	32
Multi-strategy	17	17	17	20
Long-short equity	19	19	20	20
Directional trading	29	28	27	28
Totals	100%	100%	100%	100%

Table 2.5 FoHF2

Strategy and allocations	**Q1**	**Q2**	**Q3**	**Q4**
Long-short equity	33	32	32	32
Event-driven	22	23	24	25
Arbitrage	45	45	44	43
Totals	100%	100%	100%	100%

basis of an investment objective, policies and restrictions and employ a strategy similar to those of hedge funds (see above), but may vary.

Examples of portfolio allocation by types of strategy that FoHFs might employ would be as shown in Tables 2.4 and 2.5.

HEDGE FUND VARIANTS

Our discussion to this point has focused on single-entity funds and master feeder structures established as companies, trusts or partnerships. Variants on these are described below.

Side-by-side funds

These structures resemble master feeders but the companies that are involved have their own portfolios. The assets of both pooled investment vehicles are invested in parallel, rather like the way in which managed accounts would mirror hedge funds.

Umbrella funds

Where a hedge fund will have a single portfolio and pursue a single strategy, an umbrella fund comprises two or more portfolios, each with a class of securities that in some way mirrors or reflects the type of assets in the portfolio. There are two types of such funds.

Plain vanilla umbrellas

Simple, or plain vanilla, umbrella funds are a single fund with multiple portfolios. Most FoHFs are structured this way. While this offers a simple administrative structure, it creates risk. In particular, and notwithstanding the segregation of portfolios and profits and losses in the books of the fund, a third-party creditor may attempt to satisfy its claim from the assets of more than one portfolio – particularly where the basis of the liability would cut across portfolios. Steps may be taken to address this risk, such as avoiding high-risk investments and strategies, having agreements apply by their terms to a single portfolio or by the use of intermediate companies to shield risk.

Segregated asset/portfolio companies

Segregated asset/portfolio companies (SPCs) are companies with a single legal personality but they have two or more portfolios that permit the assets and liabilities of each portfolio to be legally segregated from each other, free from credit or third-party claims. This type of company is relatively new, having been established in jurisdictions such as Jersey, Guernsey, BVI and the Cayman Islands, and in the state of Delaware.

By observing certain safeguards, investment managers of SPCs may establish and trade in multiple portfolios and avoid having the claims of creditors affect more than the portfolio in question – in contrast to the ability of creditors to claim against multiple portfolios in an umbrella fund.

Replicants

Hedge funds offer the promise of returns (what fund or investment guarantees a return?). So do many other investments, ranging from equity securities to long-only funds to SPVs. Hedge funds provide returns, as do many traditional asset classes. Investors in hedge funds seek a return greater than that which they would receive by investing directly in securities or long-only funds, known as alpha. Alpha is the reward for risk. It is the difference between what a hedge fund would make by investing on a leveraged basis and what a long-only fund would receive from buying securities without leverage. The critical question is whether it is possible for a hedge fund over a period of time to continue to generate alpha at a level sufficient to keep institutions happy with their returns – on an after-fee basis? May one achieve superior returns only via hedge funds,[13] or are there alternatives that would equal, or exceed, what a hedge fund generates post-fees?

A replicant is a quant product comprising a basket of investments – often including futures, indexes, notes and other securities. Replicants, "synthetic" hedge funds, are sold by investment firms or commercial banks as an alternative to hedge funds. The premise is that the return from the quant-driven replicant would be greater than that of the after-fee hedge fund. They are marketed as an alternative to hedge funds with their lack of transparency and high fees.

Do replicants work? Can machine outperform man? The product has been in existence for several years and attracts sufficient sums of money. Several studies have been published on the merits of replication. Some show that replicants outperform hedge funds; others do not. Some even show that FoHFs outperform replicants.

130/30 funds

A "130/30" fund is a long-only fund in which the portfolio is split into two parts: one comprises long positions; the other consists of shorts. The long positions have a weighting of 130% of the portfolio (the positive exposure) and the shorts are weighted at 30% (the negative exposure), resulting in an exposure of 100% for the fund. How do we arrive at these figures?

Assets in portfolio:	€100 million
Long positions (value):	€100 million
Short exposure:	€30 million
Reinvestment of cash from shorts into further long positions:	€30 million
Portfolio investments:	€160 million

Thus, and in our example, the manager of a 130/30 fund is able to generate an investment of €1.60 for each €1 of investor capital. The fund is capable not only of generating returns equal to or greater than the fund's benchmark, but higher, due to the presence of alpha.

130/30 funds have a fee structure akin to that of a hedge fund, comprising a management fee and a performance fee.

Side pockets

Traditionally, hedge funds used their portfolios to invest in securities. Partly as a response to the convergence of aspects of hedge funds and private equity vehicles, and as a means to achieve a diversified portfolio and increase returns, some hedge funds carve out a portion of their portfolios, or establish a separate class of securities, to be used for medium- to long-term investments. These so-called "side pockets" carry with them limitations on redemptions. Their fee structures may or may not be based on the traditional management fee/performance fee, but be fixed and based on the amounts involved. Also, the fees for the side pockets may be paid at a time different from that of the main hedge fund. Funds used in side pockets may be "reused" for more than one transaction. Hedge funds commonly limit the amount of their portfolios that may be contained in side pockets to a fixed percentage, usually between 20% and 30%.

1 Conflicts are required to be disclosed in a registered adviser's Form ADV Part II.

2 See Rule 206(4)-8 under the Advisers Act, which came into force on 10 September 2007.

3 Hedge funds may have officers such as an MLRO, but this and other positions are filled by employees of service providers such as the company secretary, the administrator or a law firm. It usually is the case that the company secretary performs such roles, to help ensure independence and to help control costs – but this must be done so as to keep this role separate from the investment manager and to ensure that the hedge fund is not taxed in the jurisdiction where the company secretary is located.

4 The Alternative Investment Managers Association (AIMA) has produced a set of due diligence questionnaires for use in evaluating hedge fund service providers and for investors in considering an investment in a hedge fund.

5 These include broadly drawn definitions of events of default and acts of insolvency, expansive definitions of what comprises margin, when margin may be called, powers on an event of details, the ability to maintain a fixed and floating charge over the entire portfolio held by the prime broker as custodian and, if an ISDA is present (as is usually the case), broad additional termination events such as fund NAV declines. A discussion of key prime broker provisions is contained in Chapter 5.

6 "Equity interests", "equity securities", "shares" and "voting shares" refer to the securities issued by a hedge fund. We call them "shares" or "voting shares" to distinguish them from non-voting shares.

7 "Restricted" refers to shares held by "Restricted Persons" as this term is defined in Rule 2790, and "Non-Restricted" refers to shares held by persons who are not Restricted Persons.

8 Short sales are "naked shorts" (the seller does not own the securities but borrows them to deliver to the buyer) or "shorts against the box" (the seller owns the securities that are sold but does not deliver them, opting to borrow for delivery to hedge the position that he

continues to hold). Naked shorting may be legitimate but is also manipulative, while shorting against the box is done more often than not to hedge existing positions.

9 A helpful description of hedge fund strategies is published by Greenwich Alternative Investments. *See* URL: www.greenwichai.com/GenPages/gvhfindex42.aspx?vNode=8&vChild=2.

10 Greenwich Report.

11 *Ibid.*

12 Hedge funds have a "base currency" which will be used as the base for all transactions and will feature in the annual audited financial statements. The portfolio will include investments priced in different currencies and it will be necessary to hedge these investments, by currency, against the base currency. This is separate from investor class hedging.

13 As is the case with investors from HNWIs to institutions, hedge funds comprise only a part of their portfolios. This is intended to achieve diversification and avoid concentration risks.

3

What's in an Articles of Association, a Limited Partnership Agreement or a Unit Trust Agreement?

Every hedge fund will be a company, unit trust or partnership. Every jurisdiction where a hedge fund is incorporated or established will have laws, rules and regulations (governing laws) providing for the establishment, operation and dissolution of a company, partnership or unit trust, as well as taxation or exemptions from taxation. These governing laws, and the court cases and administrative interpretations made about them, spell out the duties of directors, trustees or general partners (including the fiduciary duties owed) and other relevant matters. What binds hedge funds to governing laws are the Memorandum and Articles.

In this chapter, we examine the process of establishment and what comprises the Articles of a corporate hedge fund. This discussion is based on the sample articles set forth in the Appendix to this book.

SOURCES OF LAW

The Articles of a hedge fund, as is the case with the Memorandum, take their shape from local governing laws. In the case of a Cayman Islands hedge fund, this would be the Companies Law (Revised) 2004, which provides for the establishment of hedge funds, their operation and their dissolution. A related Caymans Island law that applies to hedge funds is the Mutual Funds Law (2003 Revision) (Mutual Funds Law), which provides for the registration and "regulation" of hedge funds or their exemption from registration.

Taxation is an issue critical to every hedge fund. In the Cayman Islands (and in the other offshore jurisdictions where hedge funds are incorporated), there are provisions that permit a hedge fund to qualify for or obtain an exemption from taxation. As regards the Cayman Islands, Section 6 of the Tax Concessions Law (1999 Revision) provides that a hedge fund may apply for a certificate of exemption from taxation in that jurisdiction for a period of 20 years. The scope of this would cover taxation arising from profits, income, gains or appreciation, as well as estate duties or inheritance tax payable on the securities of the hedge fund, or the offshore feeder fund and the master fund. This comes at a cost, because the entity seeking this shelter must pay an annual registration fee.

It does not mean that the hedge fund might be taxed elsewhere. For example, in the UK, investment managers must observe certain guidelines in order to help ensure that the offshore (non-UK) hedge fund that they advise is not subject to taxation in the UK. On 20 July 2007, HMRC published a Revised Statement of Practice that sets forth a number of activities that contain exemptions for UK-based investment managers of non-UK hedge funds to observe in helping the hedge funds involved remain free from UK taxation as a corporate non-resident entity.[1]

The policies behind the Statement of Practice are that "overseas investors (non-UK hedge funds) should not be charged to UK tax in relation to investment transactions conducted on their behalf and that any fees earned by a UK-resident investment manager for services performed for the non-resident should be fully chargeable to UK tax." The exemptions go to designated investment transactions, treatment of the hedge fund involved with respect to its "independent capacity" and clarification of master feeder structures, as well as providing for minor or inadvertent non-qualifying transactions.

INCORPORATION AND CAPITAL STRUCTURE

In the Cayman Islands, a hedge fund is incorporated as an exempted company under the provisions of the Companies Law (2001 Second Revision). To do this, it files documents with the Registrar of Companies. These are a Form MF1, a Section 184 Declaration, a copy of the Memorandum and Articles and a list of the first directors. Upon incorporation, the incorporator of the hedge fund would receive a Certificate of Mutual Fund Registration. The incorporator would hold an initial directors meeting, at which time it would note the incorporation and make preliminary appointments (company secretary and registered office). The shares that are issued at this point are Founders Shares (which are discussed in Chapter 2).

- A single entity hedge fund or the offshore feeder fund in a master feeder structure would register as a regulated mutual fund under Section 4(3) of the Mutual Funds Law.
- In a master feeder structure, the master fund would be incorporated with limited liability as an exempted company under the Companies Law (2004 Revision). The master fund would not register to be a regulated mutual fund. This would hold true for the corporate director of a Delaware LLC or LP onshore feeder fund.

Corporate hedge funds would have authorised share capital – as noted in Chapter 2, unit trusts would have units and limited partnerships would have interests.

A corporate Cayman Islands hedge fund would have an authorised share capital of a stated amount, reflected in the base currency. This would be divided into classes of shares with a par value. Our model hedge fund, with sterling as its base currency, would have share capital of £25,000,000 as follows:

- 10 Founders Shares of £1 par value each;
- £12,500,000, divided into 12,500,000 ordinary shares of £0.01 par value; and
- £12,500,000, divided into 25,000,000 ordinary shares of US$0.01 par value (giving effect to current exchange rates).

MEMORANDUM

The Memorandum is the constitutional document that establishes the hedge fund. It states the name of the hedge fund, gives its registered address, sets forth the powers of the hedge fund, or its "objects" (what the hedge fund can and cannot do, under and subject to its governing laws), identifies the capital and provides for the limited liability of shareholders. This document is signed by the incorporators and is lodged with the Registrar of Companies.

At the same time, the Articles, which are discussed below, are lodged.

ARTICLES

The Articles give the hedge fund its structure. They provide for its operation as regards the issuance, exchange and redemption of shares, calculating AUM and striking NAVs per class of share (and the suspension of this), suspending the issuance, exchange and redemption of shares, conferring shareholder rights, establishing the mechanism for shareholders to meet, giving a structure to directors' meetings and other relevant matters.

The remainder of this chapter is devoted to a discussion of key provisions of the Articles.

Structure

Articles are divided into sections, each composed of an operative provision. Generally, there are three types of articles: definitional, operative/procedural and substantive.

- Definitional articles define terms, such as "net asset value", class of shares", "US person", "Business Day", "Directors" and other matters.

- Operative or procedural terms state how processes are to be done. Examples are "proceedings at general meetings", "proceedings of directors" and "transmission of shares".
- Substantive articles establish requirements. They may also contain aspects of operations in them. Examples of this are "net asset value", "alternate directors", "powers of directors", and "modifications of rights".

Definitions

The defined terms in the Articles are the basis for defined terms in the Offering Materials, the material agreements and all other uses pertaining to the hedge fund. The key to understanding a hedge fund is to understand what the definitions are and how they work together.

It is crucial to get the definitions correct and ensure that they are consistent across all materials and documents. By the same token, the Directors and service providers should not be saddled with a rigid framework within which to operate. The Articles of many hedge funds define terms that are enshrined in laws or that reflect current regulatory considerations that are hard to alter to reflect changes in law or market developments. An example of this is the definition of "US person".

The term "US person" is defined not in, but *under*, the US federal securities laws. A definition appears in Regulation S under the Securities Act of 1933 (1933 Act) and in no-action letters issued by the SEC Staff. Non-US hedge funds that wish to sell their securities to US persons need to ensure that they can do so without having to register under the 1933 Act and also the Investment Company Act of 1940 (1940 Act).[2] Most non-US hedge funds define US person in their Articles and carry that definition forward into the Offering Materials and other documents.[3] This might prove burdensome if they later wish to change the definition, to reflect legal and regulatory developments.

Amending the Articles requires a lengthy and expensive process to obtain shareholder consent. Materials must be issued and proxies solicited, with an attendant waiting period involved. To avoid this, it would be better to have the definition of "US person" read "as defined in the Offering Materials from time to time", because it would be easier and less expensive to amend those documents rather than the Articles.

Other defined terms may contain an "in force" provision, such as the definition of "Law" (see Article 1 of the sample Articles) which reads, "the Companies Law (Revised)". To provide flexibility, this might be changed to read, "the Companies Law (Revised) or such other legislation that amends or replaces it".

Drafters of Articles may wish to employ either or both of these approaches to other definitions and provisions of the Articles, when and as possible.

Establishment and issuance of shares

The Articles provide for classes of shares, rights of classes and the issuance, exchange and redemption of shares. In this regard, the Articles clarify a number of points, such as whether shares can be declared to be voting or non-voting, whether rights might be changed and, if so, how, how additional classes of shares might be offered and the rights of the Founders Shares.

Shares of hedge funds are issued by the completion of the subscription documents and the payment of funds to the administrator. This procedure is not spelt out in the Articles, but the Articles provide the framework by which this process is accomplished. An important consideration in the issuance of shares is how to apportion the performance fee of the hedge fund to new investors. This is the reason why many hedge funds employ a device called "equalisation credits" and, because it is an issue that arises on subscription, this is discussed in Chapter 7.

It is the case that shares in hedge funds do not provide for pre-emption rights. Also not permitted are provisions that would options to be granted over shares.

It is the case that the Articles empower the Directors to increase or reduce the authorised share capital, divide the share capital into shares of smaller amounts or change the share capital into shares of larger amounts. Rights of share usually may not be varied save for a super-majority vote of shareholders of the class involved at a class meeting of those shares.

Operations

A significant portion of the Articles is given over to structural and operational matters, such as the procedure by which the AUM is calculated and the NAVs are struck.

AUM and NAV

The articles that comprise this portion of the Articles state what is involved in the AUM and NAV calculations, how they are done, by whom and how often. Chapter 9 of this book discusses the process of valuations that provides the framework for calculation the AUM and striking NAVs. The provisions of these Articles will, as noted in Chapter 5, appear in the Offering Materials.

These materials also set forth the mechanism when and why the two calculations would be suspended. The Articles of hedge funds differ but there are some factors that remain constant across all funds that apply to suspensions.

Generally, suspensions of striking the AUM and the NAVs per share would be done on a temporary basis and for a given period of time. This is usually 30 calendar days; this decision may be taken only by the directors, the trustee or the general partner – but they do take advice from the administrator and the investment manager.

Specific reasons must be given for a suspension. These must be set forth in the Articles. Generally, suspensions would be declared:

- when the main market for a significant portion of the portfolio assets is closed or trading is suspended or conditioned;
- in an emergency and when a redemption or sale of assets could be done but on terms that were significantly disadvantageous;
- when it is not possible to obtain prices for a material portion of the assets in the portfolio;
- when remittance of monies involved in the sale of or payment for portfolio assets cannot be carried out at normal exchange rates; and
- when proceeds of the sale or redemption of shares cannot be transmitted to or from the hedge fund's accounts.

There are limited provisions for the directors, trustee or general partner to declare a suspension.

It is important to note that these provisions do not work in isolation. When a suspension in calculating the AUM or striking NAVs is declared, there will also be a suspension in processing issuances, exchanges and redemptions of shares.

These Articles also provide for the giving of notice of a suspension and state that steps will be taken to address the factors leading to the suspension and resume normal operations. This is not what is referred to as a *force majeure* clause, but the effect is to avoid forcing incorrect AUMs and NAVs.

Compulsory redemptions and transfers

The Articles provide a means to protect the hedge fund and its investors – and directors and service providers – from having shares owned or held by persons whose holdings might cause problems. Usually, this would mean that shareholdings would subject the hedge fund to regulation in a jurisdiction that was not wanted, or jeopardise the fund's tax status. The usual situation is where having US persons holding shares might subject the hedge fund to US regulation.

The Offering Materials and subscription materials place an affirmative obligation on investors to notify the administrator of any change in status – this usually is stated in terms of requiring a notice when they cease to be an "eligible investor". In this case, the administrator will notify the directors, trustee or general partner, who will use powers contained in the Articles to redeem compulsorily the shares of the person involved. This would take place at the next dealing day following the valuation day. The investors involved would be notified of this and instructed to make arrangements to have the proceeds from the forced sale distributed to an account of its choosing.

Governance

The Articles set forth in detail how the directors are to manage the affairs of the hedge fund. (Similar provisions are contained in a unit trust or limited partnership agreement.)

These provisions state the number of directors, how meetings are to be called and held, minute and books requirements, procedures to replace directors or to appoint alternate directors and related matters. They also cross-reference other provisions in the Articles that relate to powers of the directors, including the ability to create additional classes or sub-classes of shares, to declare suspensions in operational matters (striking NAVs), seeking shareholder approval on matters and, if necessary, liquidating the hedge fund.

Shareholder rights

The Articles not only set forth the rights applicable to each class of shares, but give shareholders rights to require certain actions.

As regards rights, the provisions of the Articles that create share classes will set forth the rights applicable to each class. Related provisions will state how rights may be varied. Usually, this is done by way of amending the Articles, which requires shareholder consent. In certain, limited circumstances, rights may be varied, but only if they would not have a material adverse affect on the rights of existing shareholders. Related to this is the ability of the holder of Founders Shares to create sub-classes of shares or to alter rights if this would not have a material adverse affect on the rights of existing shareholders.

A key shareholder right is to receive notice of proposed changes to the Articles or the operation of the hedge fund, and to vote on same. Votes would be taken at an extraordinary general meeting (EGM).[4] The mechanism by which this is accomplished includes the following.

- The directors publish a notice of the proposed change, together with an explanation of the action, a discussion of the impact(s) on shareholders and the opportunity to attend the meeting at which time the proposal would be considered and acted upon.
- Proxy materials would accompany the notice.
- There would be a clear presentation of the proposed change to the Articles – usually this is done by giving the text of the current provision and the proposed new article, with redlining being used to illustrate the changed (or new) provisions.
- The materials must be provided at least a clear number of days prior to the EGM. This is usually at least seven calendar days (excluding the date of the posting of the notice and the date of the EGM).

- ❑ The procedure to conduct the EGM is stated in the Articles and must be followed.
- ❑ The results of the EGM would be communicated to all shareholders, changed Articles filed and new Articles published.

The directors, trustee or general partner may call an EGM. Also, this power is given to the shareholders, subject to a requirement that holders of a stated amount of the class of shares (usually 10% of the class) makes a request in a proper format to the directors to call such a meeting.

Increasingly, rather than engaging in hard-copy distribution of EGM materials, administrators are posting materials on a Web site or sending them out by e-mail. Also, shareholders may participate in such meetings by telephone or video conferencing, provided that they have submitted valid materials prior to the required cut-off date. This helps speeds up the process and permits more shareholders to participate in such meetings.

In terms of voting, most shareholders' votes are simply majority. The exceptions to this for items such as changes in class rights, amendments to the Article and other crucial matters is a supermajority of votes, usually 66% or even 75%.

Director indemnification, liability and insurance

Articles provide that the directors may be indemnified against those expenses, losses or liabilities that they incur in the proper exercise of their duties. The Articles state that the indemnification will come from the hedge fund – as permitted by local law. The indemnity is usually conditioned on the proper execution of duties, and states further that the director acted honestly and in good faith with a view to the best interests of the hedge fund. On occasion, it also requires that they had no reasonable cause to believe that their conduct was improper or unlawful.

Other provisions provide for limitations of liability.

Directors of hedge funds, like directors of industrial companies, seek to address their exposure through directors' and officers' insurance (D&O insurance). Policies for D&O insurance are underwritten by insurance companies in the same way as are policies for industrial companies. There are, however, some differences, owing to the nature of the hedge fund industry and the degree of regulatory and tax exposure involved. These differences manifest themselves in terms of enhanced disclosure required to obtain insurance, increased premiums for certain jurisdictions (eg, the United States for having US persons), the type of hedge fund involved (eg, long-short equity vs global derivative or credit, or event-driven or special situation) and slightly larger deductibles.

1 UK Investment Manager Exemption – Statement of Practice 1/01 revised 20 July 2007. URL: www.customs.hmrc.gov.uk/channelsPortalWebApp/channelsPortalWeb App.portal?_nfpb=true&_pageLabel=pageVAT_ShowContent&id=HMCE_PROD1_027709&propertyType=document.

2 There are two exemptions from 1940 Act registration for a non-US hedge fund. The s.3(c)(1) exemption lets a non-US fund sell its securities on a private placement basis in the US to not more than 100 US person investors. The s.3(c)(7) exemption permits a non-US fund to sell its shares in the US on a private placement basis, as long as every US investor is a "qualified purchaser" as defined in s.2(a)(51) of the 1940 Act. There is no limit in s.3(c)(7) on the number of qualified purchasers. However, a non-US hedge fund that has more than 500 investors (300 US residents) and US$10 million in assets within 120 days after the end of its most recent fiscal year must register with the SEC under s.12(g) of the Securities Exchange Act of 1934 (Exchange Act). The SEC's new foreign private issuer deregistration regime is not available for funds.

3 "US person" is defined in terms of what the investor is – individual, company, trust, partnership, foundation, endowment, etc. The definition is, today, largely one of territoriality or residence: for a trust, one would take the residence of the trustees; for a company, one would use the jurisdiction of incorporation. For individuals, there are two approaches: one uses residence, meaning that any individual (regardless of nationality) residing in the United States would be a US person; whereas the other uses this but adds in US citizens residing anywhere in the world. Caution must be taken, because there are several US laws that apply to the sale of hedge fund securities to US persons: obtaining an exemption from registration with the SEC for the hedge fund under the 1933 Act and the 1940 Act and for the investment manager under the Advisers Act. It is advisable to employ a single definition of US person for the purposes of all three Acts, to avoid confusion. As regards the 1940 Act exemptions, most non-US hedge funds use the s.3(c)(7) exemption, as this provides a greater degree of flexibility as opposed to the other exemption.

4 Increasingly, hedge funds do not hold, or are required to hold, annual general meetings.

4

Setting up the Hedge Fund

Hedge funds take their shape from the ideas of their promoters. Promoters include individuals who have previously managed hedge funds, worked at firms that managed long-only money and wish to gain experience managing long-short funds or were "captains of industry" who made career changes and desire to pursue their interests in alternative investments (AI). Promoters include institutions such as investment managers, investment firms and commercial banks – or even private equity firms.

Investment managers launch hedge funds in order to offer a range of products to their clients, increase share in existing markets or enter new markets. They also enter the arena through acquisitions. They start with an initial fund and, when they gain experience and establish a track record, launch other funds. In time, they might expand to operate managed accounts, FoHFs and other AI products.

Prime brokers may also promote hedge funds. Aside from this, they invest in hedge funds. They do this while engaging in a number of other activities (directly, through different parts of their organisations, or indirectly, via affiliates):

- financing – through margin lending or the use of derivatives, swaps or repos;
- stock lending;
- offering securities in primary and secondary offerings;
- buying, selling and structuring derivatives and structured products;
- trading;
- hedge fund M&A activity;
- syndicating loans and placing loans and/or loan participations;
- structuring SPVs, CDOs or CBOs;
- clearance and settlement of trades, effected in house or by executing brokers;
- capital introduction programmes;
- helping to secure seed capital – or even to provide it;
- start-up and consulting services – this may include office space;

- providing research, proprietary or third-party;
- record keeping;
- proprietary trading, not only in unaffiliated hedge funds but, in certain instances, its own hedge funds;
- trading derivatives as a counterparty;
- via the asset-management group, placing investors in hedge funds;
- where a hedge fund has more than one prime broker, providing consolidated reporting;
- custody or managing the relationship with sub-custodians, whether or not affiliated;
- using securities in the hedge fund's portfolio for onward hypothecation; and/or
- engaging in M&A activities, with, for or even against hedge funds.

Engaging in these activities simultaneously raises conflicts of interest. It would create regulatory issues, in particular, "soft dollar" arrangements. The issue here arises when prime brokers offer "hotel suites" and non-research and execution products to nascent hedge funds. Paying for this with "hard dollars" is permissible under applicable regulatory requirements of the US and other jurisdictions, but generally not with client money, called "soft dollars".

In order to address or avoid conflicts of interest and ensure compliance with relevant legal and regulatory requirements, prime brokers establish an arms-length relationship between themselves and the hedge funds with which they are involved, and employ information barriers (Chinese Walls) to help ensure the proper containment of information. These do not, as we will see later in this book, always ensure a complete separation, prevent conflicts or help avoid regulatory scrutiny. They may not provide comfort during periods of "market stress" such as the sub-prime/credit crisis, when hedge fund AUMs drop setting off additional termination events in ISDAs, or when investors, concerned over developments, give notice to redeem shares and are slowed or halted by the deployment of "gate" provisions, effectively locking them up. This can be exacerbated when collateral is devalued or becomes worthless. In such times, prime brokers (and, possibly, other investors) might be called on to invest in or otherwise inject capital into the hedge fund. An example of this was the investment of US$3 billion by Goldman Sachs and others into three funds, the Global Equity Opportunities Fund (GEO), the Global Alpha Fund (GAF) and the North American Equity Opportunities Fund (NAEO).[1] Investments or associations with hedge funds may require the prime broker to take difficult decisions regarding those funds, as was evident when Bear Stearns placed the Bear Stearns High-Grade Structured Credit Strategies Master Fund Ltd (BS High-Grade Structured Credit) and Bear Stearns High-Grade Structured Credit Strategies Enhanced Leverage Master Fund Ltd (BS

Enhanced High-Grade Structured Credit) in insolvency proceedings. The effects and implications of such actions are discussed in Chapter 10.

In this chapter, we discuss the process by which hedge funds go from drawing board to reality. We focus on the processes to select a strategy, identify the relevant markets and instruments and conduct requests for proposal (RFP) processes to select services. If sufficient seed capital is not available to launch and realise a break point by which the fund may begin trading, it is pointless to proceed with any steps that would incur expenses that could not be written off or amortised.

PLANNING THE HEDGE FUND

What follows is a generic timeline that shows how long each step in the formation of a hedge fund takes, and will be the basis of our discussions in this book.

Figure 4.1 Hedge fund timeline

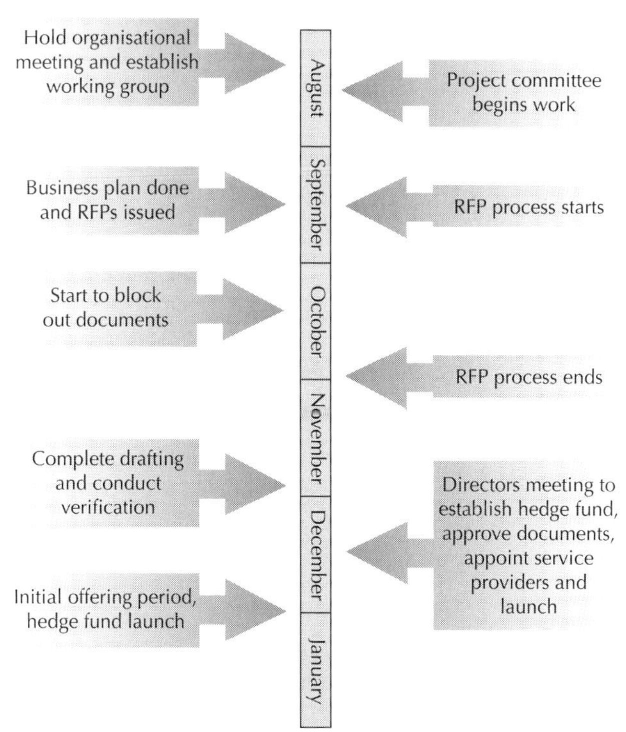

Key decisions

Hedge funds start with ideas. Their promoters go through an intensive product development process that helps them turn ideas into reality. The "key decisions" to be taken include the following:

- ❑ single entity hedge fund or master feeder structure;
- ❑ break point for launch – how much is needed to launch and be economically viable in the first year;
- ❑ whether the single entity hedge fund (or offshore feeder fund) would be listed;
- ❑ company, limited partnership or unit trust, and jurisdiction of incorporation;
- ❑ investment objective, policies and restrictions;
- ❑ parameters for capacity;
- ❑ strategy to be employed – aggressive growth, event driven, relative value, market neutral-hedging, multi strategy, special situations and so on;
- ❑ instruments to be traded and in what markets;
- ❑ types of securities and classes (and sub-classes) to be issued to investors;
- ❑ one or more prime brokers;
- ❑ policies and procedures for valuations, redemptions and NAV calculations;
- ❑ identifying where, and how, the hedge fund will be marketed;
- ❑ selecting an administrator;
- ❑ appointing the investment manager and, if applicable, an investment adviser;
- ❑ identifying and selecting other service providers; and
- ❑ sources of seed money and initial investments.

In order to be able to take these decisions, start the RFP process, select service providers and draft documents, the promoters will, as part of this process:

- ❑ examine market conditions;
- ❑ research the performance of hedge funds with strategies similar to that which they wish to adopt;
- ❑ review how prospective service providers have performed;
- ❑ review the profile of investors – institutional *vs* HNWIs and the countries where they are located – to determine whether it will be possible to market the fund to such persons, alone or through others (intermediaries, solicitors or distributors (distributors));
- ❑ meet with potential investors (prospects) to ascertain their relative degree of interest in the proposed hedge fund – but not in a manner so as to start the promotion of the hedge fund (see Chapter 7);
- ❑ meet with individuals that might be asked to serve as directors;
- ❑ identify markets for trading and securities to be bought and sold;

- review the track records of individuals to manage the portfolio (if such key individuals are not involved with promoting the hedge fund);
- query IT managers to determine whether the current systems are sufficiently robust to handle the proposed levels of activities;
- have compliance officers review the business plan (they must be involved in drafting it) to establish whether regulatory approvals must be obtained or licences and authorisations amended, and to advise on the appropriate levels of internal controls;
- consider how to market the hedge fund, and decide whether (and how) third-party distributors will be used; and
- survey executing brokers to determine whether they can effect transactions in the markets where the fund wishes to trade in a cost-effective manner while providing best execution.

It is helpful to seek advice from prospective service providers and experienced market professionals such as experts and consultants, but the extent of their involvement should be to give advice, not to make decisions. Only in extreme circumstances should this process be delegated.

The process of making decisions

The proper way to conduct the process is to appoint a committee comprising representatives from relevant departments or groups of the promoter to sit on a steering group and coordinate their activities. If this is not possible due to staffing limitations, all of those involved should sit on this committee. As regards its deliberations:

- everyone relevant to the fund and its operation – including management – must be involved, *and no one should read minutes and comment on developments;*
- one individual must take responsibility for all activities and decisions;
- a different individual should document the entire process;
- the business plan that is to form the basis of the committee's deliberations must be clear and identify specifics and measurable deliverables, dates and cost estimates;
- a process flow chart is used to note progress on each step involved – this does not end at launch but should continue through the first year of operation;
- costs must be identified and carefully controlled;
- risks must be clearly identified;
- for each risk, a control that is measurable is designed to address the risk;
- appropriate monitoring procedures are to be implemented to ensure that each control is working properly and that adequate and correct information is being generated to assess the effectiveness of the control;

- rules must be assigned; who performs what role and who makes decisions concerning fund operations – this is discussed in more detail in Chapter 8;
- most importantly, clear decisions are taken on issues that arise so that the documents that are required to launch the hedge fund may be properly drafted, reviewed and verified.[2] Catching mistakes after launch is costly and time-consuming and, in certain jurisdictions, might result in the need to offer rescission rights.

This is the time when the hedge fund takes shape. It is also the time when the foundations on which the hedge fund service provider relationships are formed. These relationships are defined not just by written agreements, but by market developments and forces and applicable legal and regulatory requirements – and how well individuals get along.

Each decision helps the promoters understand what type of service provider the hedge fund requires. For example, it may not be appropriate for a long-short European single entity fund that is managed in Europe and that wishes to use derivatives only for hedging to retain a prime broker that customarily services fixed income or global currency funds, or that is US based and SEC regulated. A global long-short fund will require a prime broker that can deliver cost-effective global custodial services and where clear apportionment of responsibility for unaffiliated third-party sub-custodians is spelt out. Making key decisions at this time, and getting them right, means getting the right service providers, attracting seed capital, launching on time, attracting further investors, achieving capacity, trading with efficiency and success, increasing the AUM, growing the NAV per share, minimising costs and operating wisely to avoid problems, such as large-scale redemptions.

It also means being able to attract funds. Investors are seeking not only a suitable return on their funds, but also stability. Increasingly, prospects are using preinvestment due diligence to enquire not just about investments, performance and strategies, but about systems and controls, compliance programmes, risk management and stress testing, the ability of the hedge fund administrator to price accurately instruments in the portfolio and strike accurate NAVs per share, free from estimates and undue influence. They want to know about gate provisions. They look, in the case of an investment manager that is running more than one hedge fund, whether it has the resources to be able to handle multiple funds – particularly as regards issues such as settlement, conflicts of interest resolution, allocation among long-short funds and long-only funds and other essential issues. They are looking at the type and quality of the collateral that is on deposit with the prime broker to ensure that, in times of market stress, the collateral will not be repriced downward or collapse, or cause the prime broker to slow or even halt lending.

All of these key decisions go into the business plan. It usually takes two to six weeks to complete the project committee stage and settle the business plan. (Some promoters bypass this and publish a business plan based on what they have used for a previous fund, revised to reflect the specifics of the proposed new fund. So, this period of time may be shorter.) It is at this point that the next stage begins.

IDENTIFYING SERVICE PROVIDERS – THE RFP PROCESS

The directors, trustee or general partner are responsible for the hedge fund and accountable to its investors – they select the service providers and oversee these relationships. (They may themselves be appointed during or at the end of the RFP process, often by an investment manager promoter.)

The prime broker is the source of securities and funds. The investment manager manages the portfolio. The administrator keeps track of activities, values the portfolio and calculates the AUM and the NAV per share for each outstanding class of shares. Executing brokers effect transactions for the hedge fund and "give up" these transactions to the prime broker. The custodian holds positions, tracks corporate actions and handles settlement. The agreements with service providers must be clear on what each is required to do. No service provider should become "first among equals". The directors, trustee or general partner must be able to exercise control and also oversight over each service provider, individually and as they relate to each other.

For the remainder of this book, and since the model of hedge fund that we will discuss is a corporate entity, we will use the term "Directors" to mean the directors of a corporate entity and, as applicable, the general partner of a limited partnership or the trustee of a unit trust.

The promoters conduct the RFP process to identify service providers for consideration and selection by the Directors. They may, if the hedge fund is not formed, negotiate documents and prepare materials for submission to the Directors for consideration and, when asked, give their views on the merits of each candidate service provider.

In many instances, the investment manager will be the promoter. Because of this, and due to the fact that the hedge fund may not yet have been established, it will fall to the investment manager to take forward the RFP process to identify the other key service providers.

It is wise not to finalise documents at this time, particularly the "material agreements".[3] The reason for this is that the offering materials must identify the service providers, state what each does and disclose the material terms of the agreements (see Chapter 5). No one can do this until the service providers are selected and the documents are agreed. There are, however, certain documents that can be prepared. These include the Memorandum and Articles, trust deed or limited partnership agreement. One may "block out" the subscription agreements and executing broker agreements, as well as the redemption and exchange forms. One may also start to draft sections of the Offering Materials such as: investment objective, policies and restrictions; subscriptions, redemptions and exchanges; calculating the AUM and the NAV per share; and other sections that are not dependent on the identification of a service provider or an agreement.

It usually takes four to seven weeks to conduct the RFP process and identify service providers for consideration by the Directors. This excludes drafting the RFP proposals that form the basis of the process (these are settled during the project committee process) and time to negotiate documents (this may take four to six weeks).

Pre-marketing may not take place until there is at least a red-herring prospectus to start soliciting prospects that has received appropriate approvals (by the Directors).

Promoters identify, but do not select, service providers. It is, however, critical that their views, as well as those of candidate service providers, be taken into account in the decision-taking process. The Directors may authorise a promoter or an investment manager to conduct an RFP process on their behalf, but service providers are formally appointed by the fund acting by its Directors. Ceding the decision-making authority not only sets a precedent by which the promoter or the investment manager "controls" the fund but may lay the groundwork for a tax authority, such HM Revenue & Customs (HMR&C), to take the position that the hedge fund is "onshore" (doing business in the jurisdiction where the investment manager is located) and to try to tax the hedge fund in that location.

Two key documents are used in the process to identify service providers, receive bids and narrow the field of candidates to two or three finalists from which to conduct negotiations and present service providers to the Directors for their consideration and selection. These are the confidentiality agreement and the RFP itself (the entire process is called the "RFP process"). It is through these that candidate service providers obtain the operating model for the hedge fund and submit their bids, bids are considered, due diligence takes place, agreements are drafted and negotiated and materials are prepared and submitted to the Directors for them to make their selections. Getting it right at this stage avoids delays, minimises costs and keeps everyone on schedule. This process may also be used to select additional service providers, including a second or third prime broker, and also replace service providers.

Confidentiality agreement

A confidentiality agreement is a document that by its terms permits two or more parties to share confidential information and maintain the confidentiality of such information. It is prudent not to release the RFP before the candidate service providers sign the confidentiality agreement. This ensures that prospective funds provide RFPs and related information to candidates without the fear of misuse or onward dissemination. It is, generally, the promoter that would sign the confidentiality agreement – unless the hedge fund is formed and the Directors are taking on this role themselves.

The person conducting the RFP process should ensure that every candidate seeking to reply to an RFP signs an identical confidentiality agreement. The confidentiality agreement should contain clear, enforceable terms. These include: a definition of what is confidential information; who states what is or is not confidential information; the names of those at the candidate (and also any affiliate) who may receive information and for what purpose; for how long the information remains confidential; the governing law and venue; narrow carve-outs for the public disclosure of information (eg, already in the public domain); when a candidate may be required or forced to provide information to third parties (by a regulator or by legal compulsion); and what remedy is available in case of a breach (usually, an injunction). A good confidentiality agreement must state what happens should the process end and the hedge fund not be launched or the candidate not be selected: the choices are to return or destroy the information and ensure that all others that received information do likewise. If for any reason confidential information is not returned or destroyed, it must remain confidential for not less than two calendar years. In all cases there must be clear prohibitions preventing any use of confidential information for any use other than that as stated in the confidentiality agreement. If a candidate wins the mandate, then, and to the extent that the provisions of the service agreement and the confidentiality agreement are inconsistent, the confidentiality agreement should remain in force during the life of the relationship – and beyond.

REQUESTS FOR PROPOSAL

The RFP is the single document used to state the hedge fund's requirements. It establishes the framework on which service providers bid for, negotiate documents and win the mandate.

A strong RFP, a complete response by the prospective service provider and meaningful due diligence help to ensure that all relevant, material issues are identified, discussed and resolved, requirements and functionality are clearly stated (and discrepancies addressed), documents are properly negotiated and correctly drafted and the relationship begins on the basis of trust and matched expectations – in the case of the prime broker-hedge fund, this should be a level playing field and not a debtor-creditor relationship. A weak RFP or no RFP may lead to wrong or conflicting expectations, misunderstandings and an unlevel playing field. It would hurt the hedge fund's ability to trade or engage in certain activities or even lead it to change service providers.

The RFP process should be driven by a number of factors, including the following.

- Identification, due diligence and shortlisting for selection, and selection itself, should be made on the basis of what the service provider can and cannot provide – and what it will cost. For prime brokers, seed capital should not be "the" determinative factor.
- The Directors have the final say. The promoter will be asked for its invaluable input on the options available (as will candidate service providers, on how they work with other service providers and their experience), but, for corporate governance purposes and to avoid adverse tax consequences, the final and formal decision rests with those responsible for the hedge fund and accountable to the investors – the Directors.
- The information in the RFP must be concise and cover all key points. Not to do this wastes time and invites delays. It would result in a bid for the mandate being inaccurate and possibly lead to a wrong choice or a decision to be taken on a factor that, when clarified, might lead to the need to amend documents including the Offering Materials, to obtain shareholder consent to effect changes or change a service provider.
- A meaningful RFP process involves due diligence reviews and competitive negotiations. The RFP process must involve interviews with candidates and hedge fund personnel, at which time queries may be answered or points clarified. The process should then move to due diligence taking place at the service provider's offices and with members other than the "selling group". This would include credit, legal and compliance, documentation, trading, "cap intro" staff and senior management. The process would conclude in a final stage in which at least two finalists engage in negotiations to agree terms of agreement. The results feed into or become part of the decision-making process.

It is prudent not to select a single finalist from among several candidates and then negotiate the agreement. Competitive negotiations prior to selection offer several advantages.

SELECTING THE PRIME BROKER

Because the PBA is the most time-consuming and difficult service provider agreement to negotiate and forms the basis for many key disclosures in the Offering Materials, the process of selecting a prime broker should begin as close as possible to the time when the decision to launch the hedge fund is taken, but in any event not later than the date that the project committee finalises the business plan. If a prime broker is appointed without an RFP process, it may not be possible to negotiate the PBA. If it occurs later, the process is bound to become complicated by having to consider fundamental issues close to the launch, renegotiate key points or amend documents – all of which take time and cost money. In either case, it might result in having to take a PBA on unacceptable or non-negotiated terms and with a promise to reconsider points later, which may never transpire.

No prime broker should be selected without an RFP process. A competitive negotiation results in a well negotiated PBA. There is no generally agreed template for an RFP, but, generally, it involves an evaluation of the following features of the prime broker:

- type of legal entity, information on the group of companies, incorporation, experience as a prime broker and general information, including regulatory history;
- summary of current hedge fund clients by location, type of structure and type of strategy – subject to confidentiality;
- transactions supported and not supported;
- lending and margining capabilities, and limitations;
- insurance coverage;
- clearing and custodial abilities – in-house, by affiliates or non-affiliates (if the latter, the prime broker should provide a sample copy of an agreement it would have in place with a non-affiliate and state whether and to what extent it takes responsibility for the actions of sub-custodians);
- corporate actions capacity;
- credit policies and requirements for ancillary documents such as ISDAs and CSAs;
- capital introduction policies, capabilities and experience – through mailings or events;
- risk management, trade and transaction reporting and controls policies and procedures;
- administrators with whom the prime broker works and has not yet worked;
- current arrangements with proposed executing brokers and administrators;
- whether affiliates will be used to trade, clear or hold derivatives and, if so, in what countries and subject to what regulations – this is important when it is time to negotiate the PBA to ensure that if affiliates are involved each is fully liable for its actions;
- business continuity requirements;
- client-support teams and abilities;
- fees, costs and charges;
- the circumstances under which it would provide seed capital and withdraw it;
- whether it has been terminated as a prime broker by other hedge funds;
- how it functions as one of two, or even three, prime brokers – this is critical when considering an "Amaranth" situation as discussed in Chapter 10;

- positions on key legal issues; and
- countries of operation and support – broken down by use of affiliates and non-affiliates.

The key issues that the prime broker needs to address in its response and as a preface to selection and negotiating the PBA include the following.

- What local country restrictions apply to the instruments the hedge fund proposes to trade? Are there restrictions on short selling, borrowing to purchase investments and securities lending and borrowing? Are certain securities hard to borrow or do they require special considerations?
- Will the prime broker also be the custodian? If not, will it use affiliated or non-affiliated custodians? How does it select unaffiliated third-party custodians or sub-custodians and to what extent does it monitor and accept responsibility for them?
- How will custodians hold securities? What are the local country risks for netting, default, insolvency and/or bankruptcy?
- What type of security interest would the prime broker wish to take over the hedge fund's assets? In what country? Would the security interest be registered? How would it be enforced? Would the charge cover only the assets the prime broker actually held, or purport to be broader? Is it a factor if the assets are held in several countries and not one of these is the jurisdiction of incorporation of the hedge fund?
- How will the prime broker calculate margin? How would margin calls be made and how much time would the fund be given to satisfy calls? How much of a "cushion" would the prime broker wish to have over and above the point at which it held a charge over the hedge fund's assets? Are there limitations on the prime broker's ability to hypothecate the fund's assets?
- Is client money protection afforded? What is the local regulatory treatment of cash? Are cash management programmes available or may the hedge fund/investment manager sweep cash out of the prime broker's account for investment elsewhere without penalty?
- Does the prime broker wish to have broad events of default and broadly drawn definitions of key terms, including acts of insolvency?
- How narrow are the execution powers to be drawn? At what point could the prime broker turn a failure to pay into an event of default and effectively close the fund?
- If there were to be an ISDA, would the prime broker require a CSA or a Master Netting Agreement? If so, what positions would the prime broker require in the way of cross default, aggregation and so on?
- Would the prime broker seek wide additional events of termination in the ISDA including AUM decline triggers or other events, credit driven or not, that would favour the prime broker?

- To what extent, if any, would the prime broker use affiliates? If this were to be the case, would the prime broker be responsible for their actions?
- How broadly would the indemnity, cross indemnity, disclaimer and liability clauses be drawn? What would be the triggers or carve-outs in or for such clauses?
- Does the prime broker agree to criteria to measure its performance? Quarterly reviews?
- How would this prime broker wish to operate *vis-à-vis* a second prime broker?
- What provisions would govern termination by one or the other party?

SELECTING THE ADMINISTRATOR

The administrator is responsible, under the supervision of the Directors and pursuant to the terms of the Administration Agreement (AA), for the administration of the hedge fund (or the master fund and the feeder funds). This includes several tasks:

- maintaining the corporate, financial and accounting books and records;
- calculating the AUM of the hedge fund (and each feeder fund) and striking the NAVs per share;
- if required, monitoring portfolio activity against the investment objective, policies and restrictions, including its strategy, and non-investment restrictions such as details of investors (US person, benefit plan investor and so on) and other matters (including, for example, German investment tax issues) agreed with the Directors;
- securing accurate price feeds and information for all positions; valuing instruments in the portfolio (and resolved issues or disputes with the prime broker and, if necessary, the Directors);
- preparing monthly financial statements and assisting the auditors in the annual audit;
- preparing, if requested and with the auditors, information for a QEF election for a US taxpaying investor;
- managing the bank accounts;
- receiving invoices and paying bills;
- gathering information, in the first instance, to address complaints and disputes – under the supervision of the Directors;
- if required, handling (or helping another service provider) with risk management and stress testing;
- reconciling trading activity on a daily basis, with the investment manager and the prime broker (and executing brokers);
- handling tax reporting and tax calculation (with the auditor);
- handling the registrar and transfer agent services for the issuance, transfer and redemption of shares;
- keeping records – to the standards required by the hedge fund;

- ❑ conducting, if required, AML checks on prospects and investors;
- ❑ calculating fees, including the management fee and the performance fee;
- ❑ performing other administrative/clerical services necessary for administration of the hedge fund;
- ❑ processing materials for Directors' insurance;
- ❑ reporting issues without delay to the Directors or their duly authorised agent; and
- ❑ doing such other tasks as required by the Directors.

The administrator does not, and should not, engage in certain other activities:

- ❑ make investment decisions or give investment advice with respect to the hedge fund's assets;
- ❑ take instructions from a distributor or the investment manager to admit or redeem investors, as only instructions from the Directors should be acted upon;
- ❑ bring the investment manager or the prime broker into the valuation process beyond what is provided for in the offering materials.

The RFP process to identify administrators should start at the same time as that for the prime broker. It may not take as long. It may not be as difficult to negotiate an AA as it is to put the PBA in place. However, the tasks that must be performed by the administrator, in many ways, are more complex than those of the prime broker; hence, this process is just as important.

The processes should not be run independent of each other. As early as possible, those conducting the due diligence exercises should "combine their efforts" to ensure several points, such as whether the administrator and prime broker have worked together and, if so, what issues have they experienced. They will also wish to confirm whether the systems of these service providers are compatible – if not, an expensive fix may be required.

The RFP process will throw up issues that require meetings between prospective service provider candidates. Such meetings should be held as early as possible to address and resolve those issues. It does no good if a candidate administrator confirms in an RFP process that it has software to handle aspects of risk management only to find that the program cannot handle certain types of derivative instruments.

What must the promoter (and others) look for in an administrator?

- ❑ Is it regulated and, if so, by whom?
- ❑ What is its regulatory track record?
- ❑ If it is a branch or subsidiary, what is the track record of its owner?
- ❑ What is the corporate and organisational structure of the candidate? Is it in good standing?

- ❑ How long has it been an administrator?
- ❑ What types of hedge funds does it serve?
- ❑ Can it handle front-office,[4] middle-office[5] and/or back-office[6] functionality?
- ❑ Does it provide services in-house or outsource activities to affiliates or third parties (and, if so, on what terms)?
- ❑ Has it handled hedge funds such as that contemplated by the promoters?
- ❑ Has it reviewed the timetable and does it agree to what is being proposed?
- ❑ Does it understand the terms of the RFP and the business plan?
- ❑ Has it agreed that all discussions, negotiations and due diligence will move forward based on the response given and that, if something goes wrong or the administrator does not deliver what it says it will, negotiations will end or if the fund is launched, it will be replaced?
- ❑ Does it agree that expenses incurred in the RFP process and negotiations, if it is successful, are its own and not those of the promoter or the hedge fund?
- ❑ What is the candidate's current "stable" of and experience with hedge funds and FoHFs by number and AUM?
- ❑ Has it been replaced as an administrator by any hedge fund or FoHF? If so, why?
- ❑ What information has it supplied about the staff that would handle the hedge fund: are they qualified, what is the rate of turnover, and so on?
- ❑ Who will be the relationship manager for the hedge fund and will that person be involved with all aspects from RFP through the first year of operations?
- ❑ What is the approach for ensuring the effective delivery of services in line with AA and a service level agreement, and how does the administrator monitor operations?
- ❑ How will the hedge fund be charged – what are the components of the fee?
- ❑ Does the accounting unit have its own integrity checks?
- ❑ How and where are records retained and are they made available on short notice and without additional cost?
- ❑ Does the administrator understand how the hedge fund will handle equalisation (if applicable), and can it handle the calculations?
- ❑ How does the administrator identify, track and escalate matters that it cannot resolve?
- ❑ What are the systems and procedures for monitoring the investment objective, policy and restrictions, escalating failed trades and any other matter?
- ❑ Can, and are, reporting obligations and filings timely made?
- ❑ What does the administrator do internally to handle its own compliance, and compliance for its clients?

- ❑ How does the administrator handle business continuity planning (BCP)?
- ❑ Has the candidate provided copies of all of its regulatory filings and audited financial statements? Is a Frag 21 or SAS 70 report produced and, if so, what does an examination of it/them reveal?
- ❑ Are the systems robust and capable of interface with the other service providers?
- ❑ Are there any conflicts of interest in taking on this hedge fund?
- ❑ Has the administrator reviewed the hedge fund's legal requirements for the AA and does it agree them?
- ❑ Can the administrator handle reconciliations as required by the hedge fund and in a manner that is consistent across service providers?
- ❑ What controls systems are in place and how recently have they been audited?
- ❑ Are there outstanding or unresolved internal audit queries or reports?
- ❑ Which document will form the basis for discussions – the candidate's own AA or that of the hedge fund? What consents or approvals are required?
- ❑ Does the administrator understand the investment objective, policies and restrictions? Has it supported funds with these or similar requirements? Are there trading strategies or instruments that it cannot support?
- ❑ Has the candidate seen the outgoing RFP proposal for prime-broker candidates (and, if there is one, that for the investment manager) and is there anything that it cannot support?
- ❑ Can the administrator provide the required type of risk modelling, risk methodology, risk management, stress testing and reporting?
- ❑ Can the administrator handle the securities and markets required by the hedge fund – for trading and hedging? How does the administrator handle stock borrowing, alone and in coordination with the prime broker?
- ❑ Can the administrator support the treasury function?
- ❑ How are corporate actions managed and handled?
- ❑ What pricing feeds are used for individual instruments for liquid markets? How does the administrator gain pricing information for illiquid instruments?
- ❑ How does the administrator handle valuations and what is its track record concerning late valuations and reporting?
- ❑ What is the track record for handling NAV calculations? When and how are estimates used? What is the track record for NAV calculation errors?

Every candidate should confirm in writing that it understands the legal requirements of the hedge fund as regards the AA. Every AA should strive to ensure that it covers the following:

- a single agreement contain all required legal provisions and disclosures in the body of the agreement with one or more schedules that set out the services actually required, in detail, and with a clear fee arrangement;
- clear and enforceable confidentiality provisions;
- reasonable liability and indemnity provisions;
- confirmation that the administrator's employees are competent and will perform their obligations with skill, care and competence;
- provisions that require the administrator to comply with the reasonable instructions of the Directors – and, if required, those of duly authorised agents of the Directors;
- procedures to meet regularly with and review the performance of the administrator;
- an enforceable service level agreements (SLA); and
- if the administrator proposes to outsource any activity, enforceable contractual provisions that hold the administrator responsible for any actions of the third party.

THE INVESTMENT MANAGER

It is the case for many hedge funds that the promoter is the investment manager. As such, there will not be an RFP process to select the service provider that will manage the hedge fund's portfolio. Nevertheless, we will review the process by which a non-investment manager promoter would seek to fill this role.

The investment manager manages the hedge fund's portfolio of assets. The investment manager conducts research, places orders to buy and sell securities for investments and hedging transactions, meets with the Directors at their meetings to provide a review of portfolio activities, interfaces with the distributor to handle due diligence queries from prospects, puts together monthly reports and other materials for investors and generally exercises control over all aspects of the hedge funds investments.

The investment manager signs the investment management agreement (IMA) with the hedge fund and, in a master feeder structure, with the master fund. Also in a master feeder structure, the investment manager may sign a feeder fund agreement with the offshore feeder fund and the master fund for the investment of the assets of the feeder fund into the master fund, but not an onshore feeder fund.

If one were to conduct an RFP process for an investment manager, the queries that one would raise would include the following.

- By whom is the investment manager regulated?
- What is its regulatory track record?
- If it is a branch or subsidiary, who is its owner and what is the track record of its owner?

- ❑ What is the corporate and organisational structure of the candidate? Is it in good standing?
- ❑ How long has it been an investment manager?
- ❑ What types of mandates does it have? Are these long only or both long and long-short? What is its client base, by type of client and location?
- ❑ What is its track record in managing hedge funds and FoHFs?
- ❑ How does it handle front-office and middle-office functionality?
- ❑ Does it rely on third parties or affiliates for any critical path activities? If so, the entities should be identified and the services described?
- ❑ Does the investment manager generate research internally or does it receive materials from third parties? Does it pay for these with hard dollars or soft dollars?
- ❑ If the desk or persons on the desk where the hedge fund is to be managed also advise long-only funds, what procedures are in place to avoid conflicts of interest? How are issues escalated when they arise?
- ❑ Has it reviewed the timetable and does it agree to what is being proposed?
- ❑ Does it understand the terms of the RFP itself – that it sets out the business plan and the requirements of the hedge fund and that all discussions, negotiations and due diligence will move forward based on the response, and that, if something goes wrong or it does not deliver what it says it will, that may be grounds to end negotiations or, if the fund is launched, replace the service provided?
- ❑ Does it realise that any expenses incurred are its own and not those of the promoter or the hedge fund?
- ❑ Has the investment manager been replaced or has a fund that it has managed experienced any issues – such as declining AUM, unusual redemptions and so on?
- ❑ What information has it supplied about the staff who would handle the hedge fund: are they qualified, what is the rate of turnover, and so on?
- ❑ What is the approach for ensuring the effective delivery of services in line with IMA and how does the candidate monitor its front- and middle-office activities?
- ❑ How will the hedge fund be charged – what are the components of the fee?
- ❑ Does the candidate have its own integrity checks (internal audit, compliance, monitoring and so on)?
- ❑ How and where are records retained and are they made available on short notice and without additional cost?
- ❑ How does the candidate identify, track and escalate matters that it cannot resolve?
- ❑ What are the systems and procedures for cooperating with the administrator (and the prime broker) to monitor the investment objective, policy and restrictions, escalate failed trades and any other matter?

- ❑ Can and are reporting obligations and filings timely made?
- ❑ What does the candidate do internally to handle its own compliance, and compliance for its clients?
- ❑ How does the candidate handle business continuity planning (BCP)?
- ❑ Has the candidate provided copies of its regulatory filings and audited financial statements? Is a Frag 21 or SAS 70 report produced and, if so, what does an examination of it/them reveal?
- ❑ Are the systems robust and capable of interface with the other service providers?
- ❑ Are there any conflicts of interest in taking on this hedge fund?
- ❑ Has the candidate reviewed the hedge fund's legal requirements for the IMA and does it agree them?
- ❑ Can it help with reconciliations as required by the hedge fund and in a manner that is consistent across service providers?
- ❑ What controls systems are in place and how recently have they been audited?
- ❑ Are there outstanding or unresolved internal audit queries or reports?
- ❑ Which document will form the basis for discussions – the candidate's own IMA or that of the hedge fund? What consents or approvals are required?
- ❑ Has this candidate supported hedge funds with these or similar requirements? Are there trading strategies or instruments that it cannot support?
- ❑ Has this candidate prepared any "paper portfolio" models that represent how it proposes to manage the portfolio? If so, what are the underlying assumptions and factors? Has this been given to third parties or prospects?
- ❑ Has the candidate seen the outgoing RFP proposal for the other service-provider candidates and are there any queries on this?
- ❑ Can the investment manager provide the required type of risk modelling, risk methodology, risk management, stress testing and reporting?
- ❑ Could the investment manager handle stock borrowing apart from the prime broker?
- ❑ How does the investment manager handle the treasury function?
- ❑ How are corporate actions managed and handled?
- ❑ What pricing feeds are used for individual instruments for liquid markets? How does the investment manager gain pricing information for illiquid instruments?
- ❑ Is the investment manager willing not to be involved in valuation issues?
- ❑ What is the track record for reviewing AUM and NAV per share calculations?

THE SELECTION PROCESS

The results of the RFP processes to review the candidate service providers and select one for each role must be documented and provided to the Directors for their consideration at a quorate meeting of the Board of Directors. These should be accompanied by the Offering Materials, the Memorandum, the Articles, the material agreements and, if required, ISDAs and CSAs with other counterparties. At this meeting, the Directors would query the proposal and address issues to ensure that their decision to appoint a prime broker is documented, well reasoned and appropriate to the needs of the fund.

The decision to select a service provider should be set forth in a resolution of the Directors. (The decision should not, unless severe exigencies are involved, be taken by one Director under a power of attorney given to him or her by the other Directors. If this is required, the Directors must receive all documents to review when they receive the power to consider and sign, and any comments they raise must be documented and, if necessary, taken into account.) That resolution should:

- ❑ refer to the documents provided to the Directors for their consideration;
- ❑ ensure that the disclosures in each document is correct, and that all documents are consistent;
- ❑ include a summary of the RFP process;
- ❑ contain a summary of the key points contained in the documents, highlighting any risks that the Directors should be aware of when making their decision – points not negotiated away, unusual provisions or costs, qualified obligations, and so on;
- ❑ state the key issues considered in the selection process;
- ❑ identify the risks (if any) involved with using this service provider;
- ❑ approve the fee schedule for at least a 12-month period and the basis on which fees would be renegotiated – up or down;
- ❑ give clear approvals – this entails approving specific documents (or, if needed, authorising a Director or an approved agent to complete negotiations on a specific document), naming authorised signatories, providing timelines within which to complete steps prior to launch, approving the opening of accounts with the prime broker and addressing required issues;
- ❑ approve disclosures about the service and the agreement in the Offering Materials; and
- ❑ authorise one Director or a duly appointed agent to give such instructions, sign such documents and take such steps as are required to address issues between the date of this meeting and the next Directors' meeting.

1 "Goldman Sachs and Various Investors Including C.V. Starr & Co, Inc, Perry Capital LLC and Eli Broad Invest $3 Billion in Global Equity Opportunities Fund", 13 August 2007, press release, URL: www2.goldmansachs.com/our_firm/media_center/articles/current_press_releases_article_070810173913.html.

2 A list of documents required to launch a hedge fund, single entity or master feeder structure, and drawn from a review of existing hedge funds, is provided in the Appendix.

3 The "material agreements" are the Prime Brokerage Agreement, the Administration Agreement, the Investment Management Agreement and the ISDA with the prime broker. Some include the executing broker agreements.

4 Trade capture, risk modelling, stress testing and reporting.

5 Trade confirmation, clearing, matching and settlement, and the "DK" process (late trades and failed trades) and also corporate actions (proxy material, dividends and so on).

6 Administration, accounting, tax calculating and reporting, registrar, transfer agent and other required services.

5

Hedge Funds and Service Providers

Hedge funds do not have officers or employees. They operate through the service providers that are retained by the Directors, which are the governing body of the fund and are fiduciaries.

The key service providers to hedge funds are the administrator, investment manager and prime broker(s) custodian. Other service providers are the executing brokers, distributor, listing sponsor (if the fund or the offshore feeder fund is listed), legal counsel, company secretary, the MLRO, auditors, trading counterparties, hardware and software providers, risk managers, non-prime broker custodians and transfer agents. (In a manner that would not raise taxation or corporate governance issues, the company secretarial and MLRO role may be performed by the administrator or by an independent service provider.) Third parties that are involved include prospects, investors, regulators, any exchange where the hedge fund is listed, tax and governmental authorities and others. All operate under the oversight of the Directors.

This chapter explores the relationships between hedge funds and their service providers. It reiterates the roles that service providers perform, summarises key points that are found in their agreements with hedge funds and identifies issues that may arise in the relationship that might affect the ability of hedge funds to operate and make money.

THE INVESTMENT MANAGER

The investment manager[1] contracts directly with the fund and/or the master fund in a master feeder structure. It may, subject to safeguards, contract with the offshore feeder fund in a master feeder structure. A non-US investment manager would not contract with an onshore feeder fund, in order to avoid the jurisdictional reach of SEC regulation.

The investment manager manages the portfolio on a fully discretionary basis in compliance with the IMA between it and the hedge fund/master fund, its own regulatory requirements, relevant provisions in the Offering Materials and exchange requirements, if the hedge fund is listed. This includes managing the portfolio, placing orders with executing brokers to effect transactions, liaising with investors when queries arise about aspects of the portfolio (subject to authorisation by the Directors), attending Directors meetings and answering queries and performing other duties as set forth in the IMA.

Non-US investment managers do not price individual positions or portfolios (they may, however, provide information to the administrator to help it perform this function), do not select, add or replace service providers (but may provide advice on this), do not take decisions or make recommendations to the Directors (in order to avoid having the hedge fund be taxed in the jurisdiction where the investment manager is located, eg, the UK), do not accept or reject investors and do not exercise oversight over the other service providers (this is a role that is to be performed by the Directors or their authorised agents). In the US model, the general partner in carrying out its duties as administrator would, subject to safeguards, perform one or more of these roles.

Key provisions of an IMA

Contents of an IMA

The IMA will reflect not only the agreement between the investment manager and the Directors, but also relevant regulatory requirements that are imposed on the investment manager if it is regulated.

IMAs may be as short as four pages or as long as 20 or more. In many ways, this is a function of whether or not the investment manager is regulated. If so, there will be certain requirements that must be included in the IMA (discussed below) or disclosures that must be made. It is also a function of the risk profile of the investment manager. In this case, the IMA would include provisions that may not necessarily relate to the management of the hedge fund's portfolio, but how this is accomplished and what requirements are necessary to deal with issues such as best execution, conflicts of interest, allocation, aggregation and so on.

The remainder of this subsection identifies and discusses key IMA provisions. This discussion does not include certain "boilerplate clauses".[2]

Definitions: key terms will be defined. Several of these will also be found in the Articles and the Offering Materials to help ensure consistency, and there will be other key terms that are used within the IMA and referenced in other material agreements.

- Terms that would appear in both the IMA and the Offering Materials include the names of the legal entities involved (including relevant service providers), references to the operative legal documents, applicable laws and regulations, the fees to be received (and key terms related to these). Other terms will relate more to the investment manager and the IMA rather than the Offering Materials, and reflect the governing law of the investment manager and market custom and practice in that jurisdiction. These include terms such as "securities" in the US and "investments" in the UK and other jurisdictions.

There are two definitions that appear in the Offering Materials, the Articles and the IMA that are of particular importance for calculating and striking the AUM and the NAVs per share, and the fees payable to the investment manager.

- "Valuation Day" is defined as the business day on which the AUM is calculated and the NAVs per share are struck. It is the last business day of each month (or the quarter, if the hedge fund operates on a quarterly cycle), unless the Directors in the exercise of their discretion and in accordance with the Articles and the Offering Materials declare a Valuation day for other purposes.
- The business day after this is called the "Dealing Day". This is the date when subscriptions, redemptions and exchanges are processed (the NAVs per share having been struck the previous day).

Another key definition, "calculation period", is the period of time on which the investment manager's performance is based.

The mandate: the operative provision in the IMA is the clause by which the hedge fund retains the investment manager to manage the assets (securities and cash) in the portfolio. For the purposes of this book, we use the term "assets" to mean the securities and cash that are held in the portfolio of the hedge fund. "Securities" means the investments that the hedge fund buys and sells, including equity and debt securities, warrants, options, futures, indexes, repos, swaps, ETFs and derivatives and other instruments (such as loans, loan participations, CFDs, CBOs and so on). The "portfolio" is held by the prime broker in its role as custodian to the hedge fund or, through the prime broker and under the PBA, third-party custodians, whether or not affiliated with the prime broker. This is not to say that the prime broker will hold all of the hedge fund's property. The administrator will hold funds in a bank account with which to pay bills and handle redemptions. Entities with which the hedge fund trades certain derivative instruments under an ISDA may hold positions.

Duties: having been retained to manage the assets in the portfolio, the investment manager must perform certain duties. These include:

- observing and complying with applicable legal and regulatory requirements;
- managing the assets in accordance with the investment objective, policies and restrictions, and in the best interests of the hedge fund;
- reporting promptly to the Directors any issues that arise that may have an impact on the hedge fund and its assets;

- ❑ liaising with the other service providers on issues such as the matching, clearance and settlement of trades, DK'd trades, dividend and interest capture and related matters;
- ❑ engaging in research with respect to the securities that are to be bought, held or sold;
- ❑ reviewing the status of assets against market conditions;
- ❑ selecting executing brokers in order to place orders to achieve best execution;
- ❑ identifying and avoiding conflicts of interest;
- ❑ maintaining confidentiality; and
- ❑ handling such other matters as are required to discharge its obligations under the IMA.

Managing the assets of the hedge fund includes many activities. It means buying and selling securities (long and short), analysing portfolio returns, keeping books and records, engaging in risk management, using margin, borrowing securities when and as required, hedging assets in the portfolio, reviewing strategies, weighting and allocations to ensure that proper investment decisions are being made, complying with applicable regulatory obligations, preparing monthly updates for investors, subscribing for securities in IPOs and rights issues, making decisions (if authorised to do so, which usually will be the case) with respect to proxies and corporate actions, giving instructions to clear, match and settle trades and borrows, voting proxies, tendering into exchange offers and making the best possible use of available cash. In short, the investment manager must exercise its discretion to ensure that the hedge fund makes money and avoids issues, but make sure that its investors are, to the fullest extent possible, kept fully informed about the hedge fund and all developments and represent its interests.

Delegation: investment managers generally do not delegate their responsibilities. However, in certain instances, this may be done, subject to safeguards. An example of this is the Asian (Hong Kong) model to work round tax or local regulatory issues or to gain expertise in certain markets. IMAs generally include a delegation clause. In these, the investment manager may delegate certain of its duties or functions, but remains liable for the acts or omissions of the person to whom it delegates any duty or function.

Apart from this, but related to it, is the ability to appoint agents. Agents are service providers to the investment manager. Agents might be retained to perform a variety of tasks, including risk management, portfolio analysis, the management of certain corporate activities (other than those carried out by the administrator) and other matters.

Specific legal/regulatory requirements: the laws and regulations of jurisdictions round the world vary in how they regulate investment managers – and, in some cases, whether investment managers need to be regulated to advise hedge funds. In certain countries, IMAs must include specific disclosures such as risk warnings concerning instruments. In other countries, IMAs must contain specific legal provisions, such as the right of the client of the investment manager to terminate the agreement at will or to notify the client of any issues that might result in the investment manager not being able to fulfil its obligations under the agreement.

Fees

While many of the clauses in an IMA are crucial to the management of the assets, the provisions about what fees the investment manager receives and how these are calculated and paid assume a special importance.

Hedge fund investment managers receive two fees: a management fee and a performance (incentive) fee.

Management fee: The management fee is a percentage of the hedge fund's AUM, excluding any accrued performance fee. Typically, this fee is one-twelfth (1/12) of a given figure, which may range from 1% to 2% of the AUM. It is calculated and paid monthly. The administrator will calculate this fee after it calculates the fund's AUM and strikes the NAV per share of any outstanding classes of shares.

Performance fee: The investment manager receives a performance fee as its incentive to achieve absolute return.

The performance fee is paid based on performance. It accrues on each Valuation Day, but is paid at the end of each calculation period (usually, a calendar year). It is, however, calculated not on the AUM, but on a per-share basis, a method of fairness so that shares are charged and pay this fee based on the actual performance of the shares in question, over the calculation period.

The following are the steps in how a performance fee would be calculated (there are many variations of this).

- The performance fee will be defined in the Articles and Offering Materials – for our hedge fund, it will be 20% of the appreciation in the NAV per share in the calculation period above the "base NAV per share" for each class of shares. The base NAV per share of each class of shares is the greater of the price at which shares of a class were initially sold and the highest NAV per share reached in the previous calculation period.
- On each Valuation Day, the administrator calculates the AUM and strikes a NAV per share for each class of shares. It then calculates and

accrues the performance fee (not deducting any accrued performance fees), based on the above.

- At the end of the calculation period, the administrator calculates the base NAV per share for that calculation period.
- The administrator then collects the accrued performance fees and pays these to the investment manager.

As can be seen, a performance fee rewards the investment manager. By the same token, a decline in performance would result in the investment manager receiving a small performance fee, or no fee at all. It is in the interests of the investment manager not only to return a strong performance for its fee, but also to provide absolute return to its investors. Weak performance translates into a diminishing asset pool with which to trade. The lower the return, the less the investment manager receives and the more likely it is that investors may redeem their shares, in part or in whole.

THE ADMINISTRATOR

The administrator values positions, handles subscriptions, redemptions and exchanges, performs due diligence and AML checks on prospects (and on investors), calculates the AUM and the NAV per share, corresponds with investors, manages aspects of the annual audit and provides monitoring services. It signs the AA with the hedge fund or the feeder funds and the master fund in a master feeder structure.

Key provisions of an AA

Like the PBA (discussed below) and the IMA, the AA contains sections that define terms, establish the relationship between (or among) the parties, provide for boilerplate legal requirements and set forth the duties and responsibilities of the administrator.

Definitions

The definitions that are used in the AA are those set forth in the Offering Materials and the Articles. There would be other definitions such as the services that the administrator would provide (in the AA, called Services), information from third parties provided by the hedge fund (third-party fund information) and data the administrator receives from its sources (administrator third-party data). These distinctions are important, not only to clarify the source of information and the duties owed, and to help clarify who pays for the data, but to help apportion liability should it transpire that information provided by any third party to the administrator is proven to be inaccurate.

Duties

Two sets of duties are provided for in the AA: those of the administrator; and those of the hedge fund (in a master feeder structure, this would be the offshore feeder fund, the master fund and the onshore feeder fund).

The hedge fund's duties: these require the hedge fund (in a master feeder structure, the above contracting entities) to provide the administrator with timely and accurate information, including financial and relevant trading and operational information) or cause third parties that have information that is required by the administrator to do the same. Without such information, the administrator would be unable to do its job.

In addition, the hedge fund is obligated to respond timely and accurately to queries, pay the administrator's fees, ensure that there are adequate funds available to pay bills and handle redemptions and respond to queries when they arise.

The administrator's duties: the administrator is the operational heart and soul of the hedge fund. It is obligated to perform key duties, or Services, such as value positions, calculate the AUM and strike the NAVs per share, keep accurate books and records, receive invoices and pay bills, handle subscriptions, exchanges and redemptions, participate and cooperate with the other service providers and ensure that all aspects of fund operations run smoothly.

The manner in which duties and services are stated is a function of drafting. Many AAs will contain a clause that specifies that the administrator will perform certain duties and provide the Services that are stated in the clause and in an appendix or annex to the AA. That appendix or annex would then list the specific duties and Services to be provided. Generally, AAs do not state the details by which Services are to be provided or benchmarks for evaluation. These are set forth in an SLA between the hedge fund and the administrator.

The SLA is the "document with the details". It generally is a document that comprises tables of figures and charts, with attendant narrative. The purpose of each entry in the SLA is to ensure that every aspect of hedge fund administration is addressed.

Administrators work with but do not necessarily sign SLAs – they view these as being detailed internal operational documents that may require frequent amendment, not as agreements between parties. Directors should endeavour to have SLAs signed so that they have a means of recourse against an administrator with a poor track record of meeting deadlines. Issues relevant to dealing with or replacing administrators and service providers are discussed in Chapter 9.

An example of how the duties clause, the services appendix and the SLA would work together as regards calculating NAVs per share would be as follows.

AA:

"The Administrator will perform the following duties and provide the Services listed below, in the Appendix and in the service level agreement ('SLA') that accompanies this Agreement and is made a part hereof. The Services include, but are not limited to: book-keeping; general fund administration; calculating the AUM of the Fund and the net asset value per share of each class of the Fund's securities ('NAV per Share')" ... "and such other duties that the Administrator and the Fund agree".

Appendix:

"... calculate the NAV per Share for each Class of Shares on each Valuation Day, subject to it receiving third party fund information and administrator third party information on a timely basis on or prior to the Valuation Day."

SLA:

"12. Calculation of the NAV

(i) Not less than five Business Days prior to the Valuation Day, the Administrator will contact every person that is a source of third party fund information and administrator third party information ("Information") to remind them that the Information that they are to give to the Administrator for it to calculate the Fund's AUM and the NAV per Share for each Class of Shares is due.

(ii) As soon as possible on the Valuation Day, the Administrator will, on the basis of the Information that it receives and the Assets in the Portfolio, together with any other information that it holds that is relevant, calculate the AUM and the NAV per Share for each Class of Shares of the Fund, and publish each NAV per Share in accordance with the instructions given to the Administrator by the Fund.

(iii) The Administrator is empowered to discuss any issues surrounding the calculation of the AUM and the NAVs per Share with any duly authorised agent of the Fund as notified to the Administrator by the Directors, but in any event the Administrator shall be solely responsible for obtaining Information, performing the calculations and publishing the NAVs per Share.

(iv) The calculation of the AUM and the NAVs per shares shall be accurate and reflect actual prices or values for the instruments that comprise the Assets. Only if the Administrator is not able to obtain a price for an instrument in the Assets would the Administrator be able to use an estimate, and in such case the Administrator shall notify the Directors at the time the estimate is used and use its best endeavours to obtain a firm price and publish the final AUM and NAV per share without delay, but in any event not later than five (5) Business Days after the Valuation Day. A NAV per Share that includes an estimate shall carry an indication of this and a statement that the final NAV per Share shall be forthcoming within the stated time frame."

Services

The administrator performs many services, as discussed above. Certain of these take on an importance greater than others. Calculating accurate AUM and NAV per share figures is critical. So, too, is the ability to obtain accurate information to price assets in the portfolio. Other critical services include the following.

Account opening: Administrators receive subscription documents/application forms, review them against the criteria for eligible investors and accept or reject applications. This process also involves the requisite AML checks for the verification of the investor's identity and source of funds.

Account opening documentation must be completed accurately and all documents provided with it complete. Original documents are required, but copies will usually be accepted if they are certified within a recent time period (30 to 60 days) by an individual who is authorised to certify that type of document, in the jurisdiction of the investor. Fax documents might be considered, but only if the originals are posted to the administrator and arrive within a designated time period. Some administrators will accept fax copies but will not process redemptions unless they have original documents. The flaw with this is that if the originals are never sent or are discarded after the faxes are sent, or if they are filed and lost and there is a substantial period of time between subscription and redemption and it is not possible to find the originals, there will not be a way to satisfy this requirement. Thus, it is better to insist that original documents arrive with the funds or within a designated time period after the copies are faxed – usually not more than five business days – and hold over any incomplete application until the next dealing day.

Match, clear and settle trades: This involves close cooperation among prime broker, investment manager and executing broker. Accuracy and timeliness are required. Investment managers place orders with executing brokers to buy or sell securities – or ETFs or loan participations. After execution, trade notifications go to the investment manager for it to review and to the prime broker for it to accept or reject the trade.[3] At the same time, the administrator must be informed of the trade for it to make appropriate entries on the fund's books and records and to ensure that it will have an accurate price feed for the instrument purchased. All three must agree on a trade.

Monitoring investment objective, policies and restrictions: It is best for the administrator to perform this role. Having the investment manager do this would result in conflicts of interest, because it might be tempted to trade out of breaches of restrictions (of any size).

THE PRIME BROKER

The prime broker provides funding and lends securities. It is the primary source of capital for hedge funds to leverage their portfolio. Prime brokers, under the PBA, perform custodial and other services related to the trading activities of the hedge fund. The prime broker–hedge fund relationship is governed not just by the PBA, but also the other documents related to the PBA and the disclosures in the Offering Materials. In a single entity structure, the prime broker contracts with the hedge fund. In a master feeder structure, the prime broker is obligated to the master fund.

Prime brokers are providers of credit. They offer enhanced services to hedge funds through capital introduction (cap intro) programmes and electronic platforms that permit, for example, multi-strategy trading in different asset classes and currencies, and that allow a hedge fund to work with more than one prime broker.[4] Multiple prime brokers may almost be a requirement for certain hedge funds. A report published by Paladyne Systems LLC, "The Need for Multi-Prime Brokers",[5] stated that increased industry demand and changing investor needs will require hedge funds that achieve certain large AUMs and that depend increasingly on technology to use multiple prime brokers.

The PBA is the document that establishes the legal relationship between the hedge fund and the prime broker. There are two basic types of PBA (and variations of each): the US model, which is driven by US legal requirements (primarily a series of no-action letters issued by the SEC) and is used by US entities (SEC registered broker–dealers and US banks);[6] and the international model that is used by non-US prime brokers. The discussion set forth below relates to non-US PBAs.

PBAs define and govern key aspects of the relationship: credit; events of default; security interest, termination; trading oversight and the cost and terms of funding. The documents that were used in the early days of hedge funds resembled, from a credit, security interest, default and termination standpoint, a series of agreements that minimised risk for the prime brokers and shifted risk almost entirely to the hedge fund. In large part, this relationship was that of debtor–creditor.

Many provisions of today's PBAs continue to be credit driven. Other provisions qualify the obligations of the parties (eg, "the prime broker may, subject to conditions, provide a borrowing facility or reserves the right to suspend financing"). Early in the relationship, prime brokers rarely negotiated PBAs. (ISDAs were negotiated but continued to reflect key terms that preserved the credit superiority of the prime broker, such as AUM triggers, key employees provisions and material changes.) The central arguments given then, and now, are that hedge funds are seekers (and prime brokers providers) of credit, that prime brokers provide services to many hedge funds at one time and need consistency in the terms of their agreements to comply with their own legal and regulatory requirements and ensure efficient operations and that prime brokers know the market and what was best for the nascent hedge fund.

The PBA is signed by the hedge fund (by its Directors or a duly authorised agent under a resolution or a power of attorney) and the prime broker. Often, in addition to a PBA, the hedge fund and the prime broker will put in place other documents, such as an ISDA (and schedule), a CSA, general terms of business, futures and options (for listed instruments), agreements, account opening documents, local market trading documents (authorisations, proxies, applications, powers and appointments), securities lending agreements, lists of authorised traders (and persons to give instructions to move funds), executing broker agreements and any other documentation. Both parties will be required to provide each other with copies of resolutions, certificates of incorporation and other documentation. It may be the case that additional materials are required, such as US Internal Revenue Service tax forms.

Normally, one entity provides prime brokerage services and signs the PBA. However, many regional and global banks and broker–dealers involve their affiliates. In that case, the prime broker signs for itself and for its affiliates "as agent and trustee". If this happens, there should be an affirmative requirement that the prime broker bring to the attention of the hedge fund any matters relevant to the performance of the agent or any change in status. It is preferable to have the prime broker sign for itself and, under a delegation clause, state what activities are to be delegated to whom and retain responsibility for all delegated activities. In addition, any charge given over the assets held in the prime brokerage account should be given solely in favour of the prime broker, and no other entity.

Key provisions of a PBA

Every PBA raises significant legal issues (these are also applicable to the offering materials and, indeed, the hedge fund's strategy). The most important of these are set out below, in the context of the non-US model. The discussion below is not exhaustive and is not intended to be or to provide definitive advice, but serves as a starting point to understand, negotiate and measure a PBA.

Definitions

Act of insolvency: Prime brokers wish this to be as wide as possible and hedge funds want to narrow this, possibly to the definition applicable in its jurisdiction of incorporation or establishment. Hedge funds should accept a definition that is concise, objective, linked to relevant jurisdictions and does not permit an act that could permit the prime broker (or others) to liquidate the portfolio.

Assets: This refers to the securities and cash that the prime broker holds for the hedge fund. It is important to ensure that this definition is linked correctly to the charge provisions, so that the prime broker takes a charge only over the assets that equals the economic amount of the hedge fund's exposure, not the entire portfolio.

Event of default: This is a pivotal term. Here, also, prime brokers wish this to be as wide as possible and hedge funds want to narrow this. The occurrence of an event of default normally gives the prime broker the ability to cease operations, liquidate the portfolio, realise its charge, and return the balance, if any, to the hedge fund. Effectively, the occurrence of an event of default would close a hedge fund. The events that should comprise an event of default are acts of insolvency, failure to pay significant amounts (not just trades that fail to settle or are DK'd), and material changes in the hedge fund's structure or finances that would directly impair the hedge fund's ability to continue to operate. Defaults or events of default in other documents should not trigger an event of default in a PBA. Any events of default should be narrowly defined.

ISDAs also contain a definition of "event of default", and caution must be taken to ensure that the definition in that agreement is, to the extent possible, identical to that in the PBA.

Margin: A clear definition of what margin is, how to calculate it and who does the calculation is important. Margin is the amount of money or securities that the prime broker requires and that becomes subject to the charge. Accordingly, there must be a margin policy, disclosure governing what is and what is not subject to the charge and disclosure of when margin is required (and all related calculations). Margin should be required when the value of the assets held by the prime broker, not all assets of the hedge fund, drops to a point at or in an agreed cushion on top of the amount of the charge. If the value of the assets held by a prime broker is, say, £240,000,000 and the prime broker has extended credit (cash and securities lent) in an amount equal to £110,000,000, the charge should cover only the amount of credit outstanding, and the point at which margin is called should be just above the £110,000,000, high enough to cover sudden or large swings in the value of assets to protect the prime broker but low enough to ensure that the hedge fund keeps unencumbered assets free of the charge and, also, free from margin calls.

AUM, NAV per share and other defined terms: PBAs often contain definitions of these and other terms (and provisions) that are used in the Offering Materials or the Articles. In such cases, definitions should be identical to those in these other documents.

How are assets to be held?

The manner in which assets are held is a function not only of what type of entity the prime broker is and how it is structured, but of the markets where assets are held, the types of assets, where the prime broker is incorporated and whether unaffiliated third parties hold cash and securities. It is preferable for the prime broker to hold cash subject to client money protection. Securities usually cannot be held in a segregated account in the name of the hedge fund; as such, they should be held in the name of the prime broker or its nominee or sub-custodian. Beneficial ownership should always remain with the hedge fund (save for jurisdictions where this is not legally possible and transfer of title is required), and the books and records of the prime broker should clearly establish the hedge fund's ownership.

Use of excess cash

The hedge fund should be able to have its excess cash held at the prime broker free of the security interest and charges, and in an interest-bearing account. The investment manager should be able to sweep excess cash without being subject to costs or increased margin rates.

Fiduciary duties

Prime brokers may not wish to owe fiduciary duties to a hedge fund client. The hedge fund should attempt to have the prime broker owe these and, if this is not possible, agree at a minimum to have the prime broker owe a general duty of care including enhanced duties for custodial functions. Duties of confidentiality should not be waived or compromised.

Hypothecation

There should be a clear statement of what assets the prime broker may hypothecate and a stated maximum percentage of the assets that may be used. The assets that the prime broker may borrow, lend, sell or otherwise transfer for its use or for the use of its customers are those assets in the portfolio that the prime broker holds, subject to the security interest. The figure of 100% of the assets encumbered by the security interest is usually the benchmark. Prime brokers require a provision that permits them to receive any fee, profit or benefit that it achieves from rehypothecation that may be a considerable amount. Hedge funds should realise that a prime broker that hypothecates assets is obligated to return "equivalent securities" (assets of an identical type, value and description).

Indemnities

Few clauses galvanise the collective attention of Directors, lawyers and investment managers than do indemnity clauses. In essence, an indemnity clause provides a form of protection to a person that, in the proper course of their operations, becomes subject to a demand, claim or suit by third party, suffers a loss and seeks reimbursement for that loss. Prime brokers wish to have indemnity clauses drafted as widely as possible. Hedge funds, naturally, wish to limit them. A good balance to achieve in an indemnity clause would be to work to achieve the following:

- ❑ limit the clause to the prime broker and its officers, directors and employees that actually perform services under the PBA (indemnified persons);
- ❑ condition the giving of an indemnity on the absence of negligence, fraud, wilful misconduct or breach of the PBA by an indemnified person;
- ❑ clarify that the indemnity is limited to actual claims or losses that arise directly from the obligations of an indemnified person under the PBA, and for reasonable legal fees;
- ❑ avoid payment on demand provisions – these require payment to be made before a claim may be established and may involve large amounts of money that, should the claim not be established, may be irrecoverable.

Limitations of liability

Both hedge funds and prime brokers wish to limit their liability. Prime brokers and/or their employees, directors or officers performing prime brokerage activities should be held liable in the event of negligence, fraud, wilful misconduct or breach of the PBA. Liability should extend to the acts or omissions of thoird parties, including affiliates, to whom the prime broker delegates its activities. Liability should also extend to third party custodians. Prime brokers accept liability for affiliates and try to narrow or eliminate liability as regards unaffiliated third parties. As the hedge fund would not be in privity of contract with the prime broker's delegatees, hedge fund Directors should not permit a prime broker to escape responsibility for the acts or omissions of third parties to whom they delegate responsibilities under the PBA.

Generally, both parties agree not to be liable for consequential or indirect losses.

Unaffiliated third-party sub-custodians

Prime brokers assume liability for affiliated sub-custodians but do not wish to assume liability for the acts or omissions (or the insolvency or bankruptcy) of unaffiliated third-party sub-custodians. Hedge fund Directors require otherwise. A compromise position is for the prime broker to be responsible for hiring and monitoring unaffiliated sub-custodians, to agree to assist the hedge fund in recovery against third-party unaffiliated sub-custodian and to assign claims that they have against such third persons. Such a critical point should not be left to be discussed and agreed after the hedge fund starts trading or be subject to carve outs on a market by market basis.

Security interest

Prime brokers require a fixed charge over the assets in the portfolio. Most take a fixed charge, while others also seek a floating charge. A fixed charge is a charge (security interest) over a particular asset. A floating charge is a charge that remains in place on a continuous basis over non-fixed assets, such as securities and cash and that permits the grantor to deal freely with the assets. A combination of a fixed and floating charge provides the maximum amount of protection to the prime broker and may prevent the most headaches to the hedge fund, in the case of an event of default. Security interests and the means to perfect, realise and enforce them vary from jurisdiction to jurisdiction. The security interest should cover only the economic value of credit actually extended.

Rights on default/execution provisions

Prime brokers wish to have a range of options available to them if an event of default occurs. These include a cessation of funding and lending activities, crystallisation of the security interest, portfolio sales/liquidation and the appointment of a receiver. No hedge fund Director should grant such wide powers. A compromise is attainable, in which both agree a threshold amount over which an event of default is declared and the rights on default come into play, and under which the sole remedy available to the prime broker is to use available cash or to agree to sell individual positions. Individual failed trades would not be events of default or give rise to rights on default. Many versions of the threshold amount formulation exist. Most involve a figure that is the "greater of" a set amount or a fixed percentage of the AUM, and usually start as a designated figure. Directors should ensure that there are provisions to reset the figure and/or percentage as the hedge fund AUM increases.

Decline triggers

AUM decline triggers, when used, appear not in PBAs but in ISDAs. These provide that, if the hedge fund's AUM declines by a stated percentage in a rolling 12-month period, the counterparty may exercise certain rights or even use such a decline to declare a termination event. AUM decline triggers also include NAV per share decline triggers. AUM decline triggers rarely appear in PBAs and should be a point to negotiate away – both in the PBA and in an ISDA.

Termination

Prime brokers like unilateral termination provisions that give them the right to close the prime brokerage account, often for no specific reason. Generally, a prime broker would use such a clause if it objected to a change in strategy or wished to curtail its activities in certain sectors, or for other reasons. Effective PBAs should have bilateral termination provisions, as hedge fund Directors, too, may wish to terminate their agreements for poor service or in the event of a change in strategy and a move to a different prime broker. Procedures should be in place to permit either party to terminate not just for cause, but when for legitimate business reasons either wishes to do so. Clear handover provisions should be in place for trading, portfolio handover, closeouts, information feeds and other matters from the time notice to terminate is served until after termination. Termination should not be an event of default and should be carved out of the definition of this term.

Representations and warranties

Just as it is important for a prime broker to receive a warranty and representation that the hedge fund is validly formed and that the PBA, once executed, will be a valid, legal and binding obligation of the hedge fund, enforceable by its terms, so, too, does the hedge fund need such representations and warranties from the prime broker. Reps and warranties, whenever possible, should be bilateral and include key points such as incorporation, valid existence, execution, enforceability, agreement to make notification if certain events transpire and so on. Certain reps and warranties are appropriate for one of the parties, such as the rep that the prime broker is duly authorised and regulated. Representations and warranties usually do not prevent significant issues but must be thought out and carefully drafted.

Cross margin, cross netting and cross default

Prime brokers, when putting in place multiple agreements (a PBA, an ISDA and/or a GMSLA), wish to achieve cross margin, cross netting and cross default. These provisions provide the greatest credit protection to the prime broker. A hedge fund, particularly a new fund, may receive benefits from cross margining, but to agree to all three impose severe risks. Today, industry practice is to provide for cross margin and possibly cross netting, but not for cross default. Default provisions should not work "upwards" so that, if an ISDA or a GMSLA is terminated, that would result in the closure of positions under these agreements but not "rise up" to terminate the PBA itself. The end of a PBA for the closure of the account due to an event of default would, if not negotiated away, result in the termination of the related agreements.

Information barriers

Prime brokers are sophisticated entities that operate on a regional or global basis. They offer many services, in addition to prime brokerage. As regulated institutions, they are required to ensure that information that one department receives is ring-fenced so that it does not, save for narrow exceptions, flow to other departments. Information about a hedge fund's trading and positions is clearly confidential, and should be available only in extremely limited instances – for compliance, internal audit, etc. PBAs and Offering Materials should make clear that the prime broker operates information barriers sufficient to ensure compliance with relevant legal and regulatory requirements and to ensure that information proprietary to the hedge fund is properly controlled.

SLAs

Hedge funds require service providers to enter into service level agreements to provide a means to measure performance. SLAs, as they are known, also contain provisions for regular reviews. Prime brokers have been reluctant to enter into SLAs with hedge funds, but the trend is in favour of having SLAs in place, particularly when there are multiple prime brokers. SLAs should be signed by the parties to ensure their enforceability.

Related documents

Offering Materials and verification notes

The Offering Materials are the primary documents used to market shares or interests of a hedge fund. This document must contain a clear statement of the material terms of the PBA, together with summary information of the prime broker. If the prime broker or an affiliate contributes seed capital, this fact might have to be disclosed.

The required disclosure should touch on the following points:

- ❑ the identity of the prime broker and any affiliate providing duties by delegation or directly;
- ❑ the actual services to be performed, eg, custody, clearing, financing and reporting;
- ❑ a statement making clear what services will not be performed, eg, investment advisory or discretionary management;
- ❑ the nature of the security interest over the assets in the portfolio;
- ❑ what monitoring, if any, is to be performed;
- ❑ events of default, and how they would be exercised;
- ❑ termination provisions;
- ❑ calculation of fees; and
- ❑ any other relevant disclosures.

Prime brokers are often asked to sign verification notes in the lead-up to the initial offering of shares or interests. Verification notes, drawn up by outside counsel, provide a means to verify statements in the offering materials and ensure that disclosures in all documents are consistent. Prime brokers usually participate in aspects of the verification process and in most instances sign the notes.

1 For purposes of this book, "investment manager" is the entity that contracts with the hedge fund (or the FoHF) to manage the assets in the portfolio. If it delegates certain of its responsibilities in an effort to gain expertise such as in a FoHF structure or the Hong Kong hedge fund model, that entity will be referred to as the adviser.

2 Examples of "boilerplate clauses" are: representations and warranties, data protection requirements, limitations of liability, indemnities, choice of law and indemnity, termination, confidentiality and general legal clauses (amendments, execution and so on).

3 PBAs give prime brokers this power. This is an important point to consider in negotiations. Generally, the power to reject a trade "in the sole discretion of the prime broker" should be conditioned on a valid reason for doing so and on prompt notice being given to the investment manager and administrator (not "when and as reasonable").

4 "Citigroup unveils new prime brokerage platform", *MarketWatch*, weekend edition, Dow Jones, 2 August 2006, URL: www.marketwatch.com/News/Story/9CrbKW296mFr9n8np Z5BxNg?siteid=mktw&dist=TNMostMailed.

5 "The Need for Multi-Prime Brokers", report by Paladyne Systems, LLC, 2 May 2006, URL: www.paladynesys.com/NewsArticles/MultiPrime-Paladyne.pdf.

6 *See* McMillan and Bergmann, "The Legal Relationship from the U.S. Perspective", *Hedge Funds and Prime Brokers* (2006), 1st ed, Chapter 2 (London: Risk Books (2006)).

6

How to Read an Offering Memorandum

In this chapter we review the components of an Offering Memorandum for a hedge fund. The document that forms the basis of our discussion is the one that is used to sell shares of an offshore feeder fund in a master feeder structure. The points that we make apply in relevant part to the PPM of an onshore feeder fund.

The Offering Memorandum carries with it liability for the Directors of the hedge fund. Prominently displayed at the top of the front cover of an Offering Memorandum is a legend stating that the Directors are responsible for the contents of this document. They can strive to eliminate their liability by conducting a verification exercise. The verification process is also discussed, below.

DRAFTING

Drafting the Offering Memorandum begins at the time the promoter's project committee is completing its deliberations, finalising the business plan and starting the RFP process to identify service providers. At this time, key decisions will have been taken that will affect not just how the hedge fund operates, but also what will have to be disclosed in the Offering Memorandum. It will not be possible to draft certain sections of the Offering Memorandum at this time, because the prime broker and administrator – and possibly other service providers – will not have been identified. The final Offering Memorandum must not only identify each of these but must also contain a description of them and also summarise the material agreements.

The Offering Memorandum is a legal document, as are the material agreements. While counsel to hedge funds normally require that they draft the Offering Memorandum, it is increasingly the case that in-house counsel to the promoter puts together the first draft of this document. This individual will be involved in all phases of the hedge fund launch and has a 360-degree view of all matters: decision-making, the RFP process, documentation requirements, the "paper portfolio", compliance requirements, marketing needs, investor profiles and other key points. Having outside counsel draft the document does help in terms of smoothing the review and verification processes, but at this point the emphasis is on ensuring that the document holds together, and there is no person better placed to do this than the promoter. Finalisation and verification must, for legal and liability reasons, rest firmly with counsel.

WHAT GOES INTO AN OFFERING MEMORANDUM?

There are no rules as to what an Offering Memorandum must contain. This is subject to the caveat that, if the fund is listed, it must satisfy listing requirements – such as those of the ISE or the CSX. The Offering Memorandum must be correct – it may not contain a material misstatement or omission. The verification process is conducted to address these concerns (primarily the latter), but verification is a "process in the round": if there is an onshore feeder fund there will be a Private Placement Memorandum and it is critical that verification cover *both* documents. A common error is to finalise the Offering Memorandum, verify it and then draft the PPM. In doing this, one may inadvertently omit disclosures from the PPM in the belief that, since the documents serve dissimilar purposes and are received by different investors,[1] information may apply to only one type of investor, eg, information in the Offering Memorandum may not be required by US tax-paying investors. In this way, errors creep in. It is verification of both documents that ensures that each is correct, that disclosures in both documents are consistent and that nothing is omitted.

An Offering Memorandum will usually contain the following sections, each of which will form a section of this Chapter:

- Important information
- Directory
- Definitions
- Summary (or key features)
- Investment objective, policy and restrictions
- Management
- Service providers: investment manager, administrator, prime broker, administrator and distributor
- Subscriptions (and distribution of securities), redemptions and exchanges
- Net asset value
- Fees and expenses
- Risk factors
- Conflicts of interest
- Reports
- For a feeder fund of a master fund, relevant issues such as the feeder fund agreement or operating agreement (and for the PPM, the way in which the capital accounts of investors are established and operated)

- ❑ Taxation
- ❑ General and statutory information
- ❑ Appendixes.

COVER PAGE

The cover page contains several disclosures. These include the name of the hedge fund, a Directors' responsibility statement, a summary of the securities being sold, the name of the investment manager, a summary of the hedge fund, key legends and, if the hedge fund is to be listed, brief information about the listing.

A Directors' responsibility statement is a statement on their responsibility for disclosures in the Offering Memorandum. It would resemble the following, but there is no "formula" for these words:

> *"The Directors named herein are responsible for this Offering Memorandum. To the best of the knowledge and belief of the Directors, who have taken reasonable care to ensure that such is the case, the information in this Offering Memorandum does not omit anything likely to affect the import of such information. The Directors accept responsibility for this document."*

The cover page names the instruments to be offered and sold and states the minimum subscription price. For example: "Investors may purchase pursuant to this offering memorandum Class A (US dollar), Class B (sterling) and Class C (euro) shares, each with a par value per share of US$0.01 (shares) of the Fund". The minimum initial investment in shares is US$250,000 (or its sterling or euro equivalent) at a price of US$100 per share (or its sterling or euro equivalent) during the Initial Offer Period and, thereafter, at the net asset value of the fund, plus any applicable equalisation credit (Offering Price)". The date of the Offering Memorandum will appear on the bottom of the page.

Finally, there may be a series of legends on the bottom of the cover page (some hedge funds place these on the inside front cover or in the next section, "Important Information"). These touch upon certain informational points, ie, the hedge fund and the Offering Memorandum are not registered with a particular regulatory authority; the Offering Memorandum should not be considered to be an offer or a solicitation in a jurisdiction where it would be unlawful to make an offer or solicitation (see Chapter 7); and, as regards the contents of the Offering Memorandum, investors must take their own advice to determine whether an investment in the shares are appropriate for them.

Depending on the jurisdictions where the prospects are located (in particular, the US), additional disclaimers will appear. These cover advertising and marketing materials, representation and warranties for returns and tax implications, the status of involvement with a compensation scheme (none, as the hedge fund will not be regulated) and the status of the investment manager being exempt from registration with the Commodity Futures Trading Commission (CFTC) as a commodity pool operator (CPO) or commodity trading advisor (CTA) and the implications of this.

Hedge fund Offering Memoranda contain "selling restrictions", which are disclosures about the status of the fund (not registered) and the offering of the securities (private placements) in the jurisdictions where the distributor of the hedge fund plans to seek investors. These may be as short as a statement that the shares have not been registered with a particular securities commission or under the laws of a country and are not available save in a private placement to certain types of investors, or lengthy as in the case of other countries with complicated private placement requirements.

These disclosures are a first indicator of the "golden thread" that runs through Offering Memorandum disclosure: the balance of disclosure versus disclaimer. Unlike the prospectus that a long-only fund would use in a public offering of securities (and save for the hedge funds that are listed on the CSX or the ISE), a hedge fund Offering Memorandum follows market standards for private placements of securities – generally, more disclaimer than disclosure. The laws of many jurisdictions provide for disclosure requirements and liability standards for public offers, but reduced information requirements and liability thresholds private placements. This follows, in some degree, the principle that institutions purchasing securities in private placements are able to fend for themselves but that retail investors buying securities in public offerings require enhanced protection. Thus, a side-by-side comparison of a prospectus with an Offering Memorandum will show the former being lengthy while the latter will be more compact – but containing greater disclaimers.

A table of contents usually follows the cover page.

IMPORTANT INFORMATION

This section contains backdrop disclosure. It starts with the clarification that the document is given on a confidential basis to a limited number of prospects to provide them with information about an investment in the hedge fund. Prospective investors should carefully read and retain this Prospectus. It also states that it must not be considered to be legal, tax, investment or other advice, and prospects must obtain their own professional advice as to various matters, including the legal requirements for investing, exchange controls, tax issues and other matters.

Another set of disclosures go to restrictions on distribution. They clarify that the hedge fund is being offered on a private placement basis (see Chapter 7) and that the document has not been approved or registered, and disclaims the delivery of the document (and usually all marketing materials) where it is not legal to market the shares of the hedge fund – in others words, if a prospect in a country where the distributor does not intend to market the hedge fund gains a copy of the Offering Memorandum despite the efforts of the distributor and others, it would be possible to refuse to permit such a person to invest and at the same time help protect the distributor, the investment manager and the Directors from claims of violating the private placement rules of the country in question.

The disclosures in this section set out in some detail the selling restrictions for key countries. These invariably include the US and certain other countries. Such restrictions take many forms and are usually settled by local counsel in the jurisdiction in question. There are many variations of these, and the following are some examples.

"Cayman Islands:	*No offer to sell Shares of the Fund to the public in the Cayman Islands may be made."*
"Portugal:	*The Comissão do Mercado de Valores Mobiliários has not approved the Fund or registered the Shares of the Fund. This offering memorandum does not constitute a public offer or solicitation to buy Shares and may not be given out or available to the public in any way. Shares may be offered only by way of private placement in Portugal."*
"United States:	*The Shares have not been and will not be registered under the US Securities Act of 1933, as amended ('1933 Act') or the laws of any state of the United States. The Shares may not be offered, sold or delivered directly or indirectly in the United States or to or for the account or benefit of any 'US Person', save under an exemption from or in a transaction that is not subject to registration under the 1933 Act and any applicable state law. In particular, only US Persons that are 'Qualified Purchasers' as this term is defined in the US Investment Company Act of 1940, as amended ('1940 Act') may purchase Shares. Each US applicant for Shares will be required to certify that it is a US Person Qualified Purchaser. The Fund will not be registered under the 1940 Act in reliance on the exemption in Section 3(c)(7) thereunder."*[2]

Additional disclosures in this section summarise the importance of the risk factors, conflicts of interest and tax advice.

DIRECTORY

The Directory is a list of the key players involved with the hedge fund. They include the Directors, mentioned by name, and the service providers, with their names and addresses. For the hedge fund, it will list the registered address. For an offshore feeder fund, there should be references to indicate whether a service provider has contracted with the master fund and the offshore feeder fund, or only one of these.

DEFINITIONS

This section is a cornerstone of the Offering Memorandum, as it sets out key terms and their definitions and gives shape to the Offering Memorandum and the operation of the hedge fund.

Drafting definitions

As a starting point, one needs to ensure that the definitions are linked to, and consistent with, the Memorandum, the Articles and the material agreements. This point will be checked during the verification process, but by ensuring that the drafting proceeds from the Memorandum and the Articles, one can build from these and not have to engage in prolonged revisions. Also, and as an operating aid, it is important to ensure that, while key operating steps are spelt out in the Articles and reflected in the Offering Memorandum and material agreements, certain key terms are referenced in the Articles and defined in the Offering Memorandum. If one keeps in mind the facts that the Articles may be changed only with shareholder approval and after a process of issuing notices and soliciting votes, whereas changing an Offering Memorandum does not require this (it requires the revision of documents, Director approval and filing with, for example, CIMA), it is easier to have the Articles name a definition, refer to the Offering Memorandum and have the term defined in that document.

From the Articles:

"US Person" *as defined in the Offering Memorandum;*

From the Offering Memorandum:

"US Person" *an individual that is resident in the United States, and for a company, partnership, trust or estate, as defined in Rule 902 of Regulation S under the 1933 Act, or [state in full the preferred definition];*

What follows in the remainder of this subsection are some key definitions and a discussion of them (they will be used throughout this book in the discussion of our model hedge fund).

Key definitions

The Definitions section will include the following:

- titles of material agreements (eg, the IMA, the AA and the PBA);
- names of the service providers;

- ❑ references to regulators (such as the CFTC, the Hong Kong Securities and Futures Authority (SFC), the MAS, the Financial Regulator, the Securities Commission, Malaysia (SC) and the SEC);
- ❑ "working terms" such as:
  - the names of related entities in a master fund structure;
  - "AUM": the total assets of the hedge fund (or a feeder fund in a master feeder structure;
  - "Base Currency": the currency of the hedge fund (and the master fund);
  - Dealing Day: the business day when the administrator processes subscriptions, exchanges and redemptions, which is the business day after the Valuation Day;
  - Gross Assets: the value of the hedge fund's investments, excluding liabilities and borrowings;
  - "Management Fee": the fee paid to the investment manager based on the assets of the hedge fund;
  - "Performance Fee: the incentive or performance fee paid by the hedge fund to the investment manager;
  - "Shares": each of the shares of the hedge fund to be issued, which will state the par value and whether this class of share carries a vote; and
  - Valuation Day": the business day when the administrator calculates the AUM and strikes the NAVs per share;
- ❑ references to laws (such as FSMA, ERISA, 1933 Act and 1940 Act).

It may be the case that a term is referenced here but defined in another section of the Offering Memorandum. An example of this would be:

> *"Subscription Price": the price per Share at which Shares may be purchased, the calculation of which is discussed in the section, "Subscriptions".*

Some hedge funds place the substance of the definition in the subscription agreements. This helps to ensure that the Offering Memorandum does not become too lengthy and locates the definition to a place where those who are affected by it can see it – and those who are not cannot. Examples of this are terms that may relate to investors in only one jurisdiction, such as "Major US Institutional Investor", Restricted Person" and "Rule 2790" – which are relevant for determining whether a non-US broker or dealer may solicit this type of investor without having to register with the SEC as a broker–dealer and whether the hedge fund may buy shares of SEC-registered IPOs of equity securities that are caught by this "hot issue" rule, respectively.

SUMMARY (OR KEY FEATURES)

This section marks the beginning of the substantive discussion of what the hedge fund is and how it operates. These disclosures focus on the establishment of the hedge fund; state the investment objective, policies and restrictions; provide key information about subscriptions, redemptions and exchanges; identify the service providers and reference to their fees; and summarise the fees and expenses of the hedge fund (and the master fund).

The disclosures in this section generally mirror the more detailed discussions that appear later in the Offering Memorandum. For example, this section will:

- give fundamental details about the establishment of the hedge fund – date of incorporation, status in the jurisdiction of establishment and its role in the master feeder structure;
- identify the classes of shares but not discuss the rights and features;
- state the fees and expenses that the investment manager will receive; it will state, but not discuss, how often the fees are calculated and paid;
- disclose the investment objective and policies and reference, but not discuss the restrictions – with the details coming in the section that bears this title; and
- reference the instruments that will be traded and name the markets involved.

INVESTMENT OBJECTIVE, POLICY AND RESTRICTIONS

In this section, the Offering Memorandum discusses in detail the hedge fund's investment objective, the policies and the restrictions. If this is an offshore feeder fund in a master fund structure, the disclosures will relate to the activities of the investment manager *vis-à-vis* the master fund. The disclosures concerning the offshore feeder fund will state that the feeder fund will invest "all or substantially all" of its assets in the master fund which will, in turn, invest with a view to achieving the investment objective.

Investment objective

The investment objective is a statement of what the hedge fund seeks to accomplish. While this may appear to be a somewhat generalised statement, it is not only the starting point for portfolio investment but also the benchmark from which to evaluate the hedge fund's performance.

A hedge fund competes against itself to deliver, regardless of market conditions, absolute return – whereas a long-only fund seeks to outperform a designated benchmark.[3]

The difference between what a hedge fund and a long-only fund would return is based on the use of leverage. The former may use leverage while the latter (unless it is a UCITS III or a 130/30 fund) may not sell short and borrow or fund purchases on margin. Thus, investing £100,000 in a hedge fund and a long-only fund would, due to the use of leverage, generate higher returns in a hedge fund, but also involve more risk. The difference between what the hedge fund would make off investing the £100,000 (and using leverage) and the gains received by the long-only fund is called alpha. Alpha is a measurement of the expression of risk: the higher the risk, the greater the return.

Examples of investment objectives are as follows:

- ❑ generating capital appreciation over the long term that exceeds the rates of return available by investing in broadly diversified equity or bond portfolios, with a low correlation to and lower volatility than those asset classes;
- ❑ achieving capital appreciation by trading investments in the fixed-income credit markets that include corporate bonds, government bonds, loan participations, high-yield bonds, convertible bonds, ABS and derivatives, deriving returns from assuming credit risk;
- ❑ achieving long-term capital growth by trading a range of equity securities, options, warrants, convertible debt securities, ETFs and other instruments on a long- and short-term basis; and
- ❑ generating growth by trading in a variety of instruments on a long- and short-term basis, including equities, debt instruments, derivatives, ETFs and structured products

Investment policies

The investment policies disclosure touches upon several topics. They include: a statement of the investment manager's belief about the strength or weakness of the market(s) in which the manager will trade; a list of the instruments and strategies to be employed and relevant details about the market(s) involved; details about the characteristics of the investments to be bought or sold, the risks involved with buying, selling or holding certain instruments; the research and investment process; and the risk-management procedures employed.

It is this section that goes from the benchmark investment objective to the specific policies. For policies, read strategies. Here, the investment manager would:

- ❑ indicate the type of issuer of equity securities that it will trade – a discussion of strong balance sheets, emerging market issuers, high levels of cash and moderate short- and long-term borrowings would indicate buys or holds, while the opposite indicators would lead to targets for short-selling or arbitrage opportunities;
- ❑ discuss its research process, state how ideas become recommendations, distinguish its investment process from those of other hedge fund managers;

- ❑ show how certain the characteristics of certain securities or non-security investments present opportunities that others do not;
- ❑ illustrate state how certain investments traded on a leveraged basis would contribute to the investment objective;
- ❑ indicate why certain strategies would work in one market, but not another, due to local legal, regulatory or tax considerations – short sales may be effected in certain jurisdictions but not others, buying UK equities attracts stamp duty (or even stamp duty reserve tax (SDRT)) but gaining the economic exposure to these instruments through certain types of derivatives might help avoid stamp duty or SDRT and reduce operating costs; and
- ❑ set out its risk management and assessment programme and procedures.

Often the discussion in this section is straightforward and sets forth examples of what issuers the investment manager would consider. A long-short equity fund would state that it would purchase the securities of issuers in certain geographic regions with strong management teams, serviceable long-term debt and a healthy cashflow, but that it would short the securities of issuers in other jurisdictions with similar characteristics. Another investment manager might disclose that its investment objective can be achieved by, for example, buying and holding investments among asset classes, industry sectors and issuers with low valuations and high potential for share price appreciation, while shorting interests in asset classes, industry sectors and issuers with the opposite characteristics.

Offering Memoranda may disclose a valuation process or measure (marketing materials would also disclose this). An example of this would be the measurement of real cash returns on capital across different asset classes, and the valuation placed upon these returns by the market. An investment manager would express this in the form of a ratio. Other valuation methods that would form the basis of an investment strategy are enterprise value-based models and instrument price-based discounted cash flow modelling.

In addition, the Offering Memorandum may also set forth indicators of value, or performance drivers. These include top-line growth (eg, share price gains), free cashflow generation, shareholder return and balance-sheet structure.

Disclosure does not stop here. Prospects will, in their due diligence exercises, query the investment manager further about the details of the valuation methods and strategies that it uses to identify investment opportunities. The responses to these supplement the disclosures in the Offering Memorandum.

Restrictions

As noted above, restrictions are the parameters imposed on hedge funds that the investment manager must observe. Restrictions are based on size and type of investment. Common restrictions are that a hedge fund may not:

- ❑ hold real estate or physically settled commodities;
- ❑ invest more than a stated percentage of the assets (or gross assets) in the securities of any one issuer or in illiquid investments;
- ❑ make loans – but it may buy or sell loan participations; or
- ❑ take control of an issuer.

Positively stated restrictions are that an investment manager must:

- ❑ comply with stated "limitations";
- ❑ observe borrowing restrictions; or
- ❑ respect "cash" investments – by this, we mean restrictions on the amount of cash invested in a particular type of money market instrument or even a prohibition on a money market fund managed by the investment manager.

Borrowing restrictions may be expressed in several ways. These include the following:

- ❑ limits on the amounts that may be borrowed – this is leverage, and the limits are set as percentages, ranging from 100% to as high as 500% of the NAV; and/or
- ❑ caps on the market value of short positions – this may be stated as a firm figure or, possibly, as an expectation (creating the possibility of drift) that short will not exceed a stated percentage of the NAV.

Other limitations are capital limits, position limits and net exposure.

MANAGEMENT

This section of the Offering Memorandum contains the disclosures about the Directors of the hedge fund – or the trustee of the unit trust or the general partner of the limited partnership.

The information about management will include a biography of each individual. Apart from this, the disclosures will mention how often the Directors meet and the fact that they receive reports from the service providers (investment manager, administrator and prime broker).

Related disclosures will indicate whether a Director holds securities in one of the key services providers – usually, the investment manager. There will also be disclosure whether a Director holds a position or directorship with another hedge fund (or master fund) managed by the investment manager. These disclosures are designed to help identify conflicts of interest.

If the offshore feeder fund (or hedge fund) is listed (eg, the ISE or CSX), additional disclosures about the Directors are required. The format required by the ISE is that it confirms that no Director:

> *"has any unspent convictions in relation to indictable offences;*
> *has been bankrupt or the subject of an involuntary arrangement, or has had a receiver appointed to any of his or her assets;*
> *has been a director of any company that, while he or she was a director with an executive function or within 12 months after he or she ceased to be a director with an executive function, had a receiver appointed or went into compulsory liquidation, creditors voluntary liquidation, administration or company voluntary arrangements, or made any composition or arrangements with its creditors generally or with any class of its creditors;*
> *has been a partner of any partnership, which while he was a partner or within 12 months after he ceased to be a partner, went into compulsory liquidation, administration or partnerships voluntary arrangement, or had a receiver appointed to any partnership asset;*
> *has had any public criticism by statutory or regulatory authorities (including recognised professional bodies); or*
> *has been disqualified by a court from acting as a director or from acting in the management or conduct of affairs of any company."*[4]

SERVICE PROVIDERS: INVESTMENT MANAGER, ADMINISTRATOR, PRIME BROKER AND DISTRIBUTOR

Investment Manager

In this part of this section, key disclosures concerning the investment manager are provided. They include information about its incorporation, regulation (if it is regulated), principal lines of business and details about affiliates (assets, types of companies and other key information).

This section will contain a summary of the material points about the IMA. It is designed to ensure that prospects or others reading and relying on the Offering Memorandum obtain a description of the IMA's material terms so that they understand not only what the investment manager will do but how they will do it.

Prime Broker

In this section, there will be a description of the prime broker with details about its incorporation, regulation, assets, lines of business and details about affiliates that would be involved in providing services to the hedge fund (or the master fund, as the case may be).

Prime brokers generally are also the primary custodian for the assets in the portfolio. In this regard, there will be a discussion of what assets the prime broker as custodian will hold, whether it will use its affiliates as sub-custodians and, also, the use of non-affiliated third parties as custodians.

This section will include a discussion of material elements of the PBA. The critical disclosures here are as follows. Certain of these may appear later as risk factors.

- What responsibility the prime broker has regarding acts or omissions of, claims against or the insolvency of unaffiliated custodians – generally, prime brokers will attempt to contract out of being liable for these. These acts might result in the inability to access positions held with sub-custodians or even the loss of such assets. At a minimum, the prime broker should be responsible for the selection of sub-custodians, the monitoring and supervision of their activities and, if claims arise, providing the hedge fund with its best endeavours in sorting out those claims or assigning its interest against such parties to the prime broker.
- The nature of the security interest over the assets held in the portfolio.
- Exactly what duties are owed and services are to be provided, and by whom – if affiliates are to be used, this must be spelt out and the affiliates named.
- The treatment of cash held by the prime broker and by other custodians (insured or uninsured, swept into money-market funds or left uninvested).
- How assets in the portfolio would be used by the prime broker or hypothecated to third parties – including affiliates – and the terms under which this would occur.
- The events of default and the remedies available to the prime broker.
- The terms of any indemnity and liability provisions in the PBA.
- What other "roles" the prime broker has or will play – eg, setting up cap intro events and providing seed capital (if so, what entity gave it and how long will it be invested).
- The confidentiality obligations imposed on the prime broker and its affiliates.
- What disclosures in the Offering Memorandum the prime broker is responsible for.
- Disclosure of any conflicts of interest that the prime broker has or may have with the hedge fund, the Directors or any service provider and how such conflicts will be resolved.
- What type of collateral will be given – the sub-prime/credit crisis makes such disclosures extremely relevant, particularly if the collateral to be posted is cardboard collateral and not liquid, exchange-traded instruments.

If there are two prime brokers, the above points must be disclosed for each. In addition, there must be a discussion of how the investment manager will use the two entities, what conflicts may arise from this and how they will be resolved. There will certainly be risk factor disclosures about the use of multiple prime brokers – one need only consider the implications of the 2006 Amaranth collapse (discussed in Chapter 10) to understand the importance of proper disclosure.

SUBSCRIPTIONS (AND DISTRIBUTION OF SECURITIES), REDEMPTIONS AND EXCHANGES

Subscriptions

The disclosures in this section set out the total number of shares available for purchase and the manner in which prospects may become investors during the "initial offering period" and thereafter in which investors may buy additional securities. Other disclosures set out the rights of each class of shares, give the minimum investment required (and the amount for additional subscriptions), define "eligible investor" (and "ineligible investor"), discuss, in light of certain tax and regulatory matters, how employment benefit plans may purchase shares, outline salient points of the AML policy concerning subscriptions and reference the subscription documents. Other disclosures are the manner in which transactions in shares would be suspended and whether there would be any restrictions on transferability.

Usually, the disclosures in this section contain a statement that the Directors may exercise their authority to waive certain requirements relating to subscriptions.

Subscriptions: Prospects buy shares in hedge funds by submitting completed subscription documents and cleared funds with the administrator by a stated time on the Valuation day prior to the Dealing day when subscriptions will be processed. Offering Memoranda make clear that if properly completed documents and cleared funds are not in by the cut-off time, they will be held over to the next Dealing day.

Closings: Offering Memoranda usually disclose that the Directors have the ability to instruct the administrator to cease accepting subscriptions. This happens in two ways:

- *soft close*: prospects that are not investors may not buy shares, but current investors may buy additional shares (newly issued shares or shares redeemed by other investors, "recycled shares"); and
- *hard close*: neither prospects nor investors may buy shares.

A soft closing or hard closing is not a suspension. Suspensions occur when circumstances require that the hedge fund temporarily cease accepting subscriptions.

The disclosures about the subscription documents will summarise key representations and warranties to be made by applicants for shares. There are many of these, and also a considerable amount of information to be provided. Generally, the "reps and warranties" go to eligibility requirements, the applicant's knowledge and expertise and awareness of the conflicts and risks involved in an investment on the shares.

Equalisation: The Offering Memorandum will disclose the equalisation credit to be applied and its calculation, if this is applicable. Equalisation is discussed in Chapter 7.

Redemptions

This section summarises the requirements that are imposed on the redemption of shares. These disclosures set out time and documentation requirements, what the redemption price would be (the NAV per share of the class of securities as of the Valuation Day prior to the Dealing Day on which the redemption would be processed), the redemption fee involved (and whether this may be waived by the Directors), how redemptions are processed by the administrator and when proceeds would be paid out.

There are also disclosures concerning how and when the Directors would declare a suspension of redemptions, under what circumstances there would be compulsory redemptions (usually, securities held by ineligible investors, which is often a defined term) and when redemptions would be restricted or postponed – gate provisions.

Gate provisions are among the most material, yet overlooked, disclosures in every Offering Memorandum. Gate provisions permit the Directors, when the hedge fund receives redemption requests that are greater than a designated amount of the number of shares of a particular class, to pro rate and grant requests that, in the aggregate, redeem shares in a total amount that equals the stated gate figure. Most gate provisions are a figure of 5–10% of AUM. Accordingly, with a gate of 5% and redemption requests totalling 9%, the administrator would reduce the requests rateably and effect redemptions that, together, equalled the 5%. The remaining redemptions would be carried over to the next Dealing Day and processed then.

Not to disclose a gate provision or to disclose its operation in an Offering Memoranda – and in the PPM of an onshore feeder fund – would be a material omission, subjecting the directors to liability and also enabling investors to seek, and probably obtain, rescission.

Gate provisions work in normal times, when hedge funds have amounts of cash sufficient to handle redemption requests (despite such requests, a fund that is soft-closed can recycle shares to current investors). What would occur in times of stress or unusual developments?

- In the sub-prime/credit crisis, redemption requests in excess of a gate provision, whether or not a hedge fund has sufficient funds to cover such redemptions, may lead to forced disclosures about such problems, which, in turn, may encourage other redemptions – a "run on the bank".
- In such situations, a hedge fund may disregard gates and redeem all investors – but doing so may reduce the hedge fund's AUM to a point that triggers a NAV decline in an ISDA with potentially widespread effects, or kick off an event of default provisions in other documents, such as a PBA. It may lead to a decline in the AUM to a point where it is not longer viable for the fund to function, leading to the closure of the fund.
- Handling large redemptions with insufficient cash positions would require the investment manager to liquidate positions to handle the redemptions. This, too, may have knock-on effects similar to those described above or adversely affect the fund's performance.
- Does a hedge fund have an obligation to disclose redemption requests that are large (from one investor) or that, if honoured, might result in a material decline in the AUM? If the fund was not ISE- or CSX-listed, there may not be such an obligation. If, however, the hedge fund was listed and required to observe continuing obligation requirements, the issue would be: when should disclosure be made, and what should be said? In all likelihood, disclosure would come at a time not when the request was received, but when the Directors decided on a course of action. What would be disclosed would be the request (it may not have to identify the investor seeking redemption, unless the holding was greater than a certain threshold – probably 10%), the amount being redeemed and the projected AUM post-redemption. The reason for the redemption would probably not require disclosure.

Exchanges

Exchanges involve the exchange of one class of share for another. Exchanges require the filing of a request with the administrator and are handled on Dealing Days, with subscriptions (if the fund is open) or redemptions. A key issue for investors is whether an exchange might result in inadvertent or undesirable tax consequences, such as having the securities exchanged being treated as a sale.

As they are empowered to suspend subscriptions or redemptions, the Directors are permitted to do the same as regards exchanges.

NET ASSET VALUE

The manner in which the hedge fund has its AUM and NAVs per share calculated is discussed in Chapter 9. The disclosures that appear in the Offering Memorandum parallel those set forth in the Articles (or the limited partnership or trust deed) and describe in detail how the AUM and the NAVs are calculated, how instruments (even cash!) are priced (valued) for the calculation, what would affect the process – suspensions, and so on. A key disclosure is that, if it is the case, the Directors may use or give approval to the administrator for it to use a valuation method other than those set forth in the documents. They would do this if they had a reasonable basis to believe that the alternative method would better reflect value and would comport with good accounting practices.

FEES AND EXPENSES

The disclosures in this section name the service providers that would receive a fee and state what fee they would receive and how it would be calculated.

Fees for service providers

Investment manager: Disclosed here are the management and performance fees. These fees and how they are calculated are discussed in Chapter 5.

Administrator: The fee paid to the administrator would be fixed or based on a percentage of the hedge fund's AUM. If a percentage fee, it would be calculated on the basis of the AUM at month end on the Dealing Day (this may or may not include redemptions and/or subscriptions). The fee may be fixed or sliding (based on the size of the fund). The administrator may or may not obtain reimbursement for certain incurred expenses.

Prime broker: There would be a description of the fees to be received by the prime broker. The disclosures would not break down the fees in detail, but would clarify that what was charged would be a combination of costs for transactions, interests costs, debit and credit balances and fees for prime brokerage. Generally, prime brokers do not charge for custodianship, but unaffiliated sub-custodians may, and if this is the case, disclosure will be made.

Other service providers: Included here would be disclosures for market counterparties, the distributor of the hedge fund's shares and a description of how executing brokers would be compensated.

Costs of launching the hedge fund

This section will contain disclosure concerning the costs of establishing the hedge fund. Such costs commonly include legal fees, filing fees, listing fees (if the hedge fund or onshore feeder fund is to be listed) and other costs incurred in setting up the fund. Additional expenses may include directors' and officers' (D&O) insurance. While each of these may not be individually identified, the total amount of these would be stated. In addition, this disclosure will state who bears the costs of establishing the fund and clarify whether the costs will be amortised over a period of time from launch, and whether some or all of the expenses would be paid for by the promoter.

How much does it cost to launch a hedge fund? There is no magic figure. A master feeder structure might incur the following setup costs:

- legal fees – £75,000;
- filing fees – approximately £2,000 per company;
- listing fees – estimated at £5,000;
- sponsor fees for the listing (estimate) – £8,500 for the first year; and
- D&O insurance for first year – estimated at £4,000 per director (three individuals by four companies, two feeder funds, one master fund and one corporate director of the onshore feeder fund).

If the £144,500 is amortised over a five-year period, the annual figure would be £36,125.

Apart from this, the fund would expect to budget for first year's running costs. These would include the fees of the service providers, transaction costs, ongoing legal fees and other expenses. In our hedge fund, we would budget for running costs of £270,000 per month, or £3,240,000 in the first year.

If we want our hedge fund to be a success and we do not want to have the initial investors bear all of the setup costs, we would aim to have enough money so that we could at least cover our first year's costs and have funds remaining for investing. To be able to launch, our hedge fund would need to raise not less than £15 million. This is a modest amount for a hedge fund, but would be large enough to ensure that our costs are covered and provide us with a reasonable amount to invest. A good track record will bring in further funds.

An issue for investment manager/promoters that pay to launch hedge funds is how they can recover their costs. In order to make this practicable, it would have to estimate the amount that it would make from its management fee and performance fee and the costs of running the fund, in order to set the figure at which the hedge fund would launch. In doing this, it would have to be mindful of the fact that the initial investors might be forced to bear the startup costs in that their proceeds would largely be used for setup costs rather than go into investable assets. Some investment managers may impose a cap on expenses in order to address this concern. The issue then becomes at what point a cap should be imposed. Through analysing figures, an amount will be set that permits the hedge fund launch with an AUM and capped costs so that initial investors are not penalised and the investment manager does not wind up underwriting the hedge fund.

RISK FACTORS

One of the key sections in any Offering Memorandum is risk factors. The disclosures in this section must be complete, timely and accurately describe the risk to investors. Risk factor disclosure is not meant to be "exculpatory". Rather, it is intended to describe the salient points of each risk so that it is understood in the context of the hedge fund's operations.

Risk factors write themselves. By this, we mean that the risks must relate to the fund and not become a general disclosure section. If a hedge fund uses derivatives only for hedging, the risk factors for derivatives should not only set this out, but state the effects of this particular type of risk. The risks in investing in certain types of equities are increased not just because the investment manager would invest in the emerging markets, but because it would use leverage to do this and might be holding illiquid instruments with sub-custodians that were not affiliated with the prime broker, and in a jurisdiction that might not provide sufficient safeguards in terms of protecting third-party assets.

What follows is a summary of some of the more readily identifiable risks found in hedge fund Offering Materials.

Investment risk: Often, hedge fund managers may have no or limited prior experience in managing this particular type of hedge fund. This would be disclosed and linked to the nature of hedge fund investment – the use of leverage.

Exposure risk and borrowing: These two risks identify and discuss the risks concerning the restrictions and limits that are placed on the investment manager in managing the portfolio assets, and the amounts borrowed to achieve leverage of an amount needed to generate an absolute return. Borrowing and short selling may result in the fund experiencing exposures that are not just greater than its AUM, but often greater by a multiple. What should be disclosed is not just this fact, but what controls are in place to address this risk.

Counterparty risk: This risk goes to the partial or complete nonperformance or wrongful performance by a counterparty of one or more transactions that would have a material impact on the fund.

Concentration: Hedge fund portfolios would rarely experience concentration risk, which is holding assets that are not diversified. However, in a master feeder structure, the feeder funds, as they would invest all of their assets in the master fund, would experience this. A significant negative event in the master fund's portfolio might have a deleterious effect on the investors.

The prime broker: Some hedge funds identify this as a risk, others do not. Depending on the terms of the PBA, disclosures would be needed as regards the ability of the prime broker to curtail or cut off borrowing or lending, or with respect to the prime broker's ability to effectively "kill" the hedge fund if it declares an act of insolvency or event of default, and liquidates the portfolio.

Currency risk: This relates to losses in the assets in the portfolio caused by currency movements – to the extent that the hedge fund holds assets in different currencies. This risk is addressed by hedging.

Short selling: Short sellers close their open positions with securities that are purchased at a later date. They "gamble" that the price of the security will have declined to a point where they can close the position and, after paying transaction costs and taking into account tax issues, they will make a profit. The risks here are not being able to obtain securities to close the short position, or the price not declining to a point where money could be made.

Investments: Different investments carry different risks. It may be that, due to factors such as volatility, the inability to hedge positions or price movements, the portfolio declines in value.

Regulatory matters: This risk factor identifies and discusses risks relevant not only to the hedge fund but also the investment manager.

Collateral: Whereas prior to the start of the sub-prime/credit crunch an Offering Memorandum might not have discussed this, depending on the type of collateral that a hedge fund (or master fund) posts, the risks related to the type of collateral and what the prime broker may do if it revalues collateral downward should be addressed. Also, if the investment manager intends to post collateral that is not exchange-traded or is illiquid, it should disclose this.

Tax considerations: The disclosures in the tax section go to the taxation of the hedge fund and/or the master fund in certain jurisdictions, as well as issues for investors in certain jurisdictions. This risk factor points out that changes in tax law might result in adverse consequences, such as not being able to recover withheld tax or losses.

Illiquidity: Shares in hedge funds are not traded on an exchange and usually there is no market for such securities; hence, an investment in such shares does not mean that an investor would be able to redeem, their shares when they wish.

CONFLICTS OF INTEREST

The very nature of hedge fund investment means that the key service providers – investment manager, prime broker, administrator and Directors – may be involved with other AI products or even manage long only products simultaneously with this hedge fund, or other hedge funds.

The disclosures in this section not only identify such conflicts (managing, receiving fees, dealing and so on) but must actually state how the entities involved intend to prevent conflicts or, if they arise, act to resolve them.

REPORTS

This section outlines the reports that investors would receive and states how often they would be made available.

MASTER FUND ISSUES

This section discusses the relationship between the offshore feeder fund and the master fund. It identifies the documents between these two entities and states how the investment manager and the Directors of each company carry out their responsibilities.

TAXATION

Taxation disclosure covers the tax implications of the operation of the fund (and the master fund) and the possible effects of investing on investors in certain jurisdictions, in particular, the US, the UK and the jurisdiction of the investment manager – in the case of our hedge fund, the Cayman Islands.

The multitude of types of hedge funds and the locations of investment managers and investors makes reproducing tax disclosures in this section of this book impossible. However, certain disclosures would in nearly all instances be addressed.

The tax treatment of the hedge fund: For a Cayman Islands fund, this means applying for and receiving a certificate of exemption under the Tax Concessions Law (1999 Revision) that, for a period of 20 years from the date of issuance, the Cayman Islands would not impose a tax on profits, income, gains or appreciation.

Investors: These disclosures would cover gains (or losses) on redemptions or other types of disposal (even, in some instances, an exchange or swap of shares in a reorganisation), dividends, death duties and inheritance tax issues.

GENERAL AND STATUTORY INFORMATION

This section of the Offering Memorandum appears at the back of the document. In it are set forth descriptive disclosures about the fund, details about its establishment and structure, its fiscal year and how it provides semi-annual and annual reports, including the audited financial statements, material agreements (the disclosures in this sub-section might duplicate earlier descriptions of key documents) and procedures governing meetings of shareholders. In many ways, this section summarises key provision of the Articles and the law of the jurisdiction of incorporation.

Other than the points noted above, certain details will appear in this section that might not appear elsewhere in the Offering Memorandum.

- ❑ Details about the Founders Shares and the rights associated with them.
- ❑ Detailed descriptions of the rights of each class of shares.
- ❑ How the Articles may be amended and how shareholder meetings (an EGM) would be called.[5]
- ❑ Details about the suspension of subscriptions, exchanges or redemptions.
- ❑ Details about the suspension of the calculation of the AUM or NAVs per share.
- ❑ Compulsory redemptions.
- ❑ Meetings of Directors.
- ❑ Where and how to inspect and/or obtain information and material agreements.
- ❑ Rights on the winding up of the hedge fund – crucial, given the issues arising out of the liquidation of the two Bear Stearns hedge funds as discussed in Chapter 10.

APPENDIXES

Appendixes will include the subscription documents and any other materials that the Directors deem to be material and for the attention of prospects or investors.

PRIVATE PLACEMENT MEMORANDUM

The disclosures in a PPM would be similar to those set forth in an Offering Memorandum. There are, however, several differences, given that this document is intended for US taxpaying investors.

The legends on the cover of this document will be orientated toward the US taxpaying investor, as this will be the only type of prospect that would receive this document. The disclosures on the inside front cover would be more extensive, due to the market practice of heavily conditioning PPMs with detailed disclaimers going toward a number of risks and addressing a number of points. These include: the document not constituting an offer or solicitation where doing this would be unlawful; disclaimer of authorisation to make representations; disclaimer of investment advice; CFTC disclaimers on status as a CPO; and a disclaimer against any part of the document being deemed to be tax advice.

Whereas an offshore feeder fund offers shares and, in the corporate model, is governed by a board of Directors, an onshore feeder fund is a company governed by an offshore corporate director (usually a Cayman Islands exempt company) and is structured around provisions of the US Internal Revenue Code of 1986, as amended (IRC). Each investor in an onshore feeder fund places his "initial capital contribution" into a "capital" account which is administered by the administrator under the oversight of the corporate director of the onshore feeder fund. Additional capital contributions may be made. In addition to completing subscription documents, each prospect signs the Operating Agreement.

The balance of the capital account reflects an investor's gains or losses. The opening value is the initial capital contribution. The balance of the capital account is adjusted to take of gains, losses, withdrawals, allocations, additional contributions and other designated events, all of which are provided for in the Operating Agreement.

As we have noted elsewhere in this book, non-US investment managers do not contract with onshore feeder funds and do not receive fees from them. This is because the performance allocation is charged and paid at the company level. The corporate director of the onshore feeder fund, called the "manager", receives this fee and, in turn, passes this to the investment manager. The mechanism by which this is done is by creating an account commonly called the "loss recovery account". In this account, the amount that the manager is to receive is subject to an amount that equals the "loss recovery amount" of each investor in the onshore feeder fund. The manner in which the recovery account functions and the calculations that are used to determine the loss recovery amount and, hence, the "manager's performance allocation", is similar to the procedure employed by the administrator in calculating the AUM and the NAVs per share in a single entity hedge fund or the offshore feeder fund. The reason why this is structured is to take advantage of provisions in the IRC that will permit US taxpaying investors holding Interests to receive tax benefits that are passed through the master fund and the onshore feeder fund to every such investor.

Other differences in a PPM as compared to an Offering Memorandum are suitability disclosures, tax disclosures, purchases by employee benefit plans (under ERISA and relevant US Department of Labor regulations) and privacy notifications. These disclosures differ in order to comply with provisions of relevant US law.

VERIFICATION

We have mentioned the role that verification plays in helping to ensure that the Offering Materials – the Offering Memorandum and the PPM – are accurate and do not contain a material misstatement or omission. The consequences of not conducting a verification exercise or missing points may lead to Director liability or, if it established that disclosures to US persons (prospects or investors) are made by the investment manager to a pooled investment vehicle, liability under Advisers Act Rule 206(4)-8.

Verification is conducted by the external lawyers to the hedge fund. This provides a degree of objectivity and validity to the exercise. Verification is, simply put, proving the correctness of every statement in the Offering Materials. This is done by identifying a source(s) for each statement that is contained in the Offering Materials. For example:

> *"Statement*
> *The Fund was incorporated as an open-ended company with limited liability in the Cayman Islands on 22 October 2007.*
>
> *Source*
> *Certificate of Incorporation of the Fund.*
>
> *Responsible*
> *The Directors of the Fund."*

The verification notes will contain a place at the front or bottom for every Director (individually) and service provider of the hedge fund to sign, attesting to the correctness of the statements contained in the verification notes that are attributable to them. The notes will also contain a reference to the Offering Materials and the material agreements used in verification. The verification notes will be tabled at the first Directors meeting, reviewed and approved, prior to their being signed.

1 Non-US persons and US tax-exempt investors receive the Offering Memorandum and buy shares of the offshore feeder fund, whereas US taxpaying investors receive the PPM and receive Interests.
2 The 1940 Act exemptions are discussed in Chapter 7.
3 For example, Ibex 35, FTSE 250, Hang Seng Index, Nikkei or the S&P500, and so on.
4 ISE Listing Rules 12.21.
5 Under Cayman Islands law, there no longer is an obligation to hold an annual general meeting. However, other jurisdictions have retained this requirement.

7

How are Shares or Interests in a Hedge Fund Marketed?

Hedge funds require capital to invest and achieve absolute return, as well as to operate. Initially, the money comes from investors and, afterwards, from gains from trading activities. Raising capital is not as simple as issuing documents, meeting with investors and receiving funds. There are many steps involved in raising capital – as there are in achieving and maintaining capacity, making wise investments, achieving a profit (and avoiding losses) and ensuring that redemptions, when they occur, do not constitute a "run on the bank" and/or require the use of gate provisions.

Raising capital is not easy, because hedge funds do not publicly offer securities but sell them in private placements, and because the legal and regulatory requirements involved in private placements vary among jurisdictions. Those selling hedge fund securities may require registration or be required to operate within restrictions. The documentation that distributors require to offer hedge fund securities may contain exacting conditions. The materials that are used beyond the Offering Materials are limited and require vetting – and there are restrictions on the type of information that may be included in them as well as conditions under which "performance data" or track records may be used. In certain instances, the materials that are used might have to be lodged with a regulator in a jurisdiction where private placements are to be made. In certain jurisdictions, private placements are not permitted.

In this chapter, we survey what is involved in identifying investors for a hedge fund, how seed capital is sought and obtained, distribution agreements and practices, the role of intermediaries, due diligence questionnaires and key aspects of private placements.

PRIVATE PLACEMENTS

What is a private placement?

Public offerings of securities require full registration and disclosure by the issuer of the securities and, after completion of the offering, continuing obligations requirements including disclosure, proxy solicitation (and content) rules, disclosure of large positions, observance of strict procedures for tender and exchange offers (best price, all holders, time-open requirements and prompt payment) and restrictions on LBOs. Public offerings are usually sold by financial intermediaries that are registered with the local regulator. Private placements are not public offerings, and these requirements generally do not apply to issuers of privately placed securities. In selling their securities in private placements, hedge fund distributors seek to avoid registration with a local regulator: this is done in reliance on an exemption from registration or the use of local registered firms, which we will call "intermediaries". A further consideration is that the investment manager will not usually be registered in the country where the private placement would take place; hence, it would need to ensure that having investors in that country would not make it amenable to any form of local registration.

There are "indicia" of private placements:

- a prohibition on general solicitation;
- limited disclosure – which is driven by the ability to avoid the disclosure requirements imposed on issuers in public offerings and by the nature of private placements with an emphasis on key disclosure;
- restrictions on the type of investor that may buy and also, as regards individuals, a limit on the number as well as, in certain instances, restrictions on the relationship of offerees to each other and the issuer; and
- a limited amount of securities are sold (this usually is not applicable in the case of hedge funds).

Generally, private placements do not require the registration of the Offering Materials or the registration of the hedge fund itself. This, however, is not the case in several jurisdictions. For example, a filing would need to be made to MAS in Singapore for the hedge fund to be recognised as a "restricted scheme".

Jurisdiction is also an issue. In this sense, this means where the offer and sale take place.

- In the United Arab Emirates (UAE), for example, registration is avoided if the sole activity carried out in that country involves an offer for sale and the sale is completed outside that jurisdiction. This means that the offer would be made from outside the country and the processing and acceptance of the Application would take place at the administrator's offices, not in this country.
- Read together, s.4(2) and s.5 of the 1933 Act provide that shares sold in a private placement need not be registered with the SEC (most hedge fund private placements in the US are done under Rule 506 of

Regulation D). However, s.5, the main registration provision of the US federal securities laws, is silent on jurisdiction. In 1990, the SEC adopted Regulation S, a safe harbour from s.5 registration for offers and sales of securities that take place outside the US, subject to the satisfaction of certain conditions. A non-US hedge fund that did not wish to accept US persons under any circumstances would use Regulation S, but a hedge fund, if it sought US money, would use Rule 506 under Regulation D.

In terms of numbers of investors, there are differing requirements.

- In Switzerland, hedge funds may be sold in a private placement or as a result of an unsolicited request of a Swiss prospect. The FBRC requirements provide that not more than 20 investors may purchase securities in a private placement.
- In the US, 1940 Act s.3(c)(1) exemption lets a non-US fund sell its securities on a private placement basis in the US to not more than 100 US persons. A second (alternative) 1940 Act exemption under s.3(c)(7) permits a non-US fund to sell its shares in the US on a private placement basis, as long as every US investor is a "qualified purchaser" (as defined in s.2(a)(51) of the 1940 Act). There is no limit in s.3(c)(7) on the number of qualified purchasers.[1]

Investor protection

Disclosure in a private placement is an important consideration. Disclosure requirements for public offerings are detailed. In addition, the liability provisions for documents that contain material misrepresentations or omission are harsh. In the US, for example, there is strict liability (no defence) for the issuer (and its directors) in the case of a prospectus in a registration statement that is declared effective by the SEC staff, if that document contains material misrepresentations or omission.

By contrast, disclosures in private placement documents are usually set by market forces and conditions. Liability is not strict liability, as is the case under 1933 Act s.11, but the antifraud rules in the 1933 Act and in the Exchange Act apply. Under these, investors that purchased securities in reliance on documents that contain material misrepresentations or omission would have a right of action to sue for damages, usually rescission. Also, the distributor of the hedge fund might face court action. In certain jurisdictions, actions that involve intent might result in a referral to a governmental agency for criminal action.

Regulators are concerned about protecting the interests of investors in all products, including hedge funds. They would be able to take action against Directors, promoters and distributors under general antifraud provisions.

One regulator even went so far as to adopt a rule that explicitly protects the interests of investors in certain pooled investment vehicles – and also prospects that consider such investments. New Rule 206(4)-8, an antifraud rule under s.206 of the Advisers Act, came into force on 10 September 2007. The new rule would, according to the SEC, ban advisers to pooled investment vehicles from "making false or misleading statements to, or otherwise defrauding, investors or prospective investors in those pooled vehicles".

In his opening remarks at the meeting when this new rule was adopted, SEC chairman Christopher Cox stated that the SEC was adopting the rule in response to *Goldstein*, the case that invalidated the "private fund" rule. New Rule 206(4)-8 permits the SEC to "look through" a pooled investment vehicle to protect the underlying investors against the fraudulent activity of the adviser. The new rule does not require SEC registration.

Rule 206(4)-8 is intended to protect investors *and* prospective investors in pooled investment vehicles. A "pooled investment vehicle" is defined as an investment company that is registered with the SEC under the 1940 Act as well as a fund that is exempt from 1940 Act registration under the s.(3)(c)(1) or the s.3(c)(7) exemptions.

The rule applies to every investment adviser to a pooled investment vehicle, whether or not the adviser is registered with the SEC under the Advisers Act.

Under this new rule, it would be unlawful for any investment adviser to make a materially false or misleading statement, to engage in a fraudulent act or to make a material omission.[2] The rule would not impose a fiduciary duty under the Advisers Act. There is not a private right of action under this rule, so an investor or prospect could not sue an adviser for a violation of the rule.

Unlike Exchange Act Rule 10b-5, which proscribes conduct "in connection with" the purchase or sale of a security, there is no such requirement in this new rule. Any fraudulent, manipulative or deceptive activity is actionable.

At the open meeting when the rule was adopted, the SEC discussed the effect of the rule on non-US advisers. Chairman Cox asked the Staff of the Division of Investment Management for its views whether the rule would change or affect the basis for the exercise of SEC jurisdiction over certain activities of non-US advisers. The Staff reaffirmed its position that the Advisers Act would not apply to the non-US activities of non-US advisers as regards their non-US clients, prospects and investors, but this act and the new rule would apply to the activities of non-US advisers as regards US prospects and investors in the funds that they advise – non-US and US alike. This position, they indicated, was consistent with the "conducts and effects" articulated in SEC Staff no-action letters[3] and used as a basis to assert jurisdiction over the US activities of non-US advisers, both Advisers Act registered and non-registered.

Under the "conducts and effects" approach, conduct inside the US or non-US conduct that had an effect in the US would suffice to permit the application of the US federal securities laws. This, coupled with the use of the "means of interstate commerce" to market non-US funds and services to US persons – telephone, post, fax, e-mail or visit – would permit the SEC to exercise jurisdiction over the activities of non-US SEC registered advisers and non-US non-SEC-registered advisers involving or affecting US persons and the pooled investment vehicles such advisers managed.

Under Rule 206(4)-8, a materially false or misleading statement in any document given to, or in a conversation with, a prospect or an investor in a fund would be actionable. So, too, would an act that constituted a fraud. Unlike other provisions of the US federal securities laws, scienter (intent) is not the test for an enforcement action under Rule 206(4)-8: negligence will suffice.

What type of statement, omission or course of conduct might be actionable?

- A materially false or misleading statement about the credentials of the adviser, the risks associated with an investment in the fund, performance data of the fund or possibly other funds managed by the adviser, or practices followed by the adviser (eg, how it allocates investment opportunities). This might occur, for example, in a meeting with a prospect or in a telephone call or e-mail. Absconding with client money would be actionable – this might result in an enforcement action under other provisions of the US federal securities laws.
- Publishing a materially false valuation or an account statement.
- A materially false or misleading statement, or a material omission, in a PPM, an RFP or any other document or publication.
- A material failure to disclose. At the meeting when the rule was adopted, the SEC Staff was asked whether the failure to disclose a side letter would be actionable. The answer was affirmative, but only if the failure to disclose the side letter breached an obligation to disclose it.
- The rule could catch a statement made to a US person prospect by a non-US, non-SEC registered adviser proposing to launch a non-US pooled investment vehicle that was to be exempt from 1940 Act registration under s.3(c)(1) or s.3(c)(7). An example of this might be an adviser, in a telephone call with a US person prospect, negligently failing to discuss a key risk factor that was contained in a private placement memorandum for this fund.

Provisions of Advisers Act s.206 apply to prospects and investors.[4] This section is conditioned on the use of the means of interstate commerce. s.206(4) serves as the authority for the new rule and satisfies a goal to extend Advisers Act protections to prospects as well as investors.

It was noted in the open meeting that advisers solicit or disseminate materials to prospects as well as investors in a fund. Advisers Act protections should apply equally to prospects and investors alike. It was also noted that advisers issue materials targeted to identifiable investors and prospects, but may publish electronic communications and post materials on Web sites which may be received or seen by many persons. Concerning enforcement actions under the rule, generally, as long as one investor may be identified a case may go forward. Since private placements involve a small number of persons to whom materials for such an offering are sent, it would be possible to identify an investor.

The effect of the new rule – all advisers, all funds and a showing of negligence – is that:

- a document with a statement by a non-US adviser that goes to a US prospect or client must be vetted to ensure that it is correct and that no material fact has been omitted – ensure that materials that are issued by affiliated and non-affiliated distributors and sub-distributors must also be properly vetted;
- a person who issues materials to a US prospect or to a client that contains a statement that is attributed to a non-US adviser should obtain the consent or approval of the non-US adviser for that statement, or have a reasonable basis to believe that the statement is correct and that no material fact has been omitted; and
- proper and regular training is essential – care should be taken in conversations with a US prospect or client to state facts clearly and correctly.

INVESTORS

Types of investors

As we noted in Chapter 1, hedge funds attract money from many sources – FoHFs, institutions, tax-exempt entities (foundations, endowments and trusts), pension plans and individuals, including HNWIs. If hedge funds offered and sold their securities in public offerings, the composition of its shareholder base might not be relevant. They do not do this – press releases about hedge funds making public offerings are not correct, as it is the investment manager that is going through registration. The nature of hedge funds and how they operate – being offshore in a jurisdiction that provides low or no taxation, having few substantive regulatory requirements, seeking money from institutions rather than individuals and being opaque as regards their activities – dictates that, to be able to continue to have these perquisites, funds be raised in private placements.

Private placements are conducted in compliance with exemptions or exceptions to public offering requirements. Requirements for private placements vary from country to country, but call for offerings to a limited number of defined types of investors with no publicity, carefully prepared documentation and, save for certain jurisdictions, no regulatory filing or clearance. Post-offering disclosure usually consists of filing amended Offering Materials and financial statements, unaudited interim and audited annual financials.

Private placements offer a benefit in that hedge funds may choose their investors. By contrast, companies conducting public offerings cannot do this and their shares are required to be freely traded on the exchanges where they are listed.[5] The types of investors that may receive Offering Materials and buy securities in private placements are "defined" in local laws and regulations. They include institutions and individuals. For individuals the requirements vary from "accredited investors" and "qualified purchasers" to "sophisticated investors". The definitions for types of individuals generally are cast in terms of assets, wealth or sophistication.

- In the US, private placements under Rule 506 of Regulation D, an exemption from registration under the 1933 Act, permits offers to an unlimited number of accredited investors and a maximum of 35 non-accredited investors. An "accredited investor" is an individual whose own net worth or joint net worth with a spouse is greater than US$1 million or whose own income exceeds US$200,000 in each of the most recent years or whose joint income with a spouse exceeds US$300,000 in each of the two most recent years. The SEC has proposed a new Rule 507 Regulation D for private placements with no restrictions on general solicitations (this proposal was pending as we went to press).
- In the UK, private placements are for persons to whom they may lawfully be issued or passed on and then only to restricted categories of recipients, investors to whom shares may be promoted without contravening FSMA s.21(1) or s.238(1) – namely, institutional investors or a maximum number of 50 individuals.
- For private placements in Hong Kong, prospects must be "professional investors" as defined in the Securities and Futures Ordinance and the Securities and Futures (Professional Investor) Rules of Hong Kong, except with the prior consent of the Directors.

Offering Materials contain a section that states the jurisdictions in which the securities of the hedge fund may be offered and the types of prospects that are eligible to become investors. The same disclosures generally appear in the distribution agreement, which is entered into by the Directors with, in many cases, the investment manager or with third parties' distributors, in the case of hedge funds that wish to sell their securities in many countries. The application materials (Application) refer to the Offering Materials and the provisions on eligibility and require prospects to warrant their status as being eligible to purchase the hedge fund's securities. Applications also make clear that prospects have an obligation to keep the administrator informed of any change in status that may affect their ability to continue to be eligible to hold securities. There is a provision in the Articles and the Offering Materials that states that the Directors have the power to redeem investors compulsorily should it be the case that they were or become ineligible to hold securities or the holding of securities would subject the hedge fund to legal, tax and regulatory sanctions.

DUE DILIGENCE QUESTIONNAIRES

Institutional investors require that hedge funds complete DDQs. These are questionnaires that supplement the disclosures make in the Offering Materials. Generally, they enquire about details of the investment manager, such as its structure, type of regulation, controls, activities, compliance procedures and other matters. Whereas a few years ago DDQs were largely taken up with queries about the investment manager's track record and the hedge fund's performance – queries that are still made – increasingly, prospects are seeking information about controls and operating procedures. Prospects, particularly institutions, care about the activities of the investment manager in terms of ensuring that its processes are robust and would not jeopardise their assets. DDQs are occasionally also given to administrators and prime brokers.

The DDQ process involves not only meetings with investors, but "road shows". In a road show, the investment manager meets prospects to discuss their interest in the hedge fund and to pursue investment interest. Road shows include one-on-one meetings as well as cap intro events sponsored by prime brokers. Cap intros involve meetings and presentations by investment managers for groups of investors. There are one-on-one meetings and also presentations. In these the investment manager is given the opportunity to make presentations to prospects.

There are regulatory concerns arising from cap intros.

- ❑ Promoters of cap intro meetings often seek an indemnity from the investment manager participants, in return for hosting the meeting and making materials available. Caution must be exercised in giving such provisions, and the sponsor of the event should covenant to provide materials only to those investors that are eligible to purchase securities in the jurisdictions where the hedge fund has taken advice and has decided to conduct a private placement.
- ❑ The participants in cap intros should ensure, prior to meeting investors, that those they meet are eligible to buy their hedge fund's securities. No one wants to go through a due diligence process only to find, at the point of sale, that the investors is for some reason not eligible.

A further consideration goes to the information contained in a DDQ. All such information must be consistent with the disclosures contained in the Offering Materials. This will help avoid potential liability issues. If this arises, it may result not just in having to offer rescission to the investors involved, but in regulatory scrutiny about false or misleading sales practices.

DISTRIBUTION

Intermediaries

Hedge funds distribute their securities through distributors. Generally, these are affiliates of the investment manager or intermediaries that are located and licensed in a jurisdiction where the hedge fund proposes to offer its shares.

On first blush, it would appear easy to have intermediaries offer securities for hedge funds. Doing this raises many issues, the most important of which follow.

Content of materials: Usually, intermediaries provide only the Offering Materials. In certain instances, those that they solicit may demand to receive more information. They seek, for example, the performance (track record) of the investment manager and, in the search for seed capital, "paper portfolio" information (the portfolio that the manager has traded during the lead up to the offering, which is used to show how the individual involved would manage this fund). Hedge fund Directors should ensure that every intermediary signed a distribution agreement with the intermediary. This should provide for, in addition to the fees to be paid – both initial fees and "trailer" fees – what materials may be used, whether the intermediary may use its own materials or those of an affiliate of the investment manager (this occurs frequently in the case of investment managers in groups of companies or with multiple funds to be sold in several jurisdictions). All materials should be reviewed and approved according to criteria established by the Directors or the investment manager if the Directors have given it consent to do this.

Compliance with selling restrictions: The intermediary must market the hedge fund's securities only in the jurisdictions where it is appointed and only to those prospects that are eligible to become investors.

Liability: Distribution agreements should provide that the liability of the Directors is curtailed, or eliminated, if the intermediary engages in bad acts or practices that give rise to liability.

Must intermediaries be registered?

A key consideration when using intermediaries to sell the hedge fund securities is whether such entities need to be registered.

In most instances, an intermediary will be registered in the country where the hedge fund proposes to sell its securities. However, there are times when distributors wish to sell hedge fund securities to investors in countries where they are not located or registered. This involves consideration of local licensing requirements.

For example, in Australia, non-Australian intermediaries that wish to sell shares of non-Australian hedge funds to Australian residents might have to register. There is a narrow exemption in Australian law that would permit non-Australian hedge funds to market their shares to certain types of Australians without having to register.

The situation in the US is different. Neither "broker" nor "dealer" is defined in terms of jurisdictional limits, but looks to a specific activity.[6] The SEC defines "solicitation" broadly to include *any* affirmative effort by a person that induces or is intended to induce transactional business for the broker–dealer or its affiliates, or develop an ongoing relationship.[7] It includes the use of broker–dealer Web sites. It also includes solicitations targeted at identifiable groups of US persons living outside the United States (eg, US embassy and military personnel).

The Exchange Act broker–dealer registration provisions apply to any broker or dealer that uses the means of interstate commerce to effect or induce transactions in securities. Thus:

- a non-US broker, dealer or bank (non-US firm) that conducts its activities totally outside the United States and with no US-based or targeted solicitations would not be required to register;
- any communication by a non-US firm into the US involving the means of interstate commerce would implicate Exchange Act broker–dealer registration.

To help determine whether a person is a "broker", the SEC asks (1) is the person engaged "in the business", (2) does the activity constitute "effecting a transaction in securities" and (3) is the activity "for the account of others". Brokers hold themselves out to be in the business of buying and selling securities for the account of others, receive transaction-based compensation and/or have access to or custody of customer funds and/or securities. The Staff of the SEC's Division of Market Regulation has stated in several no-action letters that the receipt of transaction-based compensation is key in determining whether a person is acting as a broker and that a person that received such compensation in connection with brokerage must, absent an exemption, register.

When would a non-US investment adviser or a non-US distributor of the securities of a non-US hedge fund be deemed to be a "broker" and face SEC registration as a broker–dealer?

The SEC has issued few no-action letters addressing the application of the Exchange Act broker–dealer registration provisions to investment advisers.

A person that solicits transactions, takes transaction-based compensation and effects orders for the account of others using the means of interstate commerce would be a "broker" under the Exchange Act and must register with the SEC.

If a non-US manager offered discretionary investment management to US person clients and related advisory services (including advertising, as defined in Advisers Act Rule 206(4)-1), but nothing else, it would in all likelihood be beyond the boundaries of broker–dealer registration. Adding self-directed accounts and soliciting orders to buy or sell securities using the means of interstate commerce might cause it to be a "broker" and bring it within the aegis of broker–dealer registration.

The Division of Investment Management has issued no-action letters that hold that an adviser that transmits orders to brokers or banks for execution, does not hold client funds or securities and does not receive transaction-based compensation for this would not be required to register as a broker–dealer. No-action relief was denied where the activities were more extensive eg, solicitations and/or regularly sending research. The Division of Market Regulation would take the position that doing this and receiving transaction-based compensation requires registration.

Non-US investment managers and/or distributors market non-US hedge funds to US prospects. On its face, this would appear to be a solicitation and require registration.

Rule 15a-6 under the Exchange Act is a non-exclusive safe harbour that facilitates access by US institutional investors through non-US firms to foreign securities markets and research on foreign issuers. Non-US firms can, without registration:

- effect unsolicited transactions in securities with US persons;
- with certain conditions, solicit US persons who are "major US institutional investors" by furnishing them with research reports, subject to compliance;
- solicit transactions in securities from and execute transactions with or for "US institutional investors", subject to conditions;
- solicit and execute transactions in securities directly with SEC-registered broker–dealers (whether acting as principal or agent), banks acting in a broker–dealer capacity, international entities, non-US persons temporarily present in the US with which the non-US firm has a pre-existing relationship, non-US agencies or branches of US persons permanently outside the US (if the trades occur outside the US) and US citizens resident outside the US (if the non-US firm does not direct its selling efforts toward identifiable groups of US citizens resident abroad).

Rule 15a-6 does not by its terms provide a safe harbour from broker–dealer registration for persons that are neither major US institutional investors nor US institutional investors. Thus, the solicitation of individuals that were "qualified purchasers" and eligible to buy shares of non-US hedge funds under 1940 Act s.3(c)(7) but not major US institutional investors or US institutional investors would not fall within the Rule 15a-6 safe harbour.

Rule 15a-6 is a non-exclusive safe harbour. Because of this, there are compliance controls that may be put into place to facilitate the solicitation of individuals to purchase shares of non-US hedge funds by certain non-US firms. However, such controls are extremely narrow in scope and contemplate only the offering of securities, nothing more.

The SEC is reviewing "mutual recognition" in the sense of permitting, subject to compliance with certain conditions, non-US exchanges or even broker–dealers to enter the US markets. (See "Trading Foreign Shares" by Eric Sirri, Director of the SEC's Division of Market Regulation,[8] and the June 2007 roundtable on mutual recognition.)

Given all of this, in marketing the securities of non-US hedge funds to US prospects it is prudent in the absence of clear pronouncements to:

- observe Exchange Act Rule 15a-6;
- work with SEC-registered broker–dealers when engaging in this; or
- refrain from any activity that would be a solicitation or not receive transaction-based compensation.

THE SUBSCRIPTION PROCESS

Elsewhere in this book, we discussed the process by which the administrator processes applications for shares. In this section of this chapter, we outline some of the considerations that are critical not just to the investors but to hedge funds.

Subscriptions

A hedge fund will receive subscriptions from new and existing investors if it is neither soft closed nor hard closed.

An administrator needs to perform a number of checks when it receives Applications. These include eligibility. By this we mean whether the prospect is an eligible investor as this term is defined in the Offering Materials. In addition, the administrator would perform AML checks to verify the identity of the subscriber and also confirm the source(s) of funds. Other checks that are performed would be to ensure that the prospect, if it was a US taxpaying investor seeking to buy shares in a master feeder structure, had applied for the correct feeder fund – in this case, it would be the onshore feeder fund. It is also necessary for the administrator to record certain details about the prospect as an investor so that it is able to perform certain monitoring checks to help ensure that the hedge fund avoid running foul of certain restrictions, such as ensuring that types of investors do not hold more than a certain percentage of the shares of a particular class of securities.

EQUALISATION

Hedge funds trade to generate absolute return. The more they make, the less likely it is that investors will wish to redeem their shares. By the same token, the investment manager will stand to make more money, due to the fact that it is compensated in part for its performance. Poor or no performance translates into no performance fee.

The issue of performance and performance fees is linked to the timing of investment in a hedge fund. In general, prospects that invest in a hedge fund earlier in the hedge fund's life will pay a smaller portion of the performance fee than others that invested at a later date. By way of example, our model hedge fund launched in January 2007 with an AUM of 100 and a NAV per share of £100 for the sterling voting Non-Restricted shares. At the end of June 2007, the NAV per share of this class has risen to £108. Let us presume that, at December 2007, the NAV per share of this class hits £120. During this time, the administrator has been calculating and accruing the performance fee. The performance fee is set at the rate of 20%, so the fee payable would be £3.20 per share. However, when the administrator is calculating the performance fee, it would assess the fee against the shareholders that were invested in the hedge fund on a given date. Thus, shareholders investing in the initial offering period or shortly thereafter would pay a smaller portion of their gain as performance fee to the investment manager, and those buying in later in the year would pay more.

To address this inequality, hedge funds employ "equalisation".

Using equalisation provides a number of advantages to investors and the hedge fund. First, shares that have appreciated in value pay a performance fee. Next, the employment of equalisation means that all investors have the same amount per share at risk in the hedge fund, as well as the same NAV per share. This means that the investment manager, when rewarded for its performance, receives an equal amount from among all shares involved.

There are several methods of applying equalisation. The one most commonly employed is "equalisation credit". Equalisation credit is a formula that employs certain measures:

- gross asset value per share (GAV per share);
- NAV per share;
- the high watermark (HW mark), which is the issue price of the class of shares or the highest price at the end of a calculation period – the fiscal year end;

- the equalisation credit – this occurs when the GAV per share exceeds the HW mark. The amount given as a credit is the difference between the GAV per share and the HW mark.

The equalisation credit is given for appreciation in shares, not depreciation. The process involved in using equalisation credits is, simply put, to help investors purchase new shares by using equalisation credits (or by carrying those forward to be used when there are reductions in the NAV per share of the class involved). If a prospect invests in a hedge fund when the GAV per share is below the HW mark, the investor would be charged, and have to pay, an additional performance fee relating to the difference between the current price of the shares and the HW mark.

Thus, in our example, the prospect that invested in the initial offering period and the subscribers that followed would, if equalisation were employed, pay the same amount of performance fee at year end. By the same token, if the NAV per share of the hedge fund fell in value, a prospect investing in the same class of shares as the previous two investors would, if the GAV per share fell below the HW mark, would have to pay an additional amount towards the performance fee to equalise the calculations.

1 A non-US fund that has more than 500 investors (300 US residents) and US$10 million in assets within 120 days after the end of its most recent fiscal year must register with the SEC under Exchange Act s.12(g).

2 Information is "material" if a reasonable investor would consider it significant and it would alter the total mix of information publicly available to investors. *TSC Industries, Inc. v Northway, Inc*, 426 US 438 (1976).

3 *Uniao de Bancos de Brasileiros SA* (28 July 1992). *See also Mercury Asset Management plc* (16 April 1993) and *The National Mutual Group* (8 March 1993).

4 The first two sub-sections of Section 206 are intended to protect clients and prospective clients, while the third sub-section relates solely to clients. The fourth sub-section of this rule does not reference clients or prospective clients, and gives the Commission power, by rules or regulations, to "define … and proscribe means reasonably designed to prevent … acts, practices, and courses of business as are fraudulent, manipulative or deceptive". Advisers Act Section 206(4).

5 In many jurisdictions, including the US and Japan, securities are offered for sale and sold. The regulatory regimes in these countries are based on the principle of offering securities. By contrast, in other countries such as the UK and in Hong Kong and Singapore, securities are made available by subscription, a process that permits prospects to submit completed application forms and a cheque, after which underwriters gauge the take up against the public offering materials, confirm the offering price, confirm subscriptions and offer securities.

6 A "broker" under Section 3(a)(4) of the Exchange Act is a person that is engaged in the business of effecting transactions in securities for the account of others. A "dealer" is defined in Section 3(a)(5) as any person that buys or sells securities for its own account through a broker or otherwise, but excludes a person that buys or sells securities for its own account, "individually or in a fiduciary capacity, but not as a part of a regular business" – this is the "trader" exception that hedge funds rely on to buy and sell securities.

7 "Solicitation" is not defined in a rule but was articulated in the release adopting Rule 15a-6, a safe harbour from broker-dealer registration. See Exchange Act Release 27017, 54 FR 30013, 18 July 1989.

8 URL: www.sec.gov/news/speech/2007/spch030107ers.htm.

8

How is a Hedge Fund Operated?

In previous chapters, we reviewed what hedge funds are, how they are organised, what securities they offer and how those securities are sold, the RFP process to identify service providers, who is responsible for hedge funds and the process by which hedge funds prepare for launch. In this chapter, we explore how hedge funds operate. Our discussion runs from the Directors meeting at which time documents are approved and the instructions to launch are given, through the first year of operations.

What is involved in operating a hedge fund? The steps that comprise this are the preparations for launch, the initial offering period, research and fund management, trading, prime brokerage, administration, compliance and Directors activities.

PREPARATIONS FOR LAUNCH

Many activities are required to launch a hedge fund. By "launch" we mean the start of operations following the initial offering period. These include completing the RFP process and identifying service providers, finalising documents, confirming seed capital, putting trading agreements in place and holding the initial Directors meeting.

At the initial Directors meeting, the promoters give a report on the activities involved in establishing the hedge fund and take steps to commence the initial offering period and proceed to launch. The agenda for such a meeting would include the following points:

- a report of the incorporation of the hedge fund, the establishment of the registered office and the ratification of the documents for the incorporation and registration of the hedge fund;
- the establishment of the classes of shares of the fund, together with any sub-classes;
- ratification of the issuance of the Founders Shares, the allotment of further Founders Shares and, if necessary, the transfer of these shares to the investment manager or another entity;

- ❑ key decisions, such as setting the fiscal year and the year end and appointing the auditors;
- ❑ the review and approval of the hedge fund's investment objective, policies and restrictions;
- ❑ a discussion of the Offering Memorandum and key sections of it, with an emphasis on Directors' responsibilities;
- ❑ the review and approval of the verification notes;
- ❑ the review and approval of documents necessary to offer shares of the hedge fund in the initial offering period and to launch and operate the hedge fund (*see* the list set forth in the Appendix);
- ❑ a consideration of the expenses involved in launching the hedge fund and their approval;
- ❑ the appointment of service providers;
- ❑ the approval to open accounts and name signatories – prime broker account(s), custodial accounts and bank accounts;
- ❑ the approval of a resolution to empower a Director or a duly authorised agent of a Director to take actions, sign documents, give instructions or file documents to facilitate the launch;
- ❑ provide for D&O insurance; and
- ❑ coordinate the deposit of the initial offering period proceeds with the administrator for operational purposes and the prime broker for investment.

In a master feeder structure, there will be meetings of the boards of Directors of the feeder funds and the master fund, as well as the corporate director of the onshore feeder fund (if there is one). These meetings would be held simultaneously.

At the completion of the Directors meeting, the documents that are required to operate the hedge fund will be signed by the Directors and the other entities or service providers involved (the documents would contain clauses permitting counterparty execution in more than one location). The verification notes will be signed by each Director and the service providers. Bank account mandates and other operative documents, including the Offering Materials, will be signed and delivered. If the hedge fund is listed on the ISE or the CSX, materials will be signed and delivered for filing with the exchange (and, if necessary, any local authority). When all of these steps are completed, the initial offering period starts.

INITIAL OFFERING PERIOD

As noted elsewhere in this book, a key consideration is having sufficient funds in hand to be able to launch. It costs a considerable amount of money to launch and operate a hedge fund, and because of this it is necessary to raise an amount sufficient to cover the establishment costs and provide funds sufficient to be able to trade.

The process of funding begins with the initial offering period. This is a short time period in which the distributor of the hedge fund's shares (in many instances, the investment manager or an affiliate), contacts those prospects that expressed an interest in the hedge fund and that received "red herring" Offering Materials, informs them of the approval for the launch and asks them to confirm their investment in the hedge fund. Those prospects will submit completed subscription forms to the administrator, together with supporting documents and cleared funds to cover their investment. The administrator will review the subscription forms, verify identity and source(s) of funds. When all checks have been completed successfully and cleared funds are in hand, the Directors and other service providers will be notified, funds will be transferred to the prime broker, the initial offering period will end and the hedge fund will start to trade.

RESEARCH AND FUND MANAGEMENT – AND FIDUCIARY DUTIES

At the end of the initial offering period, the administrator transfers the proceeds of the offering to the prime broker, but retains a certain amount of money in order to be able to pay the ongoing administrative expenses of the hedge fund. Certain administrators will also retain a sum of money that is sufficient to be able to handle redemption requests that are made "in the ordinary course" of operations. (Chapter 10 contains a discussion of large-scale redemption requests.) In our hedge fund, the amount of money required to launch is £25 million. The base NAV per share for each class of shares would be £100.

Prior to the launch and start of operations, the individuals that are to manage the hedge fund usually research and trade a "paper portfolio". Launch is the time when the paper portfolio is replaced by live investments. The purpose of trading a paper portfolio is to give the individuals involved experience in managing a pool of assets in accordance with the hedge fund's investment objective, policies and restrictions, and to provide a guide for prospects to gain an understanding of how these individuals might perform. (Compliance officers impose restrictions on the use of paper portfolios in the lead up to launch.) For example, in our long-short global equity fund, the paper portfolio will start with an amount of money (usually, this is the amount required to launch). The investment manager would during the RFP process "trade" this.

On launch, actual trading begins. Having traded a paper portfolio, the investment manager will use the proceeds on deposit with the prime broker to start to buy and sell investments and, shortly thereafter, trade to hedge those investments.

Research and fund management is the process by which the investment manager decides what to buy or sell, and how to hedge the portfolio. The investment manager investigates investment opportunities, internally or by reviewing research from third parties, including executing brokers. Research takes the form of a review and analysis of a listed company's performance and strategies. For example, a research report on Microsoft would review that company's performance over a given period of time, discuss its earnings history, survey its operations, discuss factors that comprise the market in which it operates, identify factors that might affect its ability to operate and give a forecast as to whether the writer of the research report believes that the company would meet, fall below or exceed its forecasts.

Research also includes meetings with company management and other senior officials, conducting surveys of the market in which the company operates, examining market trends, comparing movements in currencies and charting share prices and other indicators and economic factors that might affect performance.

Hedge fund investment managers use analytics to help identify investment opportunities, as well as for risk management purposes. Analytics are computer programs that review and compare performance data and economic indicators to help identify securities that are under- or overvalued. Internally generated research is generated on the fund management desk or in a separate research department.

External research is received and reviewed by fund managers, but there are considerations surrounding this. The key factors are how such research is paid for and how it is used to achieve "best execution". Client funds that are used to pay for research are called soft dollars or client commissions. There are restrictions placed on the ability to use client funds to pay for research or other items such as computers, travel and operating expenses. This is because an investment manager is a fiduciary and owes fiduciary duties to its clients.

Fiduciary duties are expressed in different ways in different countries, but are best understood as the legal relationship between two parties – the investment manager and the client – in which the investment manager owes duties of trust, care, obedience and skill and diligence to protect client assets and to invest them in a prudent manner, taking into account the needs of the client and its investment objectives. Investment managers as fiduciaries must avoid conflicts of interests and not take advantage of their clients. In the US, the standard under the Advisers Act was set by the Supreme Court in *SEC v Capital Gains Research Bureau*,[1] which said that this act reflects:

> *"a congressional recognition of the delicate fiduciary nature of an investment advisory relationship as well as a congressional intent to eliminate, or at least to expose, all conflicts of interest which might incline an investment adviser—consciously or unconsciously—to render advice which was not disinterested."*[2]

The US Investment Adviser Association has produced Standards of Practice, which many SEC-registered investment managers follow. Under Section I, "Fiduciary Duty and Professional Responsibility":

> [a]n investment adviser stands in a special relationship of trust and confidence with, and therefore is a fiduciary to, its clients. As a fiduciary, an investment adviser has an affirmative duty of care, loyalty, honesty, and good faith to act in the best interests of its clients. The parameters of an investment adviser's duty depend on the scope of the advisory relationship and generally include:
>
> (1) the duty at all times to place the interests of clients first;
> (2) the duty to have a reasonable basis for its investment advice;
> (3) the duty to seek best execution for client securities transactions where the adviser directs such transactions;
> (4) the duty to make investment decisions consistent with any mutually agreed upon client objectives, strategies, policies, guidelines, and restrictions;
> (5) the duty to treat clients fairly;
> (6) the duty to make full and fair disclosure to clients of all material facts about the advisory relationship, particularly regarding conflicts of interest; and
> (7) the duty to respect the confidentiality of client information.[3]

There has been a debate whether an investment manager owes fiduciary duties to the underlying investors in a hedge fund. The client of an investment manager is the fund, not the underlying investors. However, there are examples of regulators acting to protect the interests of underlying investors – one of the best known is Advisers Act Rule 206(4)-8 (discussed in Chapter 7), which proscribes fraudulent acts of investment managers towards investors and prospective investors in pooled investment vehicles. In other instances, courts in many jurisdictions will if necessary act to protect the interests of investors when investment managers engage in activities that would compromise client assets.

TRADING

Hedge funds buy and sell for investment purposes and for hedging. Trading for both purposes is accomplished by placing orders with executing brokers to purchase or sell investments.

The process of trading begins with fund management. An investment manager conducts research to identify investments suitable to achieving the stated investment objective and policies, but within the stated restrictions. The investment manager for our model hedge fund would look to identify suitable exchange-traded issuers within its strategy whose securities were underpriced or overpriced to buy or sell, respectively. When it identified such prospects, it would place orders to buy or sell. For example:

- an investment manager would place an order to buy 560,000 shares of Microsoft on the basis that the stock was undervalued and would appreciate in price;
- at the same time, the manager might place an order to sell 300,000 Apple, on the premise that this stock was overvalued and would decline in price. This trade may be done by delivering the position of Apple in the prime brokerage account or in a short sale, in which case the investment manager must arrange to borrow for delivery the shares required, from the prime broker or from another source.

After it receives an order to buy or sell securities, the executing broker would "work the order", which means that it would fill the order out of its own inventory or send the order to the market for execution. Buy or sell orders are filled in a single transaction or a series of transactions (in which case the price given to the hedge fund would be an average price).

Often, and to achieve best execution, investment managers place orders to buy or sell securities for more than one client or, in the case of an investment manager that is managing more than one hedge fund, two or more hedge fund clients. Orders, when placed this way, are "aggregated". This permits the investment manager to route an order to an executing broker to satisfy its obligation to seek best execution. When the order is filled, the investment manager will "allocate" the execution among its clients. Allocation takes place on a pre-trade basis: so, for example, an investment manager trading for three hedge funds would decide how many shares of a security each hedge fund would receive, place the order and, after confirmation, allocate to each client the amount of stock earmarked for each prior to the trade.

Trading would continue in this way as the investment manager invested the portfolio assets seeking to generate alpha and contribute toward absolute return.

If hedge funds merely bought and sold securities, the portfolios that they managed would be susceptible to movements in the prices of the assets in the portfolio. Over time – and this might be as short as a few hours, depending on market conditions – price movements might wipe out portfolio gains entirely. To do nothing would not be in the best interests of the hedge fund. For this reason, steps must be taken to ensure that the portfolio is protected. Hedging is a form of trading that is designed to minimise portfolio risk.

There are two types of hedging strategies: "static" and "dynamic". Static hedging means that an investment is put in place to protect, or hedge, an asset in the portfolio and remains in place. Dynamic hedging is an active process to protect the value of an asset in a portfolio, or the portfolio itself. In dynamic hedging, the investment manager works with a portfolio model that takes the value of all portfolio assets on a daily, interactive basis and calculates a measure of volatility inherent in the portfolio, factoring in price movements in each portfolio asset. Securities or derivatives are bought and sold that help to reduce the degree of volatility in the portfolio in such a way so as to help ensure that volatility remains at a minimum and the value of the portfolio is protected.

PRIME BROKERAGE

After the initial Directors meeting, the prime broker opens the prime brokerage account and related custodial accounts. For hedge funds trading in multiple markets this may involve accounts with affiliates of the prime broker and also accounts with unaffiliated third-party sub-custodians.

At the start of hedge fund operations, the prime broker receives the proceeds raised in the initial offering period. It has, in the process of negotiating the PBA, assigned a line of credit to the hedge fund, and it is this amount that will determine how much money it will lend the hedge fund and how much, in terms of value of securities, it is willing to lend the hedge fund.

Our model hedge fund has raised £25 million in its initial offering period. The administrator would retain £1 million for operating expenses and send £24 million to the prime broker. When this money arrives, the prime broker notifies the investment manager of the receipt of funds and the investment manager starts to trade.

Hedge funds will buy securities, buy "on margin", sell or "sell short". When a purchase is made, the executing broker will notify the prime broker that, acting on instructions from the investment manager, it has bought securities. The prime broker will check the assets that it holds and, if there are sufficient funds available to cover the trade, will inform the executing broker to "give up" the trade to it. This means that the investment manager will step out of the trade and the prime broker will settle the transaction in the hedge fund's account.

When the investment manager wishes to buy on margin, it will notify the prime broker and place the trade, borrowing funds to cover the purchase. This is using leverage. The trade will settle in the hedge fund's prime brokerage account. The prime broker will have extended credit to the hedge fund.

When securities are sold not involving a short sale, the prime broker will arrange for the delivery of securities.

When securities are sold in a short sale, the prime broker will loan the securities to the hedge fund and deliver those securities to the purchaser. If the hedge fund did not own the securities, this would be a "naked short". If the hedge fund did own the securities, the trade would be "shorting against the box". In either event, there is an extension of credit in the form of loaned securities. The hedge fund will be liable for the costs of borrowing the securities and also have to pay interest.

Borrowing funds to buy securities and securities to cover shorts involves tapping the line of credit extended to the hedge fund by the prime broker. The prime broker will on a daily basis value the assets in the portfolio to ascertain not just the overall value involved, but to determine how much credit it has extended to the hedge fund. This will be measured against the line of credit that it has extended to the hedge fund. Based on movements in the value of assets in the portfolio and other factors, in particular how much cash is in the portfolio, the hedge fund may be required to post "margin", or additional amounts of money, to ensure that the value of assets hedge securing the charge does not fall below an agreed amount.

ADMINISTRATION

The responsibilities of the administrator have been set out elsewhere in this book. There are aspects of these responsibilities that bear amplification, and these are set forth below.

From the time the initial offering period starts, the administrator will open bank accounts, process subscriptions and receive funds, set up accounts and start the process of tracking investments and monitoring portfolio activity against the hedge fund's restrictions.

The administrator will keep books and records for the hedge fund. (The official books and records are kept in the registered office of the hedge fund, which is usually in a jurisdiction other than that where the administrator is located.)

The administrator is usually delegated the responsibility to conduct and document the AML checks on prospects applying for shares. As part of this, the administrator will, in compliance with relevant law and instructions from the Directors, review the subscription documents for completeness, verify the identity of the applicant, check the source(s) of funds and, when this is completed according to established requirements, notify the distributor (and also, if requested, the investment manager) and issue a written confirmation to the prospect. The investor will be noted in the hedge fund's records.

Trades are reported on a real-time basis by the investment manager and the prime broker to the administrator. At the end of each business day, the prime broker, the investment manager and the administrator will each review and reconcile that day's trading activities. This is done to ensure the accuracy of records and as a cross-check against the other service providers. (Readers will note that, as discussed in Chapter 10, the failure to do such checks permitted Beacon Hill to misvalue assets in an effort to hide portfolio losses.)

COMPLIANCE

Compliance activities fall into several facets.

Investment management compliance involves ensuring that the investment manager satisfies the legal and regulatory obligations that are imposed on it. This does not involve monitoring the trading activities of the investment manager to ensure that it observes the investment objective, policies and restrictions: this is a role that is performed by the administrator with assistance from the risk management group in the investment manager.

Compliance is responsible for vetting promotional materials other than the Offering Materials. It does this against applicable regulatory requirements. Compliance also advises on aspects of trading, such as whether as a result of a trade a reporting threshold may be crossed, necessitating the filing of a large trading report.

Additional compliance obligations include advising on requirements to enter markets, whether instruments may be bought or sold otherwise than in conformity with the hedge fund's restrictions (this advice usually is given prior to the trade, whereas the administrator would monitor activity on a post-trade basis) and giving advice on proposed changes in applicable regulatory requirements that might affect the ability of the investment manager to trade particular securities or in certain markets.

DIRECTORS

An important facet of hedge fund governance is what activities Directors of hedge funds engage in between meetings of the board of Directors.

Good corporate governance for hedge funds requires that the Directors implement mechanisms to ensure that they are notified about material developments between meetings. It also involves ensuring that they receive complete, meaningful information at their meetings.

Directors meetings, usually held quarterly, are the opportunities not just to evaluate fund performance, but to evaluate service providers and exercise oversight.

A key aspect of fund governance is measuring the role of service providers. This involves two streams of evaluation: one concerns what information each service provider generates and how this is shared and used by the other service providers; the other addresses information "gaps".

In terms of information from service providers, the Directors should provide a format by which information is to be provided to them for their regular Directors meetings. Establishing a format will permit the Directors to review and compare the information that they receive. For example, the Directors will wish to know how many trades are DK'd and how long fails to deliver take to be rectified. They will also wish to know whether any of the key service providers is not providing information that, if forthcoming, might assist in enhancing controls or reducing costs.

In terms of gaps, not having critical path information or not sharing such information might result in the inability to spot issues before problems arise. For example, if all three key service providers regularly share information, they would be able to identify on a real-time basis a problem that one of them may have with respect to the pricing of a security. Being able to spot such issues helps ensure that accurate data is being captured to avoid, for example, inaccurate NAVs per share and other issues.

HEDGE FUND INDEXES AND INFORMATIONAL SERVICES

Investors evaluate the performance of hedge funds individually and against each other. To help them, there are services that provide information about the hedge fund industry and that compile hedge performance, analytics and statistics.

Hedge fund indexes are a helpful source of data and performance indicators. A hedge fund index is a compilation of performance indicators of hedge funds. They are used to help analyse returns by measuring performance and other key indicators against a peer group of similarly situated hedge funds. One of the most established indexes is the Credit Suisse/Tremont Hedge Index. This is comprised of a number of indexes, including the Benchmark Index, the Blue Chip Investable Index and the Sector Invest Indexes. The Website containing the indexes includes a daily news briefing and press releases. A source of information about hedge fund indexes is the Hedge Fund Marketing Alliance.[4]

HedgeFund.net is a web-based source of information with news, analytics and performance data. There are investor eligibility requirement to access this site, which contains a database of information on more than 7,800 hedge funds, funds-of-funds and commodity products. HedgePlus allows investment managers to provide quantitative and qualitative transparency. PerTrac Online is a subscription-based tool that lets subscribers sort and rank hedge funds using percentile scores, among other features. A daily bulletin, *HFN Daily Report*, contains news about hedge funds and the AI industry.

Albourne Village is an established, primary source of information about the AI industry. Available by registration, Albourne Village publishes daily and weekly news bulletins about hedge fund and private equity developments and operates a "village" where subscribers may access information about conferences, events, industry-related materials, service providers and a "data farm" that acts as a "stable for the Standard & Poor's MSCI and HedgeFund Intelligence hedge fund indexes".[5]

Hedgewire, a newsletter published by Hedgemedia Ltd, provides daily news stories, interviews, special reports and industry research and reports about the hedge fund industry.

FINalternatives is an independent database and news service for hedge funds and private equity vehicles. It is published weekly with stories posted daily on its Website.

Opalesque is a European-based source of information with news and reports about developments in hedge funds. Its daily *Alternative Market Briefing* in an online news source established as a form of "clipping service".

Eurekahedge provides a number of services. Eurekahedge Monthly provides hedge fund performance commentary, articles databases (including the Eurekahedge Alternative Investment Fund Database with fund comparisons, statistics and fund listing and graph comparisons), databases, including alternative research products, and indexes (and information about them).

1 *SEC v Capital Gains Research Bureau*, 375 US 180 (1963) ("Capital Gains Research Bureau").

2 *Capital Gains Research Bureau*, 375 US 180 at 190–192.

3 Investment Adviser Association Standards of Practice, amended 28 February, 2006, URL: www.investmentadviser.org/html/sop.html.

4 URL: www.hedgefundmarketing.org/hedgefundindexes.htm.

5 URL: www.village.albourne.com/overview.html

9

Key Issues: Valuations, Corporate Governance and Side Letters

In the previous chapter, we surveyed a number of issues that are involved in the day-to-day operations of hedge funds. There are other matters that arise on a daily basis but that take on significance due to the implications involved. These are valuations, corporate governance and side letters.

Valuations are critical because investors, prime brokers, market participants and others presume that the process of valuing positions in the portfolios from which the administrator (or general partner, in a partnership) strikes accurate AUMs and NAVs per share, will be independent, robust, free from interference and objective. Investors and regulators will not suffer weak, incorrect or intentionally wrong controls, procedures or results. Corporate governance also matters greatly. Today, hedge funds hold large positions of voting securities of issuers and would not hesitate to seek to influence management or borrow shares and vote them, whether or not "empty voting" is involved. Side letters are critical because a lack of procedures to authorise their issuance or not dealing with them properly might result in breaches of directors' duties, not treating investors equally or resulting in amendments to the Offering Materials.

Changes to service providers causes disruption and takes a considerable amount of time and effort. Here, a balance must be struck between keeping a service provider that is functioning and using efforts to improve the performance or getting rid of them – and, if the former is the route taken, being aware that liabilities might flow from inadequate or poor performance. This is a daily matter, but due to it being an event of importance, we have opted to deal with this in Chapter 10.

VALUATIONS

A hedge fund must ensure that every financial instrument in its portfolio is timely and properly priced on the date of acquisition, while held and when sold. Valuations are the basis on which the portfolio is valued, the AUM is calculated, NAVs per share are struck, shares are purchased, exchanged and redeemed and the performance fee is calculated.

Due to its importance, the valuation process must independent, robust and free from conflicts and undue influence. A related consideration is how to price assets in the portfolio – from exchanged-traded equities to the most esoteric derivatives and loan participations.

Responsibility and segregation of functions

The Articles establish the methodology by which valuations are performed. This is carried through into the Offering Materials and relevant material agreements.

The Directors are responsible for valuations. This is delegated, in nearly all instances, to the administrator.[1] This delegation does not specify how prices are to be obtained and other matters of procedure, as this is left to the responsible entity. In the case of a limited partnership, the general partner as administrator would perform this role. Only in carefully controlled situations might an investment manager handle valuations. Even then, due to the nature of the conflicts of interest that may arise, it is advisable not to permit the investment manager to value positions. Investment managers will, rightly so, provide advice on illiquid assets, particularly where they have been involved in obtaining quotes for or trading these instruments.

The other service providers would generally not have a role in the valuation process, save for being consulted in the case of the inability of the administrator to be able to value a position or where information is needed that is held (or may be obtained) by others.

As was discussed earlier in this book, the RFP materials must define the instruments and markets that will comprise the hedge fund's investment objective, policies and restrictions and state who will perform valuations. The administrator's response must make clear whether it can value positions or would require assistance or price feeds from affiliates or third parties for this. No administrator should be appointed if there is any doubt that it is not able to properly and timely value positions. Every hedge fund promoter should ensure that the due diligence process includes a walk through of the administrator's facilities. There must be clear representations and warranties in the AA that the administrator can handle this role and to the requirements imposed in the Articles and by the Directors. There should be viable alternatives so that secondary systems or service providers will spring into action should the administrator not be able to perform its duties.

How are valuations done?

The process of valuations must be spelt out in detail.

The administrator must ensure that it has accurate price feeds or sources of information for all instruments. It is frequently the case that administrators have multiple sources of prices that would be used in the case of illiquid assets. Accuracy of information, reliability of the sources and backups are critical.

As noted earlier, the Offering Materials will contain a section called "Net Asset Value" or "Valuations". This will set forth the valuation policy, the procedures by which instruments are priced, the AUM calculated, and when the NAVs per share are struck. The process follows a number of steps – all of which are specified in the Articles and Offering Materials.

- The relevant dates will be defined – Valuation Day and Dealing Day. In addition, the Directors will be empowered to declare additional Valuation Days and Dealing Days.
- The periods of time will be defined. Even though hedge funds strike NAVs per share on a monthly or quarterly basis and FoHFs strike NAVs per share on a similar time frame, underlying positions must be valued on a daily basis to assist with reconciliations, trading and portfolio valuation issues and to ensure that the figures of the main service providers – investment manager, administrator and prime broker – tally.
- The administrator will establish accounts for each class of shares and make provisions for sub-classes, as well.
- Proceeds from the sale of the hedge fund's securities (not portfolio transactions) will be entered into the accounts for each class of shares.
- Types of securities are given a means by which their value is to be derived. In general:
  - exchanged-traded equity securities would be valued by the closing (or last traded) price on the Valuation Day. The disclosure would also state how such securities would be valued if an equity security did not trade on a particular day;
  - non-listed or traded securities require a degree of flexibility. Generally, the price that is used would be cost and, after the initial valuation, at the probable realisation value as determined by the administrator;
  - certain instruments that are traded or settled through clearing firms, exchanges or financial institutions would be valued by reference to the most recently quoted official settlement price. Again, provisions would be made for instrument that fell in this category but for which no price was available;
  - even cash is valued. Here, the benchmark would be, for example, cost plus accrued interest;
  - not every instrument or deposit is carried in the base currency. A hedge fund may have, for example, securities, derivatives and other instruments in nine currencies and deposits in five currencies. All positions are "exchanged" or converted into the base currency using a defined exchange rate from an official source;
  - finally, the disclosures will give the Directors the ability to exercise their discretion should it be necessary to value an illiquid position or should information required to value a position not be available.

- Any increase or decrease in the NAV per share (excluding new subscriptions or new redemptions) are allocated to the relevant class accounts based on the previous relative NAV per share of each class of shares.
- At this point, the administrator gives every position in the portfolio a value, based on the above. In the case of a hard-to-value or illiquid position, the administrator will follow a procedure that specifies when (or if) an alternative method, or estimate, might be used. It would be at this point, and subject to the terms of this procedure, that the investment manager might be consulted. This should result in the administrator setting a price for the position.
- The AUM is calculated (in a master feeder structure, the master fund AUM is calculated and prior to the same exercise being undertaken for each feeder fund).
- The NAV per share for each class of shares is struck: the administrator divides the AUM of each class of shares by the number of outstanding shares. The administrator then publishes the NAVs per share and processes subscriptions and redemptions.

Key issues

Critical to the valuation process are ensuring the independence and integrity of the process, avoiding conflicts of interest (or having a means to declare and resolve them), keeping proper books and records, securing and working with accurate and timely price feeds for liquid assets and having a declared method to value (and understand) illiquid assets. The Asian and European unit trust and corporate hedge fund models feature separation among service providers, but the American and non-US partnership model does not, and this is where conflicts would arise. In the American model, the general partner should separate the valuation function from the investment management function and monitor all activities – this is achievable in large organisations but difficult in small shops. Regulators and investors will require adherence to strict controls to ensure that the process is free from undue influence.

Pricing liquid assets is a relatively easy proposition. The administrator will require multiple data feeds from reliable sources, and should use the information that it receives to set and confirm a price for assets. It should also engage in an active dialogue with the prime broker and the investment manager to ensure that all three service providers are working from the same databases and are arriving at figures for liquid assets that are identifiable. If not there will be mis-matches between the values that each service provider ascribes to assets, which may result in discrepancies when it comes time to calculate the AUM and NAVs per share, calculate and accrue performance fees, and trade and calculate the assets subject to the prime broker's service charge.

Pricing illiquid assets, everything from swaps and CDOs to esoteric

SPVs is a significant issue. With few exceptions, price feeds will generally not be available for illiquid investments. In this case, the administrator has several choices.

Some administrators outsource the pricing and valuation function to third parties that specialise in this. If this is done, the third party must be selected with diligence and its processes and results overseen regularly.

The administrator might ask the investment manager to provide it with information as to where it obtained the quote by which it considered acquiring the asset, and purchased it, for the administrator to use in setting the value. In other instances, particularly in the American model, the investment manager provides the price. The problem with the latter option is that it involves a degree of creativity and, on occasion, abuse. This option, "fair value accounting", lets the investment manager give an estimate for the value of illiquid securities where there is no market price. In certain instances, the estimate is given without any basis and in the absence of any readily ascertainable market value. The concern here is both with the degree of creativity involved and the likely probability that the estimated value given and a value derived from a market, had one existed, would be materially different.

In other instances, pricing models are used. Pricing models are software programs that use an algorithm to compare a number of indicators and arrive at a value. The indicators that are used are historical as well as current factors. While in many cases pricing models provide relatively reliable valuations, the indicators must be reviewed and adjusted regularly. The ability to adjust factors or override a pricing model valuation must be stated in a written procedure and used, if at all, in controlled situations.

Certain OTC instruments, such as equity and interest rate swaps or loan participations, may be easy to price. This is because, in part, there is a liquid instrument or a loan with a credit rating from which information or a price may be used to derive a value. Other instruments, such as "CDO squared" (CDOs that invest in other CDOs), depend on a credit rating (or, in the absence of a rating, on the rating of the bank packaging the instrument) to help derive a value. When ratings drop or are not present, it may not be possible to value such instruments. While CDOs squared and other packaged, highly leveraged instruments generate high yields, they may fall precipitously in value when credit ratings, if present, decline, or, when used as collateral, prime brokers discount them and call for margin.

Another consideration is "smoothing". This is a process by which hedge funds use trading strategies and other methods to even out returns. A June 2007 study published by riskdata involving 1,000 hedge funds indicated that 30% of these hedge funds were engaged in this. Using an indicator that it called "Bias Ratio", riskdata found that the more illiquid the trading strategy the more likely it was that it employed a Bias Ratio and that month-to-month returns were smoothed to help results appear less risky.[2]

The situation for US banks (and prime brokers) has changed, with the implementation in November 2007 of FASB 157. Under FASB 175, these and other institutions subject to this accounting rule will no longer be able to value Level 3 assets such as sub-prime mortgages, certain debt and other illiquid assets on the basis of assumptions or estimates. Instead, they must use market prices. How would this affect the market for CDOs? The large money centre banks and brokers that are also prime brokers are carrying large tranches of CDOs on their books. Many hedge funds have CDOs and CDOs squared in their portfolios. These institutions have already written down their assets and portfolios and, in the cases of certain hedge funds, have seen declines in AUMs and margin calls. It will probably be the case that more write downs will be forthcoming and, for hedge funds, further declines in AUMs and more margin calls. This, coupled with large-scale redemptions, might cause further strain and lead to more requests to bail out hedge funds or even result in more liquidations. "Super-SIV", a rescue fund put together to prevent further write-downs in sub-prime loans, has been described as a means to ease out losses during this second stage of the sub-prime/credit crisis. The banks leading the efforts to launch Super-SIVs are in discussions with other banks and brokers in advance of a planned December launch. Time will tell whether Super-SIVs help to alleviate the crisis and ease the burden on hedge funds and other users of services from banks and brokers.

CORPORATE GOVERNANCE

Hedge funds are shaped by, and became shapers of, corporate governance. Hedge funds trade securities and are increasingly attempting to influence the course of corporate conduct and events. As they do this, investors in hedge funds are requiring more and more information not just from investment managers on portfolio performance, but from Directors on how they are discharging their responsibilities. This portion of this chapter surveys how hedge funds have become activists in corporate activities and, in some cases, wage hostile battles for corporate control. We touch on matters critical to hedge fund corporate governance.

By corporate governance, we mean the manner in which management (officers and Directors) understand, formulate and discharge in a proper, timely, conflict-free and transparent manner their obligations towards their constituents: owners (shareholders); users; suppliers; exchanges; regulators; and the public.

Hedge funds as "shapers"

Historically, and other than in the case of special situation and event-driven hedge funds, investment managers achieved alpha due to strategic trading. They voted proxies solicited for annual general meetings and for corporate events such as exchange offers and reorganisations. Investment managers held meetings with officers and Directors to discuss current developments, earnings results and profit forecasts, and to query management on its goals and ambitions. They were not yet following in the footsteps of the corporate raiders of the 1980s who employed strategies such as greenmail, proxy contests, forcing resolutions onto agendas at AGMs or EGMs to elect their slates of directors or using acquisitions to acquire break up companies and free "crown jewels".

Hedge funds were able to use market volatility, a relatively uncrowded market space and the cloak of opacity in trading and achieve handsome returns for themselves and their investors. In 2002 the landscape changed. The Gramm–Leach–Bliley Act rescinded the 1929-era Glass–Steagall Act and let banks back into the securities business, ushering in a new era of financial engineering and easy credit.[3] Volatility began to decline in certain markets. Investors started to notice that the continuously increasing absolute returns that they were seeing from hedge funds were, in some instances, reaching a plateau or were even falling below what they might achieve from other investments. During this time, the amount of assets invested in hedge funds continued to increase. With larger numbers of hedge funds and competition increasing, new ways were required to generate returns to keep investors happy and avoid large redemptions. Investors began to "vote with their feet": they would redeem their holdings if returns did not continue to increase at a rate that outperformed other investments available to them. (Note that hedge funds traditionally did the same in the case of holdings of issuers with flat earnings or poor operations.)

The strategies employed by hedge funds to achieve even larger returns included increased derivatives activity, changed trading patterns, increasingly searching research to uncover hidden value in assets and companies and other means to increase returns. At this point, and now taking a page from the playbook of the 1980s raiders, hedge funds that were not event-driven or special situation hedge funds began to do more than query management or sell securities when they saw something that they did not like. They began to take sides when companies were put in play. They joined forces with other hedge funds or private equity vehicles or other large institutional investors to seek concessions, remove or appoint Directors or force mergers or acquisitions, or break-ups. They began to put companies into play.

The recently completed acquisition of ABN AMRO by a consortium of banks illustrates what might result when hedge funds become corporate activists and seek to influence corporate governance. In the case of ABN AMRO, the hedge fund TCI acquired a position of 1% of the Dutch bank's securities and sent it a letter demanding that the bank place a number of items on the agenda for the forthcoming AGM. Included were requests to change directors, put certain matters to shareholder vote and, most important, consider a break-up of the bank to sell assets and realise further values.

A combination of factors, including the bank's performance and share value, changes to Dutch laws and market conditions, put the institution in play. (What result TCI was actually seeking is not and may never be known.) Other institutional investors followed TCI's approach and began to take stakes. The move flushed out Barclays Bank, who announced an offer for the bank. This was followed by a bid from the consortium. Over time, hedge funds began to take an active role not just in ABN AMRO's affairs, but also in the activities of the three banks in the consortium and in the litigation surrounding ABN's proposed sale of LaSalle, a US bank. After numerous legal actions and decisions, battles for control in the press and behind-the-scenes manoeuvring, Barclays announced that it was not pursuing its proposed acquisition of the bank, leading the consortium with victory and the task of completing the transaction and moving forward.

This is one example of how one hedge fund's attempts to bring about change gave rise to more than corporate governance. In terms of pure corporate governance, however, there are many examples of how hedge funds become involved with or influence the corporate governance of issuers of securities. Prior to seeking out opportunities to influence corporate governance – adding or removing directors, seeking enhanced disclosure, forcing changes in a company's structure or other matters – one must query not just the motives involved but whether, in fact, it is proper for an investment manager to engage in such activities.

Investment managers are fiduciaries and have obligations to the investors in the hedge funds they manage. There are numerous obligations that are imposed on fiduciaries and, in the case of a hedge fund investment manager, these go not just to avoiding losses, protecting assets and achieving returns, but being responsible for their actions. It is not, however, as simple as a cost-benefit analysis. The investment manager must ask itself not only whether the benefits of the proposed action outweigh the costs but whether the action itself is proper. The wrong action may not bring about a loss, but might result in damage to reputation and redemptions.

Shaping hedge funds

Exchange-listed hedge funds will have obligations beyond preparing and circulating audited financial statements and publishing announcements. They must act in the best interests of their shareholders and treat all shareholders equally. Listing rules of the ISE and CSX impose such obligations, as do the laws of the jurisdictions where the hedge funds are incorporated. The fact that a hedge fund is unlisted will not be able to change this. The fact is that hedge funds as unit trusts, limited partnerships and companies and those that manage them are subject to strict provisions that establish governance obligations. These are in many ways identical to those imposed on industrial companies and exchanged-listed long-only funds.

In discharging their own corporate governance obligations, hedge fund Directors meet with the service providers to ensure that they operate the hedge fund in accordance with contractual, legal and regulatory obligations. At the same time, the Directors must not "delegate" key aspects of corporate governance to service providers. Oversight assumes a prominent role in the proper discharge of a Director's duties. If oversight is properly employed, Directors will not only ensure that hedge fund operations are proceeding smoothly but that information that is relevant to their own deliberations is being passed to them in a timely and complete manner.

SIDE LETTERS

Side letters are enforceable agreements between investors and hedge funds that give investors a benefit, right or concession that is not available to all investors and that could result in the investor receiving a favourable position. Provisions of side letters cover many issues, including the discolsure of portfolio and financial information: the disclosure of audited financial statements by certain dates; an exemption from early redemption fees; notification of the occurrence of certain events; "most favoured nations" status; preferable treatment when certain events arise – nearly anything that might in some way confer a degree of leverage over other investors, first notice of events, preferential treatment or an economic advantage.

Side letters reflect the following competing interests:

- ❑ investors, seeking actions, information or an advantage that helps them protect their investment;
- ❑ hedge funds, desiring to obtain large tranches of funds, particularly on start-up, and to keep these;
- ❑ other shareholders, who may not know about side letters and the conditions in them and who might legitimately believe that they are not being treated equally;
- ❑ if applicable, exchanges such as the ISE and CSX that require equal treatment for investors;
- ❑ investment managers, who may create conflicts of interest by agreeing positions with prospects that Directors may not wish to give in an effort to attract or keep funds;
- ❑ Directors who, by using side letters, must deal with issues such as authority to issue side letters, equal treatment of investors for a non-listed hedge fund and renegotiating side letters to keep investors when, in certain instances, it might be best, in the interests of all investors and in the proper execution of their fiduciary duties not to agree points and risk losing a tranche of funds. This might require the exercise of gate

provisions to avoid a large redemption that, if honoured, might lead to the consequences of forced disclosure of such a redemption and more redemptions, or a decline in AUM below an AUM decline trigger, leading to more serious consequences.

In order for a hedge fund to be able to issue a side letter, there must be appropriate authority in the Articles. If a hedge fund is listed, eg, the CSX or the ISE, the giving of a side letter may result in a breach of the requirement to treat shareholders equally. Hedge fund Directors must understand that side letters raise significant legal and corporate governance issues. Directors must consider whether granting a side letter is consistent not just with requirements in the Articles or disclosures in the Offering Materials, but with their legal obligations and the fiduciary duties that they owe. The terms of a side letter might result in an amendment to Offering Materials, and might require not just the filing of amended documents, but also the public disclosure of the side letter – which would invariably be a breach of the confidentiality terms of the side letter itself.

Regulators are turning their attention to side letters. Their concerns go not just to the effects of side letters, but their disclosure or even non-disclosure.

The SEC is concerned that side letters raise conflicts of interest and result in preferential treatment to certain investors. Prior to the adoption of Rule 206(4)-8 and in testimony in May 2006 before the Subcommittee on Securities and Investment of the US Senate Banking Committee on Banking, Housing, and Urban Affairs, Susan Ferris Wyderko, then director of the SEC's Office of Investor Education and Assistance, stated that the SEC was looking at side letters during inspections of investment managers. She testified that certain side letters

> *"are more troubling because they may involve material conflicts of interest that can harm the interests of other investors. Chief among these types of side letter agreements are those that give certain investors liquidity preferences or provide them with more access to portfolio information. Our examination staff will review side letter agreements and evaluate whether appropriate disclosure of the side letters and relevant conflicts has been made to other investors."*[4]

With the adoption of Rule 206(4)-8, the SEC has a weapon with which to attack material misrepresentations or omissions concerning side letters. In Chapter 7, we noted that the SEC Staff would consider a statement about a side letter by an adviser that constituted a breach of a fiduciary duty or a violation of a local legal or regulatory requirement to be actionable. (This rule, by its terms, would not apply to the Directors of hedge funds.) For example, in the US hedge fund model, where a general-partner investment manager is under a fiduciary duty to treat all investors equally, the representation to a US investor in a hedge fund that it manages or a prospect considering investing in that fund that the hedge fund did not issue side letters when in fact they were issued would, if material (under applicable US legal standards), violate this rule. If a non-US investment manager was not under a fiduciary or legal obligation and, when asked about provisions in side letters that the fund that it advised had issued, stated that the fund did issue side letters but failed to disclose how many letters there were or to disclose the subject matter of such letters to US prospects, *might* not, even if the statements were material, be the subject of an enforcement referral. Every case must be judged on its merits and the critical factors here are the fiduciary or local legal obligations imposed on the money manager and whether the statement was material.

The UK FSA, in its FSA feedback paper, stated that side letters might contribute to a market failure.

> *"[S]ide letters result in some, often large, investors receiving more information and preferential (early) redemption terms compared with other investors in the same share class (who may be unaware of that side letters exist and who will be denied these terms). We believe that failure by UK based hedge fund managers, to disclose the existence of these side letters is,* ***amongst other potential breaches*** *in breach of Principle 1 of our Principles for Businesses ('a firm must conduct its business with integrity'). As with valuation abuses, we will take action on this basis. As a minimum we would expect acceptable market practice to be for managers to ensure that all investors are informed when a side letter is granted and any conflicts that may arise are adequately managed. Managers that fail to inform investors will need to consider carefully their position. We have concluded that it is important to review these practices later in 2006. That work will inform our policy thinking and enable us to take action against individual firms and their senior management if appropriate [emphasis added]."*[5]

1 In a unit trust, the trustees delegate this to the administrator (in an Irish-authorised unit trust, the delegation would be from the investment manager to the administrator). In a partnership, this would be performed by the general manager.

2 "Riskdata research shows that 30% of funds trading illiquid securities smooth their returns", riskdata press release 29 June 2007. URL: www.riskdata.com, at Industry News.

3 Glass–Steagall was not longer needed because, in part, its protections were perceived to be outmoded. E-mail interview with John Sprung, 5 November 2007.

4 "Testimony Concerning Hedge Funds Before the Subcommittee on Securities and Investment of the US Senate Committee on Banking, Housing, and Urban Affairs", Susan Ferris Wyderko, Director, Office of Investor Education and Assistance, US Securities and Exchange Commission (16 May, 2006).

5 FSA feedback paper, at p. 6.

10

What Happens When Something Goes Wrong?

In this book, we have discussed what hedge funds are, how they are established, how they operate and make money and whether they should be regulated. A reader might think that this pattern would remain relatively unchanged during the hedge fund's life, despite changes in the markets, legal and regulatory developments, normal course redemptions that do not cause the Directors to exercise gate provisions and the maintenance of capacity.

What happens when something goes wrong?

By going wrong, we mean events such as the loss of key employees of the investment manager, material discrepancies in valuations and large redemptions that cannot be contained by gate provisions. This includes regulatory developments that might force the closure of hedge funds or the registration of investment managers, trading "errors" that lead to material losses, the declaration of events of default by a prime broker and even insolvency. We will also cover having to change service providers, although this is not necessarily perceived to be "something going wrong".

VALUATIONS

At several points in this book, we noted how the administrator values assets in the portfolio to help it calculate the AUM and strike NAVs per share. This, in turn, helps it perform other vital activities. The process is not free from error. Occasionally, for various reasons, certain assets may have to be repriced, which might result in changes to the AUM and the NAVs per share. These changes might fall within a threshold that would not require the administrator to have to restate NAVs per share. There are, however, situations where the new figure is materially different from what had been published. In this case, the NAVs per share will have to be restated. It might also be the case that real problems are discovered – as was the case with Beacon Hill.

As noted in Chapter 1, the Beacon Hill administrative proceeding involved, *inter alia*, the investment manager/sponsor, Beacon Hill Asset

Management, LLC (Beacon Hill), misrepresent the method that it used to value investments in the master fund's portfolio and manipulating the manner in which the AUMs of the funds that it managed were calculated. According to the Amended Complaint filed by the SEC, the officers of Beacon Hill had for a period of time been engaged in valuing portfolio assets by methods other than as set forth in the Offering Materials of the hedge funds they advised. This resulted in significant discrepancies in the value of the assets and also losses in the managed accounts that Beacon Hill was managing for unrelated third parties. Bear Stearns, the prime broker of the hedge funds that Beacon Hill managed, noticed the pricing and valuation discrepancies and "insisted that Beacon Hill address the apparent and substantial discrepancy in the net value of the Master Fund".[1] It was also discovered that Beacon Hill had engaged in trading the managed accounts to attempt to return the value of that pool of assets to profit.[2] No action was taken by Beacon Hill to address the material discrepancies; as a result, Bear Stearns notified the SEC of the discrepancy in the valuations of the portfolio and stated its concerns.[3] Beacon Hill is an example of how a single entity, when it assumes multiple functions, gets it wrong with no internal control to catch and rectify the act and how a prime broker rightly queries portfolio valuations and acts when appropriate clarification and rectification is not forthcoming.

COLLATERAL

Hedge funds use leverage to generate alpha and achieve absolute returns. Prime brokers require that hedge fund assets remain on deposit with them. A critical issue in how prime brokers administer the assets that they hold and hypothecate, and over which they maintain a charge, is how they value assets to determine the value of the portfolios that they hold to extend credit. While it is easy for the prime broker (and the administrator) to value exchange-traded equity securities and not take "haircuts"[4] over such positions, a portfolio that includes illiquid assets such as leveraged loan participations, CDOs, total return swaps and other derivatives will require a concerted effort to price each position. Haircuts will inevitably be required. The risks inherent in holding such positions – in particular, assets that are packages of other instruments, such as securities representing securitised residential mortgages – is that, if the number of defaults in the underlying mortgages increases beyond the projected default rate, the value of the securities representing the securitised assets will drop, requiring the prime broker to increase the haircut over the position and bring more previously unencumbered portfolio assets into the pool of assets that secure its charge. In the case of a global credit hedge fund with a portfolio including such assets, this could result in not only a decrease in its AUM but seeing more assets required to cover the charge. If it transpired that this would increase its borrowing exposure or even bring about a breach of the restriction, the investment manager would be required to sell assets in order to rebalance the portfolio. This would have the further effect of decreasing the AUM. If, and as is the case in the sub-prime/credit crisis, investors became nervous and redeemed their shares, the administrator might be forced to employ gate provisions to slow down or suspend redemptions. The net effect of this might be a meltdown of the hedge fund. A further complicating factor would be the combination of redemptions and the decrease in the AUM triggering an additional termination event in an ISDA and permitting an ISDA counterparty to close out all positions and net exposures, and demand the payment of a sum. This might, if the amount involved was greater than the termination amount set forth in the ISDA, constitute an event of default in the PBA, set off cross defaults in other ISDAs and empower the prime broker to utilise powers granted to it in the PBA to enforce its charge and liquidate positions, closing the hedge fund. Thus, cardboard collateral, while permitting hedge funds to achieve greater leverage, brings with it greater risks.

PRIME BROKER CONFLICTS OF INTEREST

We noted in Chapter 4 that prime brokers provide many services to hedge funds and other financial services industry participants. A critical issue to them is being able to operate their prime brokerage operations in a low risk, cost-effective way and turn a profit. In September 2006, it was reported that those that fund hedge funds stood to earn nearly US$8 billion in 2006.[5] Despite the sub-prime/credit crisis, the figures for 2007 look to be just as high.

Prime brokers receive income from many sources, including the hypothecation of assets in a hedge fund's portfolio over which it holds a charge. (Prime brokers may receive a "double dip" in that the hedge fund pays the prime broker to hold assets and the prime broker receives income from the securities that it onwards lends, or uses.) Prime brokerage does not operate in a vacuum: the investment firms and commercial banks that are engaged in prime brokerage need vast sums of money to finance their operations. All goes well in times of moderate markets. However, in times of market stress, changes in trading patterns and multiple, often large, redemption requests lead to increased demands not just on hedge funds, but on prime brokers as well. Prime brokers receive their funding from several sources, including commercial paper programmes, bankers' acceptances and the repo market. When, as is now the case, the commercial paper market contracts and it becomes not only difficult but expensive to generate funding, trading activity slows, funding becomes harder to find, assets decline in value and more collateral is required. As was noted in the *Financial Times* on Friday, 19 October, 2007 – 20 years to the day after the 1987 "market break" – the commercial paper market is shrinking. This, coupled with other economic factors, including the Northern Rock "run on the bank" and increasing interbank lending rates, is creating a financial market and economic environment that, save for one factor (the presence in certain countries of a financial banking network and a requirement for central banks to inject funds to keep market participants and the economy moving) mirrors a landscape last seen in 1929. Only time will tell whether repealing the US Glass–Steagall Act, easy lending in the residential mortgage market, encouraging financing engineering in REITs, limited partnerships and other forms of commercial property structures and relaxing controls on the type of instrument permitted as collateral in favour of cardboard collateral will result in another worldwide depression. What factor(s) will pierce the current credit/cardboard collateral bubble? The indicators do not look bullish.

LOSS OF KEY EMPLOYEES

The individuals managing hedge fund portfolios command handsome remuneration. They deserve this, because of the risks that they take. Not to reward them in a manner that is commensurate with the risks that they take would lead to a severe shortage of individuals to manage portfolios. Nearly all Offering Materials disclose as a risk factor the loss of key employees. Key individuals do leave hedge funds and take with them talented associates to form new hedge funds or to go to other funds. It may not be possible to recruit new talent. Also, gaps in coverage may lead to changes in trading patterns and decreased performance. The key element in the success of every hedge fund is the relationship between the individual managing assets on the investment manager's desk and hedge fund investors. Confidence in the individual looking after the portfolio translates not only into achieving capacity and absolute growth, but also the distant prospect of many or large-scale redemptions. A loss of confidence by, for example, individuals leaving an investment manager translates into a decline in the hedge fund and, if the situation is not addressed as a matter of urgency, a smaller hedge fund or no fund at all.

RISK MANAGEMENT

Risk management involves identifying and managing risks posed to hedge funds. These include portfolio risk, operational risk, settlement risk, liquidity risk and outsourcing risk.

Portfolio risk

Portfolio risk involves several elements: is the hedge fund trading within its stated investment objective, policies and restrictions? Is this reported adequately to investors? Are conflicts identified and addressed properly? Are the factors and data that comprise the portfolio risk model regularly reviewed and changed when required? Are all of the above being monitored on a robust, independent basis and, when issues arise, timely and properly escalated to those in control? Who controls risk management, and who governs them?

Hedge funds with one prime broker have the advantage in that they can, to the extent that all controls, information flows, pricing mechanisms and systems are working properly, rely on an administrator, their own or a third party for portfolio risk management. What happens if there are two or more prime brokers and no one can "see the whole picture"?

In September 2006, the US hedge fund Amaranth Advisors LLC announced that it suffered trading losses of US$6 billion. The losses arose from trades in natural gas futures. It was reported that trades were placed on the assumption that the spreads between certain futures prices for natural gas would widen.[6] Instead, the spreads narrowed. The SEC, the FSA and other regulators investigated the activities surrounding Amaranth's losses, as well as statements made by those connected to the hedge fund and others.

There are differences between Amaranth and Long-Term Capital Management. As pointed out in the "Big Winners" story, these included the amounts of leverage involved and the state of the debt and equity markets, and the fact that Long-Term Capital required a bailout of US$4 billion. There is also the matter of providing a remedy to those who suffered losses – and what those doing business with Amaranth may or may not have gained.

It was reported that Amaranth used "about eight prime brokers".[7] There are no indications whether having this many prime brokers was or was not a factor in the losses or the trading strategy. Certainly, each prime broker, as well as Amaranth itself, had risk management tools. Judging by the facts that market participants, prime brokers and other players took time to sort out their positions and losses and that a central bailout was not required, Amaranth did not pose systemic risk.

Amaranth, however, casts the spotlight firmly on risk monitoring. It now appears that the losses occurred because the fundamental assumptions underlying a good bet changed and no one adjusted the hedging, leading to the losses. Elements of the risk management model were not reviewed and adjusted. But the losses should not have been as great as US$6 billion: the forced closure of many positions increased the exposures involved leading to this figure as the final "damage". With hindsight, it is clear that having more robust controls for the risk management model, adjusting it and sharing information among the prime brokers involved might have helped avoid the trading losses. More information and enhanced information sharing should have resulted in the timely discovery of indicators or factors to have permitted Amaranth to adjust its trading strategy and risk management model to have minimised exposures when the trades first "turned south". It is important to ensure that hedge funds have in place robust portfolio risk management processes and make adjustments when and as required so that future situations are discovered to prevent losses and protect our markets.

Operational risk

Operational risk involves ensuring that a hedge fund's controls and procedures are functioning properly. Hedge funds must have proper IT systems, trained staff to handle research, fund management, trading, settlement, compliance, monitoring and management. There must be adequate BCP programmes in place. Risk modelling must be state of the art and regularly tested.

An important consideration is whether what a hedge fund agrees to do can be or is actually done. Many hedge funds trade CDSs and agree to settlement timetables that reflect industry norms. Backlogs in settling CDSs and other instruments due to IT issues, staffing problems (not enough, not trained) and communications issues with administrators and third parties leads to problems, such as the inability to know precisely what is in the portfolio and to be able to value it correctly. It also leads to failures to deliver and discrepancies in information held by service providers.

Liquidity risk

Liquidity risk involves having sufficient cash on hand to meet normal course redemptions and ongoing expenses. Having too little cash means that the investment manager must sell assets to generate cash. Having too much cash on hand and not investing it leads to portfolio inefficiency and affects absolute return.

Settlement risk

Settlement risk is the inability to timely or properly settle trades. A hedge fund may be experiencing operational issues settling a large number of trades of illiquid investments, such as CDSs, which, if not handled correctly, may lead to failed trades.

A key issue is to ensure that the documentation for such trades accurately reflects the agreement between the parties. Certain illiquid assets such as loan participations and SPVs require the negotiation of lengthy documents. It may be the case that an illiquid asset such as a loan participation is sold and the seller has not yet taken delivery of the asset. Unless this is clearly stated in the documentation and is understood by the buyer, or if it was discussed but not disclosed, the documents may be confirmed and the buyer may find itself demanding settlement of an asset that the seller has yet to receive. This raises not just settlement risk and operational risk problems, but AUM and accounting issues as well.

Outsourcing risk

Hedge funds do not have employees or officers. They rely on others to perform critical roles for them. They are the ultimate outsourcers. The Directors, as they are charged with oversight and fund governance, must ensure that the service providers are not only capable of what they are required to do, but that they are actually doing it. This also means that information from service providers must be consistent and complete, to permit the Directors to evaluate the performance of the service providers and make changes when and as required.

An important aspect of outsourcing is the regular review and evaluation of the service providers. Directors should ensure that agreements with service providers contain benchmarks against which to evaluate service providers and a means to address failed targets and bad performance. Directors or those that they appoint to perform oversight reviews should meet with service providers at their offices not less than twice a year (more often, if possible) to ensure that procedures are being followed and issues are being addressed or escalated.

REDEMPTIONS

In previous chapters, we touched upon the effects of redemptions on hedge funds.

Hedge funds usually keep a small portion of their assets in cash. This is intended to handle redemptions in the normal course of business. During the time between Dealing Days, the administrator will process applications for new subscriptions (unless the fund is soft or hard closed), exchanges and redemptions. Based on experience, it would anticipate that, with a small margin for error, subscriptions would match redemptions. When a hedge fund was soft closed, the administrator might move shares from investors that were redeeming to investors that wished to take up additional shares. When a hedge fund was hard closed, it would process redemptions and arrange for payments to be made to redeeming investors.

Having sufficient cash to cover redemptions becomes an issue when large or seed capital investors wish to redeem at the same time. When this occurs, the gate provisions become a factor as well as ensuring that there is sufficient cash to cover the redemptions. An equity long-short fund is capable of selling some assets to raise cash to cover redemptions beyond "normal" requirements. However, this may not be the case for credit or derivative funds. Illiquid positions may be hard to sell and settle in short time frames. It might be the case that the size of the redemptions might cause the hedge fund's AUM to decline at a level that, if disclosed, might lead remaining investors to think that the hedge fund is experiencing difficulties – which might lead to further redemption requests.

A further consideration is the use of gate provisions. A hedge fund that is not listed may not have to disclose large redemptions, but, since it will provide investors with a monthly (or quarterly) update about the hedge fund's portfolio developments, it may not be possible not to disclose this fact. Hedge funds that are listed on the ISE or CSX may be required to disclose large redemptions as well as the use of gate provisions to slow or redeem redemptions. Such disclosure would come about not when the redemption requests were received, but as early as the decision taken by the Directors to employ the gates.

ADDING OR CHANGING SERVICE PROVIDERS

Hedge funds add or replace service providers when and as their needs change or circumstances dictate. This can include adding a prime broker to handle new markets or new products, changing administrators in cases of poor performance, retaining a third party to provide enhanced portfolio risk monitoring or replacing brokers with new firms that offer better execution at lower costs.

Adding or replacing a service provider at any time or for any reason is a significant matter and requires time and attention. The decision should be taken only after the Directors review the reason(s) for the change and conduct or cause to be conducted a proper selection procedure, which should be nothing less than an RFP process similar to that when the original service providers were identified. The selection of the new service provider should be documented in the minutes of the meeting of the Directors when the change is made. If required, announcements should be made and investors notified at the earliest possible time. Prior to the time that the new service provider is engaged, it should meet with the other service providers to work out issues such as IT interface, information sharing, operational and compliance issues, to provide for a seamless start or transition. The performance of the new service provider should be reviewed for a period of time to see how it is bedding down and how it is getting along with the other service providers.

It is important, when letting a service provider go, to handle the termination within the provisions of the governing agreement. The agreements that hedge funds have with their service providers should state what services the hedge fund requires, but also provide a means to terminate the arrangement. If possible, and prior to giving notice to terminate a service provider, there should be a discussion with that entity to review its performance and provide it, if possible, with a means to address any outstanding issues. Only after this has taken place and the Directors conclude that a change is required should the RFP process to select the service provider commence.

It is an open question whether a service provider should be told that it is being released prior to the appointment of a new service provider. The arguments against this regard the premise that the interests of the hedge fund and its investors require that there be a seamless transition and that informing the outgoing service provider might result in a further decline in performance or even cause problems. An alternative when an administrator is changed is that the new administrator acts as a shadow for a couple of months unknown to investors of the original administrator, ie, calculates AUM and NAVs per share, register, etc. Telling the service provider might, in some instances, cause it to improve performance. In any event, there must be a clear, well-administered transition plan. This should be monitored by the Directors, administered by a Director or designee and provide for a quick handover with few interruptions. Relations with the outgoing service provider should, if possible, kept cordial and positive.

INSOLVENCY

The greatest, but least appreciated, risk to hedge funds today is insolvency. The insolvency proceedings of the two Bear Stearns funds seemingly combines a number of elements. including risk, valuations, illiquid assets, redemption requests and leverage.

As is well known, Bear Stearns placed two of its hedge fund master funds into insolvency. The decision was taken after the portfolios in the two master funds, comprised of illiquid instruments, declined in value. (It was reported that there were still "sufficient assets" remaining in BS High-Grade Structured Credit to "cover the US$1.4 billion" owed to Bear Stearns as the prime broker.[8]) The portfolios declined in value because they were comprised of illiquid assets and were leveraged. Bear Stearns Asset Management Inc (BSAM) sought to manage the risk in the portfolios of the two master funds by purchasing the highest-rated tranches of debt in CDOs. It was reported that during Q2 2007 the master funds increasingly employed leverage in an effort to boost returns. During this time and in the markets, the increasing number of sub-prime mortgage defaults led to decreasing credit ratings which, in turn, fuelled declines in the values of rated securities. The Bloomberg *No Value Left* Story reported that a letter dated 17 August 2007 issued to investors in the feeder funds of the two master fund structures noted that redemption requests coupled with margin calls from lenders brought on by revalued (downward) collateral brought on sales of assets, and when not enough cash was raised, creditors of the hedge funds seized and sold collateral or ended their funding of the master funds.

A further consideration, as noted in a *Business Week* article, were the facts that little cash was held (1%) to handle redemptiions, that the BS Enhanced High-Grade Structured Credit Fund employed fair value accounting, that the management of the master fund estimated the fair value of 63.10% of the securities and that the differences between the assets valued by estimate and based on a price derived from a "ready market" "could be material".[9] A further consideration was that the BS Enhanced

High-Grade Structured Credit Fund had a single equity shareholder – Barclays – while other investors gained exposure through a derivative, an unusual structure for any hedge fund. It was reported in the *Business Week* article that Barclays served notice that it wished to redeem its shares in the BS Enhanced High-Grade Structured Credit Fund. Leverage, the bringer of higher yields, hastened the steep, cyclic decline.

The two master funds that Bear Stearns placed into insolvency were Cayman Islands-incorporated exempt limited liability companies. The joint provisional liquidators (JPLs) of the two master funds petitioned the US Bankruptcy Court for the Southern District of New York (Court) for an order recognising the liquidation of the master funds in the Cayman Islands as "foreign main proceedings" or alternatively "foreign non-main proceedings" under Chapter 15 of the US Bankruptcy Code. This order, if granted, would have entitled the JPLs and the master funds to related relief – including an automatic stay in proceedings against the debtors involved. On 28 August 2007, and pending the Court's decision on the JPLs' petitions, investors sought but did not receive a court ruling to seize the assets of the two master funds. Two days later the Court handed down its decision in response to the JPLs' petitions.

To receive the order and to be able to claim relief from further and other proceedings, the JPLs required that the Court find that the Cayman Islands was the centre of main interests (COMI) for the master funds. The Court refused to grant the order, holding that the COMI of the master funds was the US, "the place where the Funds conduct the administration of their interests on a regular basis".[10] The factors cited by the Court in the BS Funds Decision were the location of the key service providers – the investment manager, the prime broker, the administrator and the executing brokers – and the places where key activities were being performed – New York, Dublin and Delaware.

The Court did leave open to the JPLs the option to place the two master funds into Chapter 7 (liquidation) or Chapter 11 (reorganisation) proceedings. Bear Stearns appealed the BS Funds Decision.

Since the BS Funds Decision was issued, the directors of the onshore feeder fund of BS Enhanced High-Grade Structured Credit Fund announced that they were winding up the fund and had appointed liquidators to handle this. At an EGM held in London on 14 November 2007, the shareholders of High-Grade Structured Credit Strategies Enhanced Leverage (Overseas) Fund (Overseas Fund), the offshore feeder fund of BS Enhanced High-Grade Structured Credit Fund, voted to remove BSAM as investment manager and controlling party and replace it with FTI Capital Advisors. Reportedly, FTI is to investigate the "circumstances of the fund's collapse".[11] It was reported that, two weeks prior to the EGM, BSAM placed Overseas Fund into voluntary liquidation and appointed KPMG as liquidator. The investors were also seeking to obtain the books and records of the hedge funds in anticipating of bringing an action against Bear Stearns and/or others. At the same time, the US investors in the onshore feeder fund petitioned Bear Stearns for the appointment of an independent inspector to monitor a vote to be taken to replace Bear Stearns as the controlling party of this feeder fund.

An analysis of the BS Funds Decision is beyond the scope of this book, but the decision taken by the Court under the US Bankruptcy Code is inconsistent with the position that hedge funds take with respect to taxation – namely, that they do not wish to be taxed in the jurisdiction where the investment manager is located. It is also inconsistent with how hedge funds have established and operated for years – namely, again, that they use the Cayman Islands or other offshore jurisdictions to incorporate but not to operate.

The resolution of the issues raised by the BS Funds Decision is critical. It raises issues about how and where a hedge fund or a master fund may be liquidated and what strategies may be employed by seeking relief in a jurisdiction other than where the fund in question is located. It raises issues about the ability of a prime broker to realise the charge that it has over the assets of the hedge fund that is placed into insolvency. In the Bear Stearns case, had the order been granted, ancillary litigation and actions would have been stayed while the prime broker unwound the positions and sold the assets to realise its charge, possibly leaving investors with no remedies and the scenario of recovering little or no part of their investments.

1 *Beacon Hill Amended Complaint*, at p. 38.
2 *Beacon Hill Amended Complaint*, at p. 40.
3 *Beacon Hill Amended Complaint*, at p. 40.
4 The term "haircut" refers to the discount applied to a position when giving it a value. It is a function of liquidity. Exchange-traded equity securities may have a small or no haircut, due to the fact that there is a liquid market for them and the position may be realised quickly, when it must be sold. By contrast, OTC derivatives, loan participations and derivatives do not have a central market where a price may be easily derived and the asset sold and settled quickly, leading the prime broker to give not full value of the position on its books, but to discount the value of the position. The discount is the haircut and reflects the illiquid nature of the instrument.
5 Christine Harper and Adrian Cox, "Amaranth May Make Goldman, Morgan Biggest Winners", Bloomberg, 25 September, 2006 ("Big Winners"). The "Big Winners" article noted that the rising earnings of investments banks were paced more by prime brokerage and derivatives trading activities, rather than underwriting and advisory activities.
6 Jenny Anderson, "Betting on the Weather and Taking an Ice-Cold Bath", *New York Times*, 29 September, 2006.
7 "Big Winners".
8 "Bear Stearns Tells Fund Investors 'No Value Left' (Update 6)", Bloomberg.com, 18 August 2007 ("Bloomberg *No Value Left* Story"). URL: www.bloomberg.com/apps/news?pid=20670001&refer=home&sid=aiMUHwcg.
9 "Bear Bets Wrong", Matthew Goldstein and David Henry, *Business Week*, 22 October 2007,

pp. 50–56, at 52 (quoting the auditor's note in the 2006 audited financial statements of the BS Enhanced High-Grade Structured Credit Fund (*Business Week* article).

10 In re Bear Stearns High-Grade Structured Credit Strategies Master Fund, Ltd. (In Provisional Liquidation); Case No. 07–12383; In re Bear Stearns High-Grade Structured Credit Strategies Enhanced Leverage Master Fund, Ltd. (In Provisional Liquidation); Case No. 07–12384, Decision and Order Denying Recognition (Bankr. SDNY 30 August 2007); Amended Decision and Order Denying Recognition (Bankr. SDNY 5 September 2007) (BS Funds Decision).

11 "Bear Stearns in new US$1.2bn write down", James Quinn, Wall Street Correspondent, 15 November 2007. URL: www.telegraph.co.uk/money/main.jhtml?xml=/money/2007/11/15/cnbear115.xml.

Appendix 1

Articles provided by courtesy of Ogier

COMPANIES LAW (REVISED)
COMPANY LIMITED BY SHARES
ARTICLES OF ASSOCIATION
OF
ABC FUND, LTD.
(Adopted by Special Resolution passed on [ ], 200[ ])

Preliminary

1. The regulations contained in Table A in the First Schedule of the Law shall not apply to the Company and the following regulations shall be the Articles of Association of the Company.
2. In these Articles:
   (a) the following terms shall have the meanings set opposite if not inconsistent with the subject or context:

"Administrator"	any person appointed and for the time being acting as administrator of the Company;
"allotment"	shares are taken to be allotted when a person acquires the unconditional right to be included in the Register in respect of those shares;
"Articles"	these articles of association of the Company as from time to time amended by Special Resolution;
"Auditors"	the auditors for the time being of the Company;
"Business Day"	such day or days as the Directors may from time to time determine;
"Class"	a class of shares designated by the Directors pursuant to these Articles;

"clear days"	in relation to a period of notice means that period excluding both the day when the notice is given or deemed to be given and the day for which it is given or on which it is to take effect;
"Company"	the above-named company;
"Directors"	the directors for the time being of the Company or, as the case may be, those Directors assembled as a board or as a committee of the board;
"dividend"	includes a distribution or interim dividend or interim distribution;
"electronic"	has the same meaning as in the Electronic Transactions Law (Revised);
"electronic communication"	a communication sent by electronic means, including by fax;
"electronic record"	has the same meaning as in the Electronic Transactions Law (Revised);
"electronic signature"	has the same meaning as in the Electronic Transactions Law (Revised);
"executed"	means any mode of execution;
"Fiscal Period"	in relation to a Portfolio, a period which commences on each of (A) in respect of the initial Fiscal Period, the date shares relating to such Portfolio are first issued and (B) thereafter on (i) the first day of each Performance Period in respect of such Portfolio, (ii) the day next following any Redemption Day on which shares relating to such Portfolio are redeemed, (iii) each Subscription Day on which shares relating to such Portfolio are issued, (iv) the day next following any date on which dividends are declared in respect of shares relating to such Portfolio or as of which any amount is credited or debited against any Record of such Portfolio pursuant to these Articles, (v) any other date that the Directors select in their discretion, and the prior Fiscal Period will end on the day immediately preceding the first day of a new Fiscal Period;

"Gross Negligence"	in relation to a person means a standard of conduct beyond negligence whereby a person acts with reckless disregard for the consequences of his action or inaction;
"holder"	in relation to any share, the Member whose name is entered in the Register as the holder of the share;
"Incentive Fee"	the incentive fee payable to the Investment Manager pursuant to the Investment Management Agreement or, if calculated pursuant to some other agreement or document approved by the Directors, then the incentive fee payable to the Investment Manager pursuant to such other agreement or document;
"Initial Offering Period"	in respect of shares of each Class, Sub-Class and Series, the initial period during which the shares of that Class, Sub-Class and Series are offered for subscription as determined by the Directors pursuant to these Articles;
"Investment Management Agreement"	the agreement for the time being in force between the Company and the Investment Manager;
"Investment Manager"	any person appointed and for the time being acting as investment manager of the Company;
"Investments"	means, but shall not be limited to, securities and other financial instruments held directly or by any Master Fund, including, without limitation, capital stock; all manner of equity securities (whether registered or unregistered, traded or untraded); shares of beneficial interest; partnership interests and similar financial instruments; bonds, notes and debentures (whether subordinated, convertible or otherwise); currencies; interest rate, currency, equity and other derivative products, including, without limitation: (i) futures contracts (and options thereon) relating to stock indices, currencies, United States Government securities, securities of non-U.S. governments, other financial instruments and all other commodities and (ii) swaps

(including credit default swaps), options, rights, warrants, when-issued securities, caps, collars, floors, forward rate agreements, and repurchase and reverse repurchase agreements and other cash equivalents; (iii) spot and forward currency transactions; and (iv) agreements relating to or securing such transactions; leases, including without limitation, equipment lease certificates; equipment trust certificates; loans; accounts and notes receivable and payable held by trade or other creditors; trade acceptances and claims; contracts and other claims; executory contracts; participations; mutual funds; U.S. and non-U.S. money market funds and instruments; obligations of the United States, or any state thereof, non-U.S. governments and instrumentalities of any of them; commercial paper; certificates of deposit; bankers' acceptances; trust receipts; letters of credit; money market instruments; accounts payable; puts; other bankruptcy claims and bank debt; and other obligations and instruments or evidences of indebtedness of whatever kind or nature; in each case, of any person, corporation, government or other entity whatsoever, whether or not publicly traded or readily marketable;

"Islands"	the British Overseas Territory of the Cayman Islands;
"Law"	the Companies Law (Revised);
"Master Fund"	ABC Master Fund, Ltd.;
"Member"	has the same meaning as in the Law;
"Memorandum"	the memorandum of association of the Company as from time to time amended;
"month"	a calendar month;
"Net Asset Value"	when used with reference to the Company or to a particular Portfolio or to a particular Class, Sub-Class or Series means the aggregate of the Net Asset Value per Share of all shares of the Company or that Portfolio or that Class, Sub-Class or Series, as the case may be;

"Net Asset Value per Share"	in respect of shares of each Class, Sub-Class or Series, the net asset value per share of such Class, Sub-Class or Series, as determined in accordance with these Articles;
"Net Loss"	any amount by which the Net Asset Value of the Company or, if applicable, Portfolio as of the first day of a Fiscal Period exceeds the Net Asset Value of the Company or, if applicable, Portfolio as of the last day of the same Fiscal Period;
"Net Profit"	any amount by which the Net Asset Value of the Company or, if applicable, Portfolio as of the last day of a Fiscal Period exceeds the Net Asset Value of the Company or, if applicable, Portfolio as of the first day of the same Fiscal Period;
"Non-qualified Person"	any person who holds or owns shares in breach of the restrictions contained in or imposed pursuant to these Articles or in respect of whom any warranty required pursuant to these Articles was not true when made or has ceased to be true;
"Offering Memorandum"	the current private placement memorandum, confidential memorandum, prospectus, or any other explanatory document setting forth, *inter alia*, the investment objectives of the Company, as may be amended or supplemented from time to time;
"officer"	includes a Director or a Secretary;
"Operational Currency"	in relation to each Class, such currency as the Directors may determine in accordance with these Articles;
"Ordinary Resolution"	a resolution of a duly constituted general meeting of the Company passed by a simple majority of the votes cast by, or on behalf of, the Members entitled to vote present in person or by proxy and voting at the meeting and includes a unanimous written resolution;
"paid up"	means paid up as to the par value and any premium payable in respect of the issue of any shares and includes credited as paid up;

"Participation Percentage"	in respect of each Class, a percentage established for each Class on the Company's books as of the first day of each Fiscal Period. The Participation Percentage of a Class for a Fiscal Period shall be determined by dividing the amount of the Record attributable to such Class as of the beginning of the Fiscal Period by the sum of the Records of all of the Classes relating to the same Portfolio as of the beginning of the Fiscal Period. The sum of the Participation Percentage of all Classes relating to the same Portfolio for each Fiscal Period shall equal 100%; in respect of each Sub-Class, a percentage established for each Sub-Class on the Company's books as of the first day of each Fiscal Period. The Participation Percentage of a Sub-Class for a Fiscal Period shall be determined by dividing the amount of the Record attributable to such Sub-Class as of the beginning of the Fiscal Period by the sum of the Records of all of the Sub-Classes of that Class as of the beginning of the Fiscal Period. The sum of the Participation Percentage of all Sub-Classes of that Class for each Fiscal Period shall equal 100%; in respect of each Series, a percentage established for each Series on the Company's books as of the first day of each Fiscal Period. The Participation Percentage of a Series for a Fiscal Period shall be determined by dividing the amount of the Record attributable to such Series as of the beginning of the Fiscal Period by the sum of the Records of all of the Series of that Class or Sub-Class, as the case may be, as of the beginning of the Fiscal Period. The sum of the Participation Percentage of all Series of that Class or Sub-Class, as the case may be, for each Fiscal Period shall equal 100%; for the avoidance of doubt and solely for purposes of calculating Participation Percentages, accruals for any Incentive Fee not yet earned shall be added back to the value of each Record;

"Performance Period"	the period of time by reference to which the Incentive Fee in respect of any Class or Sub-Class is calculated;
"Portfolio"	a portfolio of Investments held by the Company on behalf of a particular Class (or if applicable, particular Classes having identical investment objectives and investment strategies);
"Recognised Interest"	a security interest in shares recognised by the Company pursuant to these Articles;
"Record"	a separate record maintained in the books of the Company in respect of any Class, Sub-Class or Series of shares pursuant to these Articles;
"Redemption Day"	in respect of each Class, Sub-Class and/or any particular shares, such day or days as the Directors may from time to time determine either generally or in any particular case;
"Redemption Price"	the price at which shares shall be redeemed determined in accordance with these Articles;
"Redemption Request"	has the meaning ascribed thereto in these Articles;
"Register"	the register of Members required to be kept pursuant to the Law;
"Seal"	the common seal of the Company including every duplicate seal;
"Secretary"	any person appointed by the Directors to perform any of the duties of the secretary of the Company, including a joint, assistant or deputy secretary;
"Series"	a series of any Class or Sub-Class (as the case may be) designated by the Directors pursuant to these Articles;
"share"	a redeemable participating share of $0.01 par value (including a fraction of such a share) of any Class, Sub-Class or Series in the capital of the Company having the rights set out in these Articles. Such shares may be divided into different Classes, Sub-Classes and Series, in the discretion of the Directors. In these Articles the term "share" shall embrace all

	Classes, Sub-Classes and Series except when reference is made to a specific Class, Sub-Class or Series;
"signed"	includes an electronic signature and a signature or a representation of a signature affixed by mechanical means;
"Special Resolution"	has the same meaning as in the Law and includes a unanimous written resolution of all Members entitled to vote expressed to be a special resolution;
"Sub-Class"	a sub-class of any Class of shares designated by the Directors pursuant to these Articles;
"Subscription Day"	in respect of each Class, Sub-Class and/or any particular shares, such day or days as the Directors may from time to time determine either in any particular case or generally;
"Subscription Price"	the price at which shares shall be issued determined in accordance with these Articles;
"United States"	the United States of America, its territories and possessions including each State and the District of Columbia;
"Valuation Day"	in respect of each Class, Sub-Class or Series, such day or days as the Directors may from time to time determine either in any particular case or generally; and
"written" and "in writing"	includes all modes of representing or reproducing words in visible form including in the form of an electronic record;

(b) unless the context otherwise requires words or expressions defined in the Law shall have the same meanings herein but excluding any statutory modification thereof not in force when these Articles become binding on the Company;

(c) unless the context otherwise requires:
   - (i) words importing the singular number shall include the plural number and vice-versa;
   - (ii) words importing the masculine gender only shall include the feminine gender; and
   - (iii) words importing persons only shall include companies or associations or bodies of persons whether incorporated or not;

(d) in each reference to a determination or exercise by the Directors of a discretion under these Articles it shall be implied that such discretion shall be exercised by the Directors in their sole and absolute discretion either generally or in any particular case;

(e) the word "may" shall be construed as permissive and the word "shall" shall be construed as imperative;

(f) any phrase introduced by the terms "including", "include", "in particular" or any similar expression shall be construed as illustrative and shall not limit the sense of the words preceeding those terms;

(g) reference to a "dollar" or "dollars" (or "$") are references to dollars of the currency of the United States;

(h) the headings herein are for convenience only and shall not affect the construction of these Articles;

(i) references to statutes are, unless otherwise specified, references to statutes of the Islands (and such reference shall be taken to be to the short title applicable to such statute) and, subject to paragraph (b) above, include any statutory modification or re-enactment thereof for the time being in force;

(j) in these Articles section 8 of the Electronic Transactions Law (Revised) shall not apply; and

(k) where an Ordinary Resolution is expressed to be required for any purpose, a Special Resolution is also effective for that purpose.

Commencement of Business

3. The preliminary expenses incurred in the formation of the Company and the initial issue of shares shall be paid by the Company and may be amortised over such period as the Directors may determine and the amount so paid shall in the accounts of the Company be charged against income and/or capital as the Directors shall determine.

4. The business of the Company may be commenced as soon after incorporation as the Directors think fit, notwithstanding that only some of the shares may have been allotted.

Situation of offices of the Company

5. The registered office of the Company shall be at such address in the Islands as the Directors shall from time to time determine. The Company, in addition to its registered office, may establish and maintain such other offices, places of business and agencies in the Islands and elsewhere as the Directors may from time to time determine.

Share Capital

6. The authorised share capital of the Company is $50,000 divided into 5,000,000 shares.
7. Subject to these Articles, all shares for the time being unissued shall be under the control of the Directors who may issue, allot and dispose of or grant options over the same to such persons, on such terms and in such manner as they may think fit.
8. The Directors may in their discretion refuse to accept any application for shares and may accept any application in whole or in part.
9. Before the allotment of any share, the Directors:
   (a) shall designate the Class to which such share shall belong, the Operational Currency of such Class and, if applicable, the Portfolio into which the subscription proceeds of shares of such Class shall be invested. On the designation of any Class, the Directors, or any duly authorised agent of the Company, shall determine the manner in which shares of such Class shall differ from shares of any other Class including, without limitation, as to the amount of fees payable to the Investment Manager to be charged against shares of such Class and any variation of terms of such Class;
   (b) on the issue of any shares of any Class, may, in their discretion (whether on the first or a subsequent issue of shares of such Class), divide such Class into Sub-Classes. Once the Directors have determined that a Class shall be divided into Sub-Classes, further Sub-Classes may be created following the first issue of shares of that Class or in the event that shares of an existing Class are subsequently divided into Sub-Classes, the shares of that Class then in issue shall automatically be designated the first Sub-Class of that Class, and further Sub-Classes of such Class may be created. On the designation of any Sub-Class, the Directors or any authorised agent of the Company, may agree to vary certain terms generally applicable to holders of shares of the Class from which the Sub-Class is designated;
   (c) in respect of the first issue of shares of any Class or Sub-Class (as the case may be), shall determine whether shares of that Class or Sub-Class (as the case may be) will be issued in Series, and if so, shall designate such shares as the first Series of the relevant Class or Sub-Class (as the case may be); and
   (d) in respect of the issue of any Class or Sub-Class (as the case may be) for which shares of the first Series have been issued, shall designate the Series to which such share will belong. All subsequent Series shall be designated sequentially.
10. (a) Any of the foregoing designations made by or on behalf of the

Directors before the allotment of any share may be cancelled by subsequent resolution of the Directors before the allotment of a share, and such share shall after such cancellation be available for allotment and issue as a part of any other Class, Sub-Class or Series of shares, and subject to the foregoing may be subsequently redesignated in like manner.

(b) Any issued shares of a Class may, from time to time, be redesignated by a resolution of the Directors provided that:

(i) all issued shares of the same Class are so redesignated;

(ii) except for the change of designation of the Class, the designations of the Sub-Classes or Series within such Class shall not be affected; and

(iii) no terms (except the then current designation) or rights attaching to any such shares shall be affected by such redesignation.

11. The different Classes, Sub-Classes and Series of shares, confer upon the holders the same rights and rank *pari passu* in all respects, except as otherwise provided in these Articles.

12. (a) The Directors may impose such restrictions and require such warranties as they consider necessary or desirable for the purpose of ensuring that no shares are held by or for the benefit of (i) any person in breach of the law or requirements of any country or governmental authority; (ii) any person who has given representations in a subscription agreement which were not true when given or have ceased to be true; or (iii) any person or persons in circumstances (whether directly or indirectly affecting such person or persons and whether taken alone or in conjunction with any other person or persons, connected or not, or any other circumstances appearing to the Directors to be relevant) in which the Directors determine the continuing ownership of shares by such person or persons would cause (1) an undue risk of adverse tax or other consequences to the Company, any Master Fund or any of the Members; and/or (2) the Company to be required to comply with any registration or filing requirements in any jurisdiction with which it would not otherwise be required to comply.

(b) A holder of shares shall, upon becoming aware that he is, or is holding shares for the benefit of, a Non-qualified Person, promptly either deliver to the Company a written request for the redemption of the shares so held by him in accordance with these Articles or transfer the same to a person who is not, and would not thereby be, a Non-qualified Person.

(c) If it shall come to the attention of the Directors that any shares are held by or for the benefit of a Non-qualified Person, the Directors may by written notice require redemption or transfer in accordance with these Articles of the shares so held.

13. The Company may on any issue of shares pay such brokerage, underwriting, sales or commission charges as may be lawful.

14. (a) Except as required by law, no person shall be recognised by the Company as holding any share upon any trust, and the Company shall not be bound by or recognise (even when having notice thereof) any equitable, contingent, future or partial interest in any share, or (save only as by these Articles otherwise provided or as by law required) any other right in respect of any share except an absolute right thereto in the registered holder.

(b) Notwithstanding the preceding sub-Article (a) the Company may (but shall not be obliged to) recognise a security interest of which it has actual notice over shares. The Company shall not be treated as having recognised any such security interest unless it has so agreed in writing with the secured party.

15. The Directors shall keep or cause to be kept a Register as required by section 40 of the Law.

16. The Directors in each year shall prepare or cause to be prepared an annual return and declaration setting forth the particulars required by section 187 of the Law and deliver a copy thereof to the registrar of companies in and for the Islands.

Issue of Shares

17. Subject as hereinafter provided, on receipt by the Company or its authorised agent of an application in writing (unless the Directors shall otherwise agree) in such form as the Directors may from time to time determine, and such information as the Directors may from time to time require in their discretion, the Company may:

(a) on such day or days as the Directors may determine, make the initial issue of shares of any Class, Sub-Class or Series at such initial Subscription Price per share as the Directors may determine; or

(b) subject as hereinafter provided, after the Initial Offering Period, (or, if there is no Initial Offering Period in respect of shares of any Class, Sub-Class or Series after the initial issue of shares of that Class, Sub-Class or Series), issue further shares of any existing Class, Sub-Class or Series on any Subscription Day and such shares shall be issued at a Subscription Price per share of not less than the total of:

(i) an amount equal to the nominal value of a share; and

(ii) a premium calculated by deducting from the Net Asset Value per Share of a share of the relevant Class, Sub-Class or

Series on the applicable Valuation Day, the nominal value of a share and rounding the amount so obtained up or down to the nearest convenient unit of the Operational Currency of the Class concerned.

18. The Directors may, in their discretion, allot and issue shares of any Class, Sub-Class or Series against the vesting in the Company of any Investments or other property of whatsoever nature and wheresoever situate and in connection therewith the following provisions shall apply:
    (a) the number of shares to be issued shall be not more than that number which would have fallen to be issued for cash as hereinbefore in this Article provided on the day of issue against the payment of a sum equal to the value of the Investments or other property, as the case may be, so vested in the Company;
    (b) the Directors may provide that the whole or any part of expenses arising in connection with the vesting of the Investments or other property in the Company shall be paid by the Company or by the person to whom the shares are to be issued or partly by the Company and partly by such person; and
    (c) the value of the Investments or other property to be vested in the Company shall be determined by the Directors on the basis of the principles related to the determination of Net Asset Value provided in these Articles.

19. The Directors may require an applicant for any shares to pay to the Company or the Investment Manager or introducing brokers, placement agents or any such other specified persons, or to the Company for the benefit of the Investment Manager or introducing brokers, placement agents or any other specified persons, such sales charge or placement or underwriting fee as the Directors may determine from time to time in respect of (if applicable) the relevant Class, Sub-Class or Series. The Directors may differentiate, in their discretion, between applicants as to the amount of such sales charges

20. Shares may be issued in such minimum numbers as the Directors may specify either generally or in any particular case. The Directors may from time to time also prescribe an amount as the minimum subscription amount either generally or in any particular case.

21. Unless the Directors determine to accept Investments or other property as consideration for shares, shares shall be issued only upon payment in full of the Subscription Price in respect thereof in the relevant Operational Currency or in such other currency or currencies as the Directors may determine to be appropriate either generally or in relation to a particular Class or in any specific case.

22. Where subscription monies (or Investments to be vested in the Company) will not produce an exact number of shares, the Company

may issue fractions of shares and, save as otherwise herein provided, any such fraction of a share shall be subject to and carry the corresponding fraction of liabilities (whether with respect to nominal or par value, premium, contribution or otherwise howsoever), limitations, preferences, privileges, qualifications, restrictions, rights or other attributes of a whole share of the relevant Class, Sub-Class or Series. The Company shall not issue fractions of a share that exceed such number of decimal places as the Directors may determine, and in the absence of such determination such fractions shall be rounded down to two decimal points and any monies represented by the amount by which those fractions have been rounded down shall be retained as part of the Record for the relevant Class, Sub-Class or Series.

23. No shares of any Class, Sub-Class or Series shall be issued during any period when the determination of the Net Asset Value per Share of the relevant Class, Sub-Class or Series is suspended.
24. The Company may decline to allot shares to satisfy any application unless cleared funds in payment of the Subscription Price (or Investments to be vested in the Company) and any applicable charges have been received by the Company by close of business on the Valuation Day immediately preceding the relevant Subscription Day or by such earlier time as the Directors may in their discretion determine.
25. Payment for shares shall be made at such time and place and to such person on behalf of the Company as the Directors may from time to time determine.

Records

26. The Directors shall establish in the books of the Company a separate Record for each Class, Sub-Class and Series of shares, and the following provisions shall apply thereto:
    (a) the proceeds from the allotment and issue of each Class, Sub-Class and Series of shares shall be applied in the books of the Company to the Record established for that Class, Sub-Class and Series of shares and assets required to satisfy any redemption of shares or paid as dividends, shall be accounted for out of the relevant Record;
    (b) subject to paragraphs (c) and (d) below, as of the last day of each Fiscal Period any Net Profit or Net Loss for the Fiscal Period shall be allocated among and credited to or debited against the Records of firstly, the Classes relating to the relevant Portfolio, secondly the Sub-Classes and thirdly the Series in proportion to their respective Participation Percentages for that Fiscal Period;

(c) if any assets of the Company are used for currency hedging in relation to a particular Class, the Directors may in their discretion deduct the cost of such hedging from the Record of such Class and the assets and liabilities and income and expenditure attributable thereto shall be applied to such Record;

(d) where any event takes place which may affect the proportion of the Net Profit and Net Loss attributable to a Record, the Directors may in their discretion make such adjustment to the allocations made pursuant to this Article as they deem appropriate to ensure that any Net Profit or Net Loss of the Company is properly and fairly attributable to the Records; and

(e) in the case of any asset or liability (including any expense) of the Company which the Directors do not consider is attributable to a particular Record, the Directors shall allocate such asset or liability among the Records in proportion to respective Participation Percentages of each Class, Sub-Class and Series.

Determination of Net Asset Value per Share

27. Net Asset Value of the Company shall be determined as at close of business on each Valuation Day. The calculation shall be made in accordance with the provisions of this Article by adding the value of all the assets of the Company and deducting therefrom the total liabilities of the Company. The Net Asset Value of a Class, Sub-Class or Series will then be calculated by adding the value of all the assets attributable to the relevant Record and deducting therefrom the total liabilities attributable to such Record. The Net Asset Value per Share will be calculated by dividing the Net Asset Value of a Class, Sub-Class or Series by the number of shares of the relevant Class, Sub-Class or Series in issue and deemed to be in issue on such Valuation Day. Net Asset Value per Share shall be rounded to the nearest cent or such other amount as the Directors may determine and the benefit of such roundings may be retained by the Company.

28. For the purposes of this Article:

(a) shares for which application has been made shall be deemed to be in issue and the full Subscription Price to have been received at the beginning of the Subscription Day on which they are issued; and

(b) shares to be redeemed shall be deemed to remain in issue until and including the close of business on the Redemption Day on which they are to be redeemed, and from that time until paid the Redemption Price shall be deemed to be a liability of the Company.

29. For the purposes of this Article the net assets of the Company shall

be determined (except for amortisation of organisational costs) on the accrual basis of accounting using the International Financial Reporting Standards issued by the International Accounting Standards Board (or such other standards as the Directors shall in their discretion determine) as a guideline and in accordance with the following:

(a) the assets of the Company shall be deemed to include, without limitation, (1) all cash on hand or on deposit, including any interest accrued thereon, (2) all bills and demand notes and accounts receivable (including proceeds of Investments and other assets sold but not delivered), (3) all Investments and other assets owned or contracted for by the Company, (4) the Company's interest in any Master Fund, (5) all dividends and distributions payable in stock, cash or other property receivable by the Company, provided that the Company may make adjustments with respect to fluctuations in the market value of Investments caused by trading ex-dividend or ex-rights or by similar practices, (6) all interest accrued on any interest-bearing instruments owned by the Company, except to the extent that the same is included or reflected in the valuation of such instruments, and (7) all other assets of every kind and nature, including prepaid expenses (it being understood that goodwill shall be deemed to have no value);

(b) the liabilities of the Company shall be deemed to include, without limitation, (1) all loans, bills and accounts payable, (2) all accrued or payable expenses and fees chargeable to the Company including dividends declared but unpaid (provided that expenses of a regular or recurring nature may be calculated on an estimated figure for yearly or other periods in advance and accrued over any such period) and accrued fees payable to the Investment Manager, (3) gross acquisition cost of Investments and other property contracted to be purchased, (4) such sum (if any) as the Directors consider appropriate to allow for brokerage, stamp duty and any other governmental tax or charges, (5) dividends declared on shares of any Class, Sub-Class or Series, but not yet paid, and (6) all other liabilities, including unknown or unfixed contingencies, preliminary expenses incurred in or about the formation and establishment of the Company (apportioned in accordance with Article 3) and such reserves as the Directors may reasonably deem advisable. In the event any liability is not payable until some future time after the Valuation Date, the Directors may from time to time make such allowance as is considered appropriate to reflect the true current value thereof; and

(c) the assets of the Company shall be valued in accordance with such policies as the Directors may determine, including such policies as the Directors may approve from time to time and cause to be set out in the Offering Memorandum.

30. Without prejudice to their general powers to delegate their functions, the Directors may delegate any of their functions in relation to the calculation of Net Asset Value per Share to any other person. All valuations of the Company's assets and liabilities made by the Directors (or their delegate) pursuant to the preceding Article shall be final and conclusive.

31. Where for the purposes of these Articles or for any other purpose any amount in one currency is required to be converted into another currency, the Directors may effect such conversion using such rate of exchange as they consider appropriate, in their discretion.

32. In determining Net Asset Value per Share, the Directors may consult with and rely upon, without independent investigation, the advice of the Investment Manager, the Administrator, the Company's brokers or investment advisers or the custodian.

Suspension of Determination of Net Asset Value per Share

33. The Directors may, from time to time, in their discretion and for any reason, declare a suspension of the determination of Net Asset Value per Share of any Class and the issue and redemption of shares of such Class. These circumstances may include, but shall not be limited to, such circumstances as the Directors may approve from time to time and cause to be set out in the Offering Memorandum.

34. Any such suspension shall take effect at such time as the Directors shall declare but not later than the close of business on the Business Day next following the declaration and thereafter there shall be no determination of Net Asset Value per Share of the affected Class until the Directors shall declare the suspension to be at an end.

35. Whenever the Directors shall declare a suspension of the determination of the Net Asset Value per Share, then as soon as may be practicable after any such declaration the Directors shall cause a notice (in such manner as they may determine) to be given to the holders of the shares of the affected Class stating that such declaration has been made, and at the end of any period of suspension the Directors shall cause another notice to be given to the holders of shares stating that the period of suspension has ended.

Repurchase of Subscriber Share

36. As soon as the Directors determine that it is lawful for the Company to do so, the Company shall purchase from the subscriber to the Memorandum the one share agreed to be taken by such subscriber. Such share shall be repurchased for cash at its par value and the Company may make a payment out of capital in respect of such purchase price.

Redemption of Shares

37. (a) Subject to the provisions of the Law and these Articles a Member may request the Company to redeem all or some only of his shares as of any Redemption Day in accordance with the following provisions of this Article. If a Member redeeming shares has subscribed for shares at different times and is not redeeming all of his shares, those shares which have been in issue for the longest period of time will be redeemed first unless determined otherwise by the Directors.

(b) The Directors may in their discretion, prescribe an initial period or periods from the date of issue of shares during which the redemption of shares of any Class or Sub-Class is not permitted. Any such restriction on redemptions may be prescribed, waived or modified by the Directors in their discretion generally or in respect of any group of Members or a specific Member.

(c) Any redemption request (a "Redemption Request") shall be in writing, shall specify the number of shares (and the Class, Sub-Class and Series) to which it relates or indicate the manner in which the number of shares to be redeemed is to be determined and shall be signed by the holder thereof (or, in the case of joint holders, by all such joint holders).

(d) Unless the Directors otherwise determine in their discretion, a Redemption Request shall not be satisfied where such Redemption Request relates to (i) a number of shares less than such number as the Directors shall from time to time determine, or (ii) shares having an aggregate value by reference to their Net Asset Value per Share of less than such amount as the Directors may from time to time determine.

(e) If a Redemption Request is received from a Member which would, if satisfied, result in such Member holding (i) a number of shares less than such number as the Directors shall from time to time determine, or (ii) shares whose aggregate value by reference to their Net Asset Value per Share is less than such amount as the Directors may from time to time determine, the Directors may in their discretion treat such Redemption Request as a request for the entire holding of such Member or as a request for a partial redemption only up to such minimum holding amount and the Company may thereupon effect the redemption of such shares whether or not the Company shall have received certificate(s) in respect of such shares.

(f) A Redemption Request and any certificate(s) representing the shares to which it relates must be lodged with the Company or its authorised agent at such time and place before the Redemption Day for which the redemption is requested as the Directors may from time to time determine in respect of each Class, Sub-Class or Series and if they are not so received the redemption may be effected on the next following Redemption Day provided always that the Directors shall, where a certificate has not been issued, and otherwise may at their option dispense with production of any certificate which shall have become lost or destroyed, in the latter case upon compliance by the holder with the like requirements for replacement of a lost or destroyed certificate pursuant to these Articles.

(g) Redemption Requests may be submitted by fax to the Company or its authorised agent provided that the original signed Redemption Request is received by the Company or its authorised agent before the relevant Redemption Day and provided further that the Member making the Redemption Request complies with such conditions as may be set out in the Offering Memorandum. The Company, its Directors and agents may rely upon any Redemption Request believed by them in good faith to be genuine.

(h) A Redemption Request, once given, may only be withdrawn with the consent of the Directors, following consultation with the Investment Manager.

(i) The right of redemption of any Class, Sub-Class or Series of shares may be suspended during any period when the determination of Net Asset Value per Share of the relevant Class, Sub-Class or Series is suspended.

(j) If one or more Redemption Requests are received in respect of any one Redemption Day that would, if satisfied, result in the redemptions of an amount equal to more than [20]% of the total net asset value of the Company, the Directors may determine in their discretion to reduce the amount of each Redemption Request pro rata so that Redemption Requests represent in aggregate an amount equal to no more than [20]% of the total net asset value of the Company. The partial amounts of the Redemption Requests which remain unsatisfied shall be carried forward to the next Redemption Day and satisfied in priority to any Redemption Requests received in relation to such subsequent Redemption Day until the prior Redemption Requests shall have been satisfied in full.

38. (a) The Directors may at any time by notice in writing to any Non-qualified Person compulsorily redeem all or any of the shares held by such person upon a day which shall be not less than nor more than such number of days as the Directors may, in their discretion, from time to time determine from the date of such notice. Upon such day, such shares shall be redeemed in all respects as if the holder thereof had submitted a Redemption Request whether or not the Company shall have received any certificate(s) in respect of such shares.

(b) The Directors, in their discretion, with or without cause, may at any time by notice in writing to any Member compulsorily redeem all or any of a Member's shares on any Redemption Day which shall be not less than such number of days as the Directors may, in their discretion, from time to time determine from the date of the notice. Upon such day, such shares shall be redeemed in all respects as if the holder thereof had submitted a Redemption Request whether or not the Company shall have received any certificate(s) in respect of such shares.

(c) The Directors may at any time redeem shares to effect a conversion in the manner described in these Articles.

(d) Any restrictions imposed pursuant to these Articles on redemptions made at the option of the Members shall not apply to any compulsory redemption of shares by the Company.

(e) All costs incurred in a compulsory redemption of shares shall be for the account of the Member thereof and may be deducted from the proceeds of the redemption.

(f) The procedure for determining which shares will be compulsorily redeemed in any particular case is subject to change at the discretion of the Directors. In exercising discretion and in making determinations as to whether to compulsorily redeem shares, and in determining which Members shall be subject to compulsory redemption, the Directors may act upon the basis of such information as may be known to them, without any obligation to make special enquiries, and may rely upon the advice of counsel. In no event shall the Company be liable to any Member for any consequence of any determination made by the Directors with respect to such compulsory redemption.

39. The following provisions shall apply to all redemptions of shares:

(a) The Redemption Price for each share shall be the total of:

(i) an amount equal to the nominal value of a share; and

(ii) a premium equal to an amount calculated by deducting from the Net Asset Value per Share of a share of the relevant Class, Sub-Class or Series on the relevant Redemption Day the nominal value of a share and rounding the amount so obtained up or down to the nearest convenient unit of the Operational Currency of the Class concerned.

(b) The nominal value of shares shall be redeemed out of the proceeds arising from the issue of an equal number of shares and the premium (if any) on such shares shall be paid from the relevant share premium account provided always that at the discretion of the Directors such shares may be redeemed out of the profits of the Company which would otherwise have been available for dividend and any premiums thereon may be paid out of the profits of the Company or, if permitted by the Law, out of capital.

(c) The Directors may, if appropriate disclosure has been made in the Offering Memorandum or the relevant Member has otherwise agreed, levy a charge of such amount as they may from time to time determine on the redemption of shares of any Class, Sub-Class or Series which are redeemed within such periods of the date of issue or in such other circumstances as the Directors may from time to time determine and the amount of such charge shall be deducted from the relevant Redemption Price. Such charge may be waived by the Directors in their absolute discretion generally or in respect of a specific Member. Such charge may be paid to the Company or to such other person as the Directors may determine.

(d) Unless the Directors refuse to make a redemption payment in accordance with these Articles, payment of the Redemption Price shall be made in such manner as the Directors may from time to time determine in respect of each Class, Sub-Class and Series, and may cause such determination to be set out in the Offering Memorandum from time to time. If any shares are redeemed without provision by the Member of appropriate payment instructions, the Directors may deposit in a separate bank account the aggregate Redemption Price of all shares held by the Member which are so redeemed. Upon such deposit the person whose shares have been so redeemed shall have no interest in or claim against the Company or its assets except the right to receive (subject to the provisions of these Articles as to a redemption of shares that may result in a breach or violation of any applicable laws or regulations) the moneys so deposited (without interest).

(e) Payment of the Redemption Price may, at the discretion of the Directors, be satisfied in whole or in part by the transfer of assets of the Company provided that the Company shall transfer to a redeeming Member that proportion of the assets of the Company which is then equivalent in value to the Redemption Price of the shares to be redeemed (or such redeemed part thereof which is being so satisfied).

(f) Notwithstanding any other provisions of these Articles, the Company may, in the discretion of the Directors, refuse to make a redemption payment to a Member if the Directors suspect or are advised that the payment of any redemption proceeds to such Member may result in a breach or violation of any applicable laws or regulations (including, without limitation, any anti-money laundering or anti-terrorism laws and regulations) by the Company or any other person in any relevant jurisdiction, or such refusal is necessary to ensure the compliance by the Company, its Directors, the Investment Manager or the Administrator and their respective affiliates, subsidiaries or associates or any of the Company's other service providers with any such applicable law or regulation in any relevant jurisdiction. In such circumstances, and until otherwise instructed by the relevant authority, the Directors may deposit such redemption proceeds in a separate bank account. If the Directors are given permission to pay out such redemption proceeds to the relevant Member, such Member's only right against the Company shall be the right to receive the moneys so deposited (without interest).

(g) Upon the date of redemption of a share, the holder shall cease to be entitled to any rights in respect thereof (except for the right to receive (i) the Redemption Price therefor and (ii) any dividend which had been declared in respect thereof before such redemption being effected) and accordingly his name shall be removed from the Register with respect thereto and the share shall be cancelled.

Conversion of Shares

40. Subject to the provisions of the Law and these Articles and to any restrictions imposed by the Directors:

(a) immediately after the close of business on the last day in each Performance Period, all shares of each Class or Sub-Class (as the case may be) issued in Series, other than (1) the oldest Series of shares of that Class or Sub-Class (as the case may be) which have been charged an Incentive Fee in respect of the immediately preceding Performance Period and (2) any Series of shares of that Class or Sub-Class (as the case may be) in respect of which no Incentive Fee has been charged for the immediately preceding

Performance Period, shall be converted into the oldest Series of shares of that Class or Sub-Class (as the case may be) which have been charged an Incentive Fee in respect of the immediately preceding Performance Period;

(b) a holder of shares of a Class, Sub-Class or Series may at any time submit a written request to the Company that all or any of his shares be converted into shares of a different Class, Sub-Class or Series, and in each case the Directors may in their discretion refuse any such request and may accept any such request in whole or in part and on such terms as the Directors may determine;

(c) (i) any conversion effected pursuant to this Article shall be treated as a simultaneous redemption of the relevant shares (the "Old Shares") and the allotment and issue of the new Class, Sub-Class or Series of shares (the "New Shares") with the application of the proceeds of such redemption to the purchase of the New Shares;

(ii) for the purposes of this Article, the relevant Redemption Day shall be a Valuation Day for the purpose of calculating the Redemption Price of the Old Shares and the Subscription Price of the New Shares; and

(iii) the conversion of Old Shares for New Shares shall in all other respects be treated as a redemption to which the provisions of these Articles (other than those provisions relating to payment) shall apply (whether or not the Company shall have received any certificate(s) in respect of such shares), the Redemption Price being satisfied by the issue of the New Shares;

(d) except in relation to a conversion pursuant to paragraph (a) above, the Directors may make such adjustments to the Redemption Price of the Old Shares and to the terms relating to the issue of New Shares as they in their discretion deem necessary to ensure that, for the purpose of calculating any Incentive Fee, such New Shares are treated for such purposes as if they were the Old Shares.

Transfer of Shares

41. The instrument of transfer of a share may be in any usual form or in any other form which the Directors may approve and shall be executed by or on behalf of the transferor.

42. Except in the case of shares which are subject to a Recognised Interest, the Directors may, in their absolute discretion and without giving any reason, refuse to register the transfer of a share to any

person. The Directors shall not, without the consent of the secured party, register any transfer of shares which are the subject of a Recognised Interest if such transfer appears to the Directors to be inconsistent with the terms of such Recognised Interest, and, subject to the following Article, shall register any transfer of shares which are the subject of Recognised Interest upon enforcement by the secured party of such Recognised Interest.

43. The Directors shall decline to register any transfer of a share:
   (a) to or for the benefit of a person who is or would, upon registration, be a Non-qualified Person; or
   (b) if the instrument of transfer relates to more than one Class or Sub-Class of shares.

44. If the Directors refuse to register a transfer of a share, they shall within two (2) months after the date on which the transfer was lodged with the Company send to the transferee notice of the refusal.

45. The registration of transfers of shares or of shares of any Class or Sub-Class may be suspended at such times and for such periods (not exceeding thirty (30) days in any year) as the Directors may determine.

46. No fee shall be charged for the registration of any instrument of transfer or other document relating to or affecting the title to any share.

47. The Company shall be entitled to retain any instrument of transfer which is registered, but any instrument of transfer which the Directors refuse to register shall be returned to the person lodging it when notice of the refusal is given.

Transmission of Shares

48. If a Member dies the survivor or survivors where he was a joint holder, and his personal representatives where he was a sole holder or the only survivor of joint holders shall be the only persons recognised by the Company as having any title to his interest; but nothing in the Articles shall release the estate of a deceased Member from any liability in respect of any share which had been jointly held by him.

49. A person becoming entitled to a share in consequence of the death or bankruptcy of a Member may, upon such evidence being produced as the Directors may properly require, elect either to become the holder of the share or to have some person nominated by him registered as the transferee. If he elects to become the holder he shall give notice to the Company to that effect. If he elects to have another person registered he shall execute an instrument of transfer of the share to that person. All the Articles relating to the transfer of shares shall apply to the notice or instrument of transfer as if it were an

instrument of transfer executed by the Member and the death or bankruptcy of the Member had not occurred.

50. A person becoming entitled to a share by reason of the death or bankruptcy of a Member shall have the rights to which he would be entitled if he were the holder of the share, except that he shall not, before being registered as the holder of the share, be entitled in respect of it to attend or vote at any meeting of the Company or at any separate meeting of the holders of any class of shares in the Company.

Share certificates

51. Every person, upon becoming the holder of any shares, shall, if he can demonstrate to the Directors or any authorised agent of the Company that he is legally required to hold certificated shares, or if the Directors otherwise permit, be entitled without payment to one (1) certificate for all the shares of each Class, Sub-Class or Series held by him (and, upon transferring a part of his holding of shares of any Class to a certificate for the balance of such holding) or several certificates each for one (1) or more of his shares upon payment for every certificate after the first of such reasonable sum as the Directors may determine. Every certificate shall specify the number, class and distinguishing numbers (if any) of the shares to which it relates and the amount or respective amounts paid up thereon. A certificate may be sealed with the Seal or executed in such other manner as the Directors may prescribe. The Company shall not be bound to issue more than one (1) certificate for shares held jointly by several persons and delivery of a certificate for a share to one (1) joint holder shall be a sufficient delivery to all of them.

52. If a share certificate is defaced, worn-out, lost or destroyed, it may be renewed on such terms (if any) as to evidence and indemnity and payment of the expenses reasonably incurred by the Company in investigating evidence as the Directors may determine but otherwise free of charge, and (in the case of defacement or wearing-out) on delivery to the Company of the old certificate.

Variation of Terms

53. Notwithstanding any other provision of these Articles, the Company (acting through the Directors or any duly authorised agent) may enter into a written agreement with an existing or a prospective Member in respect of shares of a certain Class or Sub-Class providing for offering terms that vary from those applicable to other Members of the same Class or Sub-Class including, without limitation, the

waiver or reduction of fees payable in respect of such shares and different redemption terms, and in such circumstances the Directors may issue shares of the same Class or Sub-Class to such Member or may determine to issue a separate Class or Sub-Class of shares to such Member.

Modification of Rights

54. Subject to the following Article, the rights attached to any Class of shares may be varied or abrogated either whilst the Company is a going concern or during or in contemplation of a winding up, with the consent in writing of two thirds of the Members affected by the proposed variation or abrogation of rights or with the sanction of a resolution of such Members holding not less than two thirds of the shares of the relevant Class present in person or by proxy at a separate general meeting of the Members holding shares of that Class but not otherwise. For such purposes the Directors may in their discretion treat all Classes of shares as forming one Class, if they consider that they would all be affected in the same way by the proposals under consideration and that there would be no conflict of interest between them, but in any other case shall treat them as separate Classes, as the case may be. To every such separate meeting all the provisions of these Articles relating to general meetings of the Company or to the proceedings thereat shall, *mutatis mutandis*, apply except that the necessary quorum shall be one person holding or representing by proxy at least one-third in nominal amount of the issued shares of the Class (but so that if at any adjourned meeting of such holders a quorum as above defined is not present, those holders who are present shall be a quorum) and that every holder of shares of the Class shall on a poll have one vote for each share of the Class held by him.

55. (a) The rights conferred upon the holders of the shares shall be deemed to be varied by the creation or issue of any shares ranking ahead of the shares with regard to participation in the profits or assets of the Company. A Class, Sub-Class or Series to which different levels of fees are payable to the Investment Manager or different redemption rights apply (including the imposition of, absence of, or different level of, a redemption fee) shall not be deemed to rank in priority to any other Class, Sub-Class or Series as regards shareholder rights or participating in the profits or assets of the Company.

(b) The rights attached to the shares shall be deemed not to be varied or abrogated by:

(i) the issue of shares of any Class, Sub-Class or Series;

(ii) the redemption or repurchase of any share;
(iii) the conversion of shares of one Class, Sub-Class or Series into shares of another Class, Sub-Class or Series;
(iv) the redesignation of a Class of Share by the Directors pursuant to these Articles;
(v) the exercise by the Directors or any liquidator of any of their discretions specified in these Articles; or
(vi) the Company entering into any written agreement with a prospective member providing for offering terms that vary from those applicable to other Members of the same Class or Sub-Class;

Alteration of Capital

56. (a) Subject to and in so far as permitted by the provisions of the Law, the Company may from time to time by Ordinary Resolution alter or amend the Memorandum to:
(i) increase its share capital by such sum as the resolution shall prescribe and with such rights, priorities and privileges annexed thereto as set out in such Ordinary Resolution;
(ii) consolidate and divide all or any of its share capital into shares of larger amounts than its existing shares;
(iii) convert all or any of its paid-up shares into stock and reconvert that stock into paid-up shares of any denomination;
(iv) sub-divide its existing shares, or any of them, into shares of smaller amounts than is fixed by the Memorandum; and
(v) cancel any shares which, at the date of the passing of the resolution, have not been taken or agreed to be taken by any person, and diminish the amount of its share capital by the amount of the shares so cancelled.

(b) Except so far as otherwise provided by the conditions of issue, the new shares shall be subject to the same provisions with reference to transfer, transmission, forfeiture and otherwise as the shares in the original share capital.

57. Whenever as a result of a consolidation of shares any Members would become entitled to fractions of a share, the Directors may, on behalf of those Members, sell the shares representing the fractions for the best price reasonably obtainable to any person (including, subject to the provisions of the Law, the Company) and distribute the net proceeds of sale in due proportion among those Members, and the Directors may authorise some person to execute an instrument of transfer of the shares to, or in accordance with the directions of the purchaser. The transferee shall not be bound to see to the application of the purchase money nor shall his title to the shares be affected by

any irregularity in or invalidity of the proceedings in reference to the sale.

58. The Company may by Special Resolution reduce its share capital and any capital redemption reserve in any manner and with, and subject to, any incident, consent, order or other matter required by law.

General Meetings

59. The Directors may, whenever they think fit, convene a general meeting of the Company. If at any time there are not sufficient Directors capable of acting to form a quorum, any Director or any one (1) or more Members holding in the aggregate not less than one-half of the par value of the Company entitled to vote may convene a general meeting in the same manner as nearly as possible as that in which meetings may be convened by the Directors. The Directors shall, upon the requisition in writing of one (1) or more Members holding in the aggregate not less than one-tenth of such par value of the Company as at the date of the requisition carries the right to vote at general meetings, convene a general meeting. Any such requisition shall specify the object of the meeting proposed to be called, and shall be left at the registered office of the Company. Any such requisition may consist of several documents in like form signed by one (1) or more of the requisitionists and a requisition by joint holders of shares must be signed by all of such joint holders. If the Directors do not proceed to convene a general meeting within seven (7) days from the date of such requisition being left as aforesaid, the requisitionists or any of them may convene a general meeting in the same manner as nearly as possible as that in which meetings may be convened by the Directors, but no meeting so convened shall be held more than three (3) months after the expiry of such seven (7) days. The requisitionists shall be reimbursed by the Company for all reasonable expenses incurred by them as a result of the failure by the Directors to convene the general meeting.

60. At least seven (7) clear days' notice specifying the place, the day and the hour of each general meeting and the general nature of the business to be transacted thereat shall be given in the manner hereinafter provided, or in such other manner (if any) as may be prescribed by Ordinary Resolution, to such persons as are entitled to vote or may otherwise be entitled under these Articles to receive such notices from the Company; but with the consent of holders of ninety per cent (90%) in par value of the shares entitled to receive notice of some particular meeting, that meeting may be convened by such shorter notice or without notice and in such manner as those Members may think fit.

61. Subject to the provisions of the Articles and to any restrictions imposed on any shares, the notice shall be given to all the Members, to all the persons entitled to a share in consequence of the death or bankruptcy of a Member and to the Directors. Where the notice of meeting is published on a web-site in accordance with these Articles, it shall continue to be published in the same place on that web-site from the date of the notification until the conclusion of the meeting to which the notice relates.

62. The accidental omission to give notice of a meeting to, or the non-receipt of notice of a meeting by, any person entitled to receive notice shall not invalidate the proceedings at that meeting. Where a notice of meeting published on a web-site in accordance with these Articles is by accident published in different places on the web-site or published for part only of the period from the date of the notification until the conclusion of the meeting to which the notice relates, the proceedings at such meeting are not thereby invalidated.

Proceedings at General Meetings

63. No business shall be transacted at any meeting unless a quorum is present; save as herein otherwise provided, one or more Members holding in the aggregate not less than one-third of the voting shares present in person or by proxy and entitled to vote shall be a quorum.

64. If such a quorum is not present within half an hour from the time appointed for the meeting, or if during a meeting a quorum ceases to be present, the meeting shall stand adjourned to the same day in the next week, at the same time and place or to such day and at such time and place as the Directors may determine, and if at the adjourned meeting a quorum is not present within half an hour from the time appointed for the meeting the Members present shall be a quorum.

65. A person may participate in a general meeting through the medium of conference telephone, video or similar form of communications equipment if all persons participating in the meeting are able to hear and speak to each other throughout the meeting. A person participating in this way is deemed to be present in person at the meeting and is counted in the quorum and entitled to vote. All business transacted in this way at the meeting is for the purpose of the Articles deemed to be validly and effectively transacted at the meeting although fewer than two (2) persons are physically present at the same place. The meeting is deemed to take place where the largest group of those participating is assembled or, if there is no such group, where the chairman of the meeting then is.

66. The chairman, if any, of the board of Directors or in his absence some other Director nominated by the Directors shall preside as chairman

of the meeting, but if neither the chairman nor such other Director (if any) is present within fifteen (15) minutes after the time appointed for holding the meeting and willing to act, the Directors present shall elect one (1) of their number to be chairman and, if there is only one (1) Director present and willing to act, he shall be chairman.

67. If no Director is willing to act as chairman, or if no Director is present within fifteen (15) minutes after the time appointed for holding the meeting, the Members present and entitled to vote shall choose one (1) of their number to be chairman.

68. A Director shall, notwithstanding that he is not a Member, be entitled to attend and speak at any general meeting and at any separate meeting of the holders of any class of shares in the Company.

69. The chairman may, with the consent of any meeting at which a quorum is present (and shall if so directed by the meeting), adjourn the meeting from time to time and from place to place, but no business shall be transacted at any adjourned meeting other than business which might properly have been transacted at the meeting had the adjournment not taken place. When a meeting is adjourned for fourteen (14) days or more, at least seven (7) clear days' notice shall be given specifying the time and place of the adjourned meeting and the general nature of the business to be transacted. Otherwise it shall not be necessary to give any such notice.

70. A resolution put to the vote of the meeting shall be decided on a show of hands unless before, or on the declaration of the result of, the show of hands a poll is duly demanded. A poll may be demanded:
    (a) by the chairman; or
    (b) by any Member or Members present in person or by proxy holding at least ten per cent in par value of the shares giving a right to attend and vote.

71. Unless a poll is duly demanded, a declaration by the chairman that a resolution has been carried or carried unanimously, or by a particular majority, or lost, or not carried by a particular majority and an entry to that effect in the minutes of the meeting shall be conclusive evidence of the fact without proof of the number or proportion of the votes recorded in favour of or against the resolution.

72. The demand for a poll may, before the poll is taken, be withdrawn but only with the consent of the chairman and a demand so withdrawn shall not be taken to have invalidated the result of a show of hands declared before the demand was made.

73. A poll shall be taken in such manner as the chairman directs and he may appoint scrutineers (who need not be Members) and fix a place and time for declaring the result of the poll. The result of the poll shall be deemed to be the resolution of the meeting at which the poll was demanded.

74. In the case of equality of votes, whether on a show of hands or on a poll, the chairman shall be entitled to a casting vote in addition to any other vote he may have.
75. A poll demanded on the election of a chairman or on a question of adjournment shall be taken immediately. A poll demanded on any other question shall be taken either immediately or at such time and place as the chairman directs not being more than 30 days after the poll is demanded. The demand for a poll shall not prevent the continuance of a meeting for the transaction of any business other than the question on which the poll was demanded. If a poll is demanded before the declaration of the result of a show of hands and the demand is duly withdrawn, the meeting shall continue as if the demand had not been made.
76. No notice need be given of a poll not taken immediately if the time and place at which it is taken are announced at the meeting at which it is demanded. In any other case at least seven (7) clear days' notice shall be given specifying the time and place at which the poll is to be taken.
77. A resolution in writing executed by or on behalf of each Member who would have been entitled to vote upon it if it had been proposed at a general meeting at which he was present shall be as effectual as if it had been passed at a general meeting duly convened and held and may consist of several instruments in the like form each executed by or on behalf of one (1) or more Members. If a resolution in writing is described as a Special Resolution or as an Ordinary Resolution, it has effect accordingly.
78. If and for so long as the Company has only one (1) Member entitled to vote:
    (a) in relation to a general meeting, the sole Member or a proxy for that Member or (if the Member is a corporation) a duly authorised representative of that Member is a quorum and these Articles are modified accordingly,
    (b) the sole Member may agree that any general meeting be called by shorter notice than that provided for by the Articles; and
    (c) all other provisions of the Articles apply with any necessary modification (unless the provision expressly provides otherwise).

Votes of Members

79. Subject to any rights or restrictions attached to any shares, on a show of hands every Member who (being an individual) is present in person or by proxy or (being a corporation) is present by a duly authorised representative not being himself a Member entitled to vote, shall have one (1) vote, and on a poll every Member entitled to

vote and every person representing a Member entitled to vote by proxy shall have one (1) vote for every share of which he is the holder.

80. In the case of joint holders, the vote of the senior who tenders a vote, whether in person or by proxy, shall be accepted to the exclusion of the votes of the other joint holders; and seniority shall be determined by the order in which the names of the holders stand in the Register.

81. A Member in respect of whom an order has been made by any court having jurisdiction (whether in the Islands or elsewhere) in matters concerning mental disorder may vote, whether on a show of hands or on a poll, by his receiver, *curator bonis* or other person authorised in that behalf appointed by that court, and any such receiver, *curator bonis* or other person may, on a poll, vote by proxy. Evidence to the satisfaction of the Directors of the authority of the person claiming to exercise the right to vote shall be received at the registered office of the Company, or at such other place as is specified in accordance with the Articles for the deposit or delivery of forms of appointment of a proxy, or in any other manner specified in the Articles for the appointment of a proxy, not less than forty eight (48) hours before the time appointed for holding the meeting or adjourned meeting at which the right to vote is to be exercised and in default the right to vote shall not be exercisable.

82. No Member shall, unless the Directors otherwise determine, be entitled to vote at any general meeting or at any separate meeting of the holders of any Class of shares in the Company, either in person or by proxy, in respect of any share held by him unless all moneys presently payable by him in respect of that share have been paid.

83. No objection shall be raised to the qualification of any voter except at the meeting or adjourned meeting at which the vote objected to is tendered, and every vote not disallowed at the meeting shall be valid. Any objection made in due time shall be referred to the chairman whose decision shall be final and conclusive.

84. On a poll, votes may be given either personally or by proxy. Deposit or delivery of a form of appointment of a proxy does not preclude a Member from attending and voting at the meeting or at any adjournment of it.

85. A Member holding more than one share need not cast the votes in respect of his shares in the same way on any resolution and therefore may vote a share or some or all of such shares either for or against a resolution and/or abstain from voting a share or some or all of the shares and, subject to the terms of the instrument appointing him, a proxy appointed under one or more instruments may vote a share or some or all of the shares in respect of which he is appointed either for or against a resolution and/or abstain from voting.

86. Subject as set out herein, an instrument appointing a proxy shall be in writing in any usual form or in any other form which the Directors may approve and shall be executed by or on behalf of the appointor save that, subject to the Law, the Directors may accept the appointment of a proxy received in an electronic communication at an address specified for such purpose, on such terms and subject to such conditions as they consider fit. The Directors may require the production of any evidence which they consider necessary to determine the validity of any appointment pursuant to this Article.

87. The form of appointment of a proxy and any authority under which it is executed or a copy of such authority certified notarially or in some other way approved by the Directors may:

(a) in the case of an instrument in writing, be left at or sent by post to the registered office of the Company or such other place as is specified in the notice convening the meeting or in any form of appointment of proxy sent out by the Company in relation to the meeting at any time before the time for holding the meeting or adjourned meeting at which the person named in the form of appointment of proxy proposes to vote;

(b) in the case of an appointment of a proxy contained in an electronic communication, where an address has been specified by or on behalf of the Company for the purpose of receiving electronic communications:

(i) in the notice convening the meeting; or

(ii) in any form of appointment of a proxy sent out by the Company in relation to the meeting; or

(iii) in any invitation contained in an electronic communication to appoint a proxy issued by the Company in relation to the meeting,

be received at such address at any time before the time for holding the meeting or adjourned meeting at which the person named in the form of appointment of proxy proposes to vote;

(c) in the case of a poll taken more than forty eight (48) hours after it is demanded, be deposited or delivered as required by paragraphs (a) or (b) of this Article after the poll has been demanded and at any time before the time appointed for the taking of the poll; or

(d) where the poll is not taken immediately but is taken not more than forty eight (48) hours after it was demanded, be delivered at the meeting at which the poll was demanded to the chairman or to the Secretary or to any Director;

and a form of appointment of proxy which is not deposited or delivered in accordance with this Article is invalid.

88. Any corporation or other non-natural person which is a Member may

in accordance with its constitutional documents, or in the absence of such provision by resolution of its directors or other governing body, authorise such person as it thinks fit to act as its representative at any meeting of the Company or of any class of Members, and the person so authorised shall be entitled to exercise the same powers on behalf of the corporation which he represents as the corporation could exercise if it were an individual Member.

89. A vote given or poll demanded by proxy or by the duly authorised representative of a corporation shall be valid notwithstanding the previous determination of the authority of the person voting or demanding a poll unless notice of the determination was received by the Company at the registered office of the Company or, in the case of a proxy, any other place specified for delivery or receipt of the form of appointment of proxy or, where the appointment of a proxy was contained in an electronic communication, at the address at which the form of appointment was received, before the commencement of the meeting or adjourned meeting at which the vote is given or the poll demanded or (in the case of a poll taken otherwise than on the same day as the meeting or adjourned meeting) the time appointed for taking the poll.

Number of Directors

90. Unless otherwise determined by Ordinary Resolution, the number of Directors (other than alternate Directors) is not subject to a maximum and the minimum number is one (1) provided always that there will be no Directors until the first Director(s) are appointed by the subscriber(s) to the Memorandum.

Alternate Directors

91. Any Director (other than an alternate Director) may without the approval of the Directors appoint any person willing to act, whether or not he is a Director, to be an alternate Director and may remove from office an alternate Director so appointed by him.

92. An alternate Director shall be entitled to receive notice of all meetings of Directors and of all meetings of committees of Directors of which his appointor is a member. An alternate Director may waive the requirement that notice be given to him of a meeting of Directors or a committee of Directors, either prospectively or retrospectively. Notice of a board meeting is deemed to be duly given to an alternate Director if it is given to him personally or by word of mouth or by electronic communication to an address given by him to the Company for that purpose or sent in writing to him at his last known

address or another address given by him to the Company for that purpose. An alternate Director shall be entitled to attend and vote at any such meeting at which the Director appointing him is not personally present, and generally to perform all the functions of his appointor as a Director in his absence but shall not be entitled to receive any remuneration from the Company for his services as an alternate Director.

93. An alternate Director shall cease to be an alternate Director if his appointor ceases to be a Director.

94. Any appointment or removal of an alternate Director shall be by notice to the Company signed by the Director making or revoking the appointment or in any other manner approved by the Directors. Any such notice may be left at or sent by post or facsimile transmission to the office or such other place as may be designated for the purpose by the Directors.

95. Save as otherwise provided in the Articles, an alternate Director shall be deemed for all purposes to be a Director and shall alone be responsible for his own acts and defaults and he shall not be deemed to be the agent of the Director appointing him.

Proxy Directors

96. A Director may be represented at any meetings of the Directors by a proxy appointed by him in which event the presence or vote of the proxy shall for all purposes be deemed to be that of the Director. The provisions of these Articles as to the appointment of proxies by the Members shall *mutatis mutandis* apply to the appointment of proxies by Directors. Any person appointed as a proxy Director shall be the agent of the Director appointing him, and not an officer of the Company.

Powers of Directors

97. Subject to the provisions of the Law, the Memorandum and to any directions given by Ordinary Resolution, the business of the Company shall be managed by the Directors who may exercise all the powers of the Company which are not required by these Articles or by law to be exercised or done by the Company. No alteration of the Memorandum or Articles and no such direction shall invalidate any prior act of the Directors which would have been valid if that alteration had not been made or that direction had not been given. The powers given by this Article shall not be limited by any special power given to the Directors by the Articles and a meeting of Directors at

which a quorum is present may exercise all powers exercisable by the Directors.

Delegation of Directors' powers

98. The Directors may, by power of attorney or otherwise, appoint any person to be the agent of the Company for such purposes and on such conditions as they determine, including authority for the agent to delegate all or any of his powers. In particular and without prejudice to the foregoing sentence:
   (a) the Directors may appoint the Administrator and may confer on the Administrator so appointed any of the powers exercisable by them as Directors upon such terms and conditions including the right to remuneration payable by the Company and with such restrictions and with such powers of delegation as they think fit and either collaterally with or to the exclusion of their own powers; and
   (b) the Directors shall appoint the Investment Manager and may confer upon the Investment Manager so appointed any of the powers exercisable by them upon such terms and conditions, including the right to remuneration payable by the Company and with such restrictions and powers of delegation as they think fit and either collaterally with or to the exclusion of their own powers.
99. The Directors may by power of attorney or otherwise appoint any company, firm, person or body of persons, whether nominated directly or indirectly by the Directors, to be the attorney or authorised signatory of the Company for such purpose and with such powers, authorities and discretions (not exceeding those vested in or exercisable by the Directors under these Articles) and for such period and subject to such conditions as they may think fit, and any such powers of attorney or other appointment may contain such provisions for the protection and convenience of persons dealing with any such attorneys or authorised signatories as the Directors may think fit and may also authorise any such attorney or authorised signatory to delegate all or any of the powers, authorities and discretions vested in him.
100. The Directors may delegate any of their powers to any committee consisting of one (1) or more Directors. They may also delegate to any managing Director or any Director holding any other executive office such of their powers as they consider desirable to be exercised by him. Any such delegation may be made subject to any conditions the Directors may impose, and either collaterally with or to the exclusion of their own powers and may be revoked or altered. Subject to any

such conditions, the proceedings of a committee with two (2) or more members shall be governed by the provisions of the Articles regulating the proceedings of Directors so far as they are capable of applying. Where a provision of the Articles refers to the exercise of a power, authority or discretion by the Directors and that power, authority or discretion has been delegated by the Directors to a committee, the provision shall be construed as permitting the exercise of the power, authority or discretion by the committee.

101. The Directors may establish any committees, local boards or agencies or appoint any person to be a manager or agent for managing the affairs of the Company and may appoint any person to be a member of such committees or local boards. Except in relation to the appointment of a Director as managing Director or to a committee of Directors pursuant to the preceding Article any such appointment may be made subject to any conditions the Directors may impose provided that such appointment is not to the exclusion of the Directors' powers and may be revoked or altered by the Directors at any time. Subject to any such conditions, the proceedings of any such committee, local board or agency shall be governed by the Articles regulating the proceedings of Directors so far as they are capable of applying.

Appointment, disqualification and removal of Directors

102. The first Director(s) shall be appointed in writing by the subscriber to the Memorandum.
103. There is no age limit for Directors of the Company.
104. The shareholding qualification for Directors may be fixed by Ordinary Resolution and unless and until so fixed no shareholding qualification shall be required.
105. The Company may by Ordinary Resolution, remove a Director from office and may by Ordinary Resolution appoint a person who is willing to act to be a Director either to fill a vacancy or as an additional Director.
106. The Directors may appoint any person who is willing to act to be a Director, either to fill a vacancy or as an additional Director, provided that the appointment does not cause the number of Directors to exceed any number fixed by or in accordance with the Articles as the maximum number of Directors.
107. The office of a Director shall be vacated if:
    (a) he becomes prohibited by law from being a Director;
    (b) he becomes bankrupt or makes any arrangement or composition with his creditors generally;

(c) he dies, or is, in the opinion of all his co-Directors, incapable by reason of mental disorder of discharging his duties as Director;
(d) he resigns his office by notice to the Company; or
(e) he has for more than six (6) consecutive months been absent without permission of the Directors from meetings of Directors held during that period and his alternate Director (if any) has not during such period attended any such meetings instead of him, and the Directors resolve that his office be vacated; or
(f) he is removed from office by notice addressed to him at his last known address and signed by all his co-Directors.

Remuneration of Directors

108. The Directors shall be entitled to such remuneration as they shall themselves determine and, unless the resolution provides otherwise, the remuneration shall be deemed to accrue from day to day.
109. A Director who, at the request of the Directors, goes or resides outside of the Islands, makes a special journey or performs a special service on behalf of the Company may be paid such reasonable additional remuneration (whether by way of salary, percentage of profits or otherwise) and expenses as the Directors may decide.

Directors' Expenses

110. The Directors may be paid all travelling, hotel and other expenses properly incurred by them in connection with their attendance at meetings of Directors or committees of Directors or general meetings or separate meetings of the holders of any class of shares or of debentures of the Company or otherwise in connection with the discharge of their duties.

Directors' Appointments and Interests

111. The Directors may appoint one (1) or more of their body to the office of managing Director or to any other executive office under the Company, and may enter into an agreement or arrangement with any Director for his employment by the Company or for the provision by him of any services outside the scope of the ordinary duties of a Director (other than the office of auditor). Any such appointment, agreement or arrangement may be made upon such terms as the Directors determine and they may remunerate any such Director for his services as they think fit. Any appointment of a Director to an executive office shall determine if he ceases to be a Director but

without prejudice to any claim to damages for breach of the contract of service between the Director and the Company.

112. If he has disclosed to the Directors the nature and extent of any material interest of his, a Director notwithstanding his office:
   (a) may be a party to, or otherwise interested in, any transaction or arrangement with the Company or in which the Company is otherwise interested;
   (b) may be a director or other officer of, or employed by, or a party to any transaction or arrangement with, or otherwise interested in, any body corporate promoted by the Company or in which the Company is otherwise interested; and
   (c) shall not, by reason of his office, be accountable to the Company for any benefit which he derives from any such office or employment or from any such transaction or arrangement or from any interest in any such body corporate and no such transaction or arrangement shall be liable to be avoided on the ground of any such interest or benefit.

113. For the purposes of the preceding Article:
   (a) a general notice given to the Directors that a Director is to be regarded as having an interest of the nature and extent specified in the notice in any transaction or arrangement in which a specified person or class of persons is interested shall be deemed to be a disclosure that the Director has an interest in any such transaction of the nature and extent so specified; and
   (b) an interest of which a Director has no knowledge and of which it is unreasonable to expect him to have knowledge shall not be treated as an interest of his.

Proceedings of Directors

114. Subject to the provisions of the Articles, the Directors may regulate their proceedings as they think fit. A Director may, and the Secretary at the request of a Director shall, call a meeting of the Directors. Every Director shall receive notice of a meeting. Notice of a board meeting is deemed to be duly given to a Director if it is given to him personally or by word of mouth or by electronic communication to an address given by him to the Company for that purpose or sent in writing to him at his last known address or other address given by him to the Company for that purpose. A Director may waive the requirement that notice be given to him of a meeting of Directors or a committee of Directors, either prospectively or retrospectively. Questions arising at a meeting shall be decided by a majority of votes. A Director who is also an alternate Director shall be entitled in the

absence of his appointor to a separate vote on behalf of his appointor in addition to his own vote.

115. A Director or his alternate Director may participate in a meeting of Directors or a committee of Directors through the medium of conference telephone, video or similar form of communications equipment if all persons participating in the meeting are able to hear and speak to each other throughout the meeting. A person participating in this way is deemed to be present in person at the meeting and is counted in a quorum and entitled to vote. All business transacted in this way by the Directors or a committee of Directors is for the purpose of the Articles deemed to be validly and effectively transacted at a meeting of the Directors or of a committee of Directors although fewer than two (2) Directors or alternate Directors are physically present at the same place. The meeting is deemed to take place where the largest group of those participating is assembled or, if there is no such group, where the chairman of the meeting then is.

116. The quorum for the transaction of the business of the Directors may be fixed by the Directors and unless so fixed at any other number shall be two (2). A person who holds office only as an alternate Director shall, if his appointor is not present, be counted in the quorum.

117. The Directors may appoint one (1) of their number to be the chairman of the board of Directors and may at any time remove him from that office. Unless he is unwilling to do so, the Director so appointed shall preside at every meeting of Directors at which he is present. But if there is no Director holding that office, or if the Director holding it is unwilling to preside or is not present within five (5) minutes after the time appointed for the meeting, the Directors present may appoint one (1) of their number to be chairman of the meeting.

118. All acts done by a meeting of Directors, or of a committee of Directors, or by any person acting as a Director shall, notwithstanding that it be afterwards discovered that there was a defect in the appointment of any Director or that any of them were disqualified from holding office, or had vacated office, or were not entitled to vote, be as valid as if every such person had been duly appointed and was qualified and had continued to be a Director and had been entitled to vote.

119. A Director who is present at a meeting of the Directors at which action on any Company matter is taken shall be presumed to have assented to the action taken unless his dissent shall be entered in the minutes of the meeting or unless he shall file his written dissent from such action with the person acting as the secretary of the meeting before the adjournment thereof or shall forward such dissent by registered mail to the Company immediately after the conclusion of

the meeting. Such right to dissent shall not apply to a Director who voted in favour of such action.

120. A resolution in writing signed by all the Directors entitled to receive notice of a meeting of Directors or of a committee of Directors shall be as valid and effectual as if it has been passed at a meeting of Directors or (as the case may be) a committee of Directors duly convened and held and may consist of several documents in the like form each signed by one (1) or more Directors; but a resolution signed by an alternate Director need not also be signed by his appointor and, if it is signed by a Director who has appointed an alternate Director it need not be signed by the alternate Director in that capacity.

121. If and for so long as there is a sole Director of the Company:
   (a) he may exercise all the powers conferred on the Directors by the Articles by any means permitted by the Articles or the Law;
   (b) the quorum for the transaction of business is one (1); and
   (c) all other provisions of the Articles apply with any necessary modification (unless the provision expressly provides otherwise).

122. Provided that a Director has disclosed his material interest pursuant to the Articles, a Director may vote at any meeting of Directors or of a committee of Directors on any resolution concerning a matter in which he has, directly or indirectly, an interest or duty. The Director shall be counted in the quorum present at a meeting when any such resolution is under consideration and if he votes his vote shall be counted.

Secretary and other officers

123. The Directors may by resolution appoint a Secretary and may by resolution also appoint such other officers as may from time to time be required upon such terms as to duration of office, remuneration and otherwise as they may think fit. Such Secretary or other officers need not be Directors and in the case of the other officers may be ascribed such titles as the Directors may decide. The Directors may by resolution remove any Secretary or other officer appointed pursuant to this Article.

124. No person shall be appointed or hold office as Secretary who is:
   (a) the sole Director of the Company; or
   (b) a corporation the sole Director of which is the sole Director of the Company; or
   (c) the sole Director of a corporation which is the sole Director of the Company.

Minutes

125. The Directors shall cause minutes to be made in books kept for the purpose:
   (a) of all appointments of officers made by the Directors; and
   (b) of all proceedings of meetings of the Company, of the holders of any Class of shares in the Company, and of the Directors, and of committees of Directors, including the names of the Directors present at each such meeting.

Seal

126. (a) The Company may, if the Directors so determine, have a Seal. The Seal shall only be used by the authority of the Directors or of a committee of Directors authorised by the Directors. The Directors may determine who shall sign any instrument to which the seal is affixed, and unless otherwise so determined every such instrument shall be signed by a Director and by the Secretary or by a second Director.
   (b) The Company may have for use in any place or places outside the Islands a duplicate Seal or Seals, each of which shall be a facsimile of the Seal of the Company and, if the Directors so determine, shall have added on its face the name of every place where it is to be used.
   (c) The Directors may by resolution determine (i) that any signature required by this Article need not be manual, but may be affixed by some other method or system of reproduction or mechanical or electronic signature and/or (ii) that any document may bear a printed facsimile of the Seal in lieu of affixing the Seal thereto.
   (d) No document or deed otherwise duly executed and delivered by or on behalf of the Company shall be regarded as invalid merely because at the date of the delivery of the deed or document, the Director, Secretary or other officer or person who shall have executed the same or affixed the Seal thereto, as the case may be, for and on behalf of the Company shall have ceased to hold such office and authority on behalf of the Company.

Dividends

127. The Directors may from time to time declare dividends on the shares of any Class or Sub-Class provided that no such dividend shall be paid otherwise than out of the assets of the Company relating to such Class or Sub-Class legally available for distribution by way of dividend.

128. No dividend shall be paid from share premium account, unless immediately following the date on which the dividend is proposed to be paid, the Company shall be able to pay the debts of the Company as they fall due in the ordinary course of business.

129. The Directors may, before paying any dividend on any Class or Sub-Class of shares, set aside out of the profits of the Company such sums as they think proper as a reserve or reserves which shall, at the discretion of the Directors, be applicable for meeting contingencies, or for equalising dividends, or for any other purpose to which the profits of the Company may be properly applied, and pending such application may, at the like discretion, either be employed in the business of the Company (in which case the Directors shall not be bound to keep such sums separate from the Company's other assets) or be invested in such investments as the Directors may from time to time think fit (in which case the Directors may from time to time deal with and vary such investments and dispose of all or any part thereof for the benefit of the Company as they think fit).

130. Any dividend or other moneys payable on or in respect of a share may be paid by wire transfer to such bank account as the holder or other person entitled thereto may in writing direct, or by cheque or warrant sent by post to the registered address of the person entitled or, if two (2) or more persons are the holders of the share or are jointly entitled to it by reason of the death or bankruptcy of the holder, to the registered address of that one (1) of those persons who is first named in the Register or to such person and to such address or bank account as the person or persons entitled may in writing direct. Subject to any applicable law or regulations, every cheque shall be made payable to the order of the person or persons entitled or to such other person as the person or persons entitled may in writing direct and payment of the cheque shall be a good discharge to the Company. Any joint holder or other person jointly entitled to a share as aforesaid may give receipts for any dividend or other moneys payable in respect of the share.

131. The Directors may declare that any dividend on any Class or Sub-Class is paid wholly or partly by the distribution of specific assets attributable to the relevant Record and in particular of paid-up shares, debentures or debenture stock of any other company or in any one or more of such ways, and the Directors shall give effect to such resolution, and where any difficulty arises in regard to such distribution, the Directors may settle the same as they think expedient, and in particular may issue fractional shares and fix the value for distribution of such specific assets or any part thereof and may determine that cash payments shall be made to any Members upon the footing of the value so fixed in order to adjust the rights of all

parties, and may vest any such specific assets in trustees as may seem expedient to the Directors.

132. No dividend or other moneys payable in respect of a share shall bear interest against the Company unless otherwise provided by the rights attached to the share.

133. Any dividend which cannot be paid to a Member and/or which remains unclaimed after six months from the date of declaration of such dividend may, in the discretion of the Directors, be paid into a separate account in the Company's name, provided that the Company shall not be constituted as a trustee in respect of that account and the dividend shall remain as a debt due to the Member. Any dividend which remains unclaimed after a period of six years from the date of declaration of such dividend shall be forfeited and shall revert to the Company.

Record Dates

134. Subject to the rights attached to shares, the Directors may fix any date as the record date for a dividend, allotment or issue. The record date may be on or at any time before or after a date on which the dividend, allotment or issue is declared, made or paid.

Accounts

135. No Member shall (as such) have any right of inspecting any accounting records or other book or document of the Company except as authorised by statute or authorised by the Directors or by Ordinary Resolution.

136. Any accounts, Directors' report or auditors' report required or permitted to be sent by the Company to any person pursuant to any statute shall be treated as sent to such person if:
    (a) sent by electronic communication to an address for the time being notified to the Company by that person for that purpose;
    (b) published on a web-site, provided that the following conditions are met:
        (i) the Company and that person have agreed that such documents may be accessed by him on a web-site (instead of their being sent by post or otherwise delivered to him); and
        (ii) that person is notified, in a manner for the time being agreed for the purpose between him and the Company of:
            (A) the publication of the documents on a web-site;
            (B) the address of that web-site;
            (C) the place on that web-site where the documents may be accessed; and

(D) how such documents may be accessed.

137. Documents treated as sent to any person in accordance with the preceding Article are to be treated as sent to him not less than five (5) days before the date of the meeting at which copies of those documents are to be laid if, and only if:
   (a) the documents are published on the web-site throughout a period beginning at least 5 days before the date of the meeting and ending with the conclusion of the meeting; and
   (b) the notification is given not less than 5 days before the date of the meeting.

138. Where accounts, Directors' reports and auditors' reports that are to be published on a website in accordance with the preceding Article are by accident published in different places on the web-site or published for part only of the period from the date of the notification until the conclusion of the meeting to which the notice relates, the proceedings at such meeting are not thereby invalidated.

Audit

139. The Directors shall by resolution appoint the Auditors on such terms as to duration of office, remuneration or otherwise as they may think fit. The Directors may at any time by resolution remove the Auditors and if so, the Directors shall appoint replacement Auditors. The Directors shall appoint Auditors to replace Auditors that resign.

140. No person shall act as Auditor at a time when he knows that he is disqualified to act as such, and if an Auditor to his knowledge becomes so disqualified during his term of office he shall thereupon vacate his office and give notice in writing to the Company that he has vacated it by reason of such disqualification.

141. The Auditors shall examine such books, accounts and vouchers as may be necessary for the performance of their duties.

142. The Auditors shall make a report to the Members on the accounts examined by them and on every balance sheet prepared by them during their tenure of office and the report shall state:
   (a) whether they have audited the accounts in accordance with approved auditing standards;
   (b) the accounting basis upon which the accounts have been prepared; and
   (c) whether in their opinion the accounts present fairly the financial position of the Company at the date of the accounts and the results of its operations and the changes in its net assets for the period then ended.

143. The Auditors shall be furnished with a list of all books kept by the Company and shall at all times have the right of access to the books

and accounts and vouchers of the Company and shall be entitled to require from the Directors and officers of the Company such information and explanations as may be necessary for the performance of their duties.

Capitalisation of Profits

144. The Directors may:
    (a) subject as provided in this Article, resolve to capitalise any undivided profits of the Company relating to a Class, Sub-Class or Series not required for paying any preferential dividend (whether or not they are available for distribution) or any sum standing to the credit of the share premium account or capital redemption reserve maintained by the Company in respect of such Class, Sub-Class or Series;
    (b) appropriate the sum resolved to be capitalised to the Members who would have been entitled to it if it were distributed by way of dividend and in the same proportions and apply such sum on their behalf, in paying up in full unissued shares of the Company of the relevant Class, Sub-Class or Series of a nominal amount equal to such sum, and allot the shares credited as fully paid to those Members, or as they may direct, in those proportions;
    (c) make such provision by the issue of fractional certificates or by payment in cash or otherwise as they determine in the case of shares becoming distributable under this Article in fractions; and
    (d) authorise any person to enter on behalf of all the Members concerned into an agreement with the Company providing for the allotment to them respectively, credited as fully paid, of any shares to which they may be entitled upon such capitalisation, any agreement made under such authority being binding on all such Members.
145. Notwithstanding the provisions of these Articles as to capitalisation of profits, if the Investment Manager, for the benefit of a particular Member, waives all or any part of the fees due to it, the Company may apply an amount equal to the amount so waived to pay up additional shares of the same Class, Sub-Class or Series for distribution to such Member on the next Subscription Day at the Subscription Price then ruling.

Share Premium and Reserve Accounts

146. The Directors shall establish in respect of each Class, Sub-Class and Series an account to be called the share premium account and shall carry to the credit of that account from time to time a sum equal to

the amount or value of the premium paid on the issue of any shares of the relevant Class, Sub-Class and Series.

147. There shall be debited to the share premium account on the redemption of a share of any Class, Sub-Class and Series the difference between the nominal value of such share redeemed and the Redemption Price unless such sum has been paid out of the profits of the Company or, if permitted by section 37 of the Law, out of capital.

148. The Company shall at all times comply with the provisions of the Law in relation to the share premium account and the premiums attaching to the shares and in relation to the redemption of the shares.

149. The Directors may set aside out of the profits of the Company attributable to a Record and carry to the credit of any reserve account relating to such Record, such sums as they think proper, which shall, at the discretion of the Directors, be applicable for any purpose to which the profits or reserves may be properly applied and pending such application may at the like discretion either be employed in the business of the Company or be invested in such Investments as the Directors may from time to time think fit. The Directors may also carry forward to the accounts of the succeeding year or years any balance of profits which they shall not think fit to place to reserve.

Notices

150. Any notice to be given to or by any person pursuant to the Articles (other than a notice convening a meeting of the board of Directors or of a committee of the board of Directors) shall be in writing or in an electronic communication to an address for the time being notified for that purpose to the person giving the notice.

151. Subject to the preceding Article, the Company may give any notice to a Member either personally or by sending it by post in a prepaid envelope addressed to the Member at his registered address, or by leaving it at that address, or by sending it using electronic communications to an address for the time being notified to the Company by such Member for that purpose. In the case of joint holders of a share, all notices shall be given to the joint holder whose name stands first in the Register in respect of the joint holding and notice so given shall be sufficient notice to all the joint holders. Any Member whose registered address is not within the Islands shall be entitled to have notices given to him at that address or at an address specified by him to which notices may be sent using electronic communications.

152. A notice of general meeting may be given to a Member by the Company by publishing the notice on a web-site, provided that the following conditions are met:

(a) the Member and the Company have agreed that notices of general meetings may be accessed by him on a web-site; and
(b) the Member is given a notification, in the manner agreed for the time being between the Member and the Company, containing the following information:
  (i) the fact that the notice has been published on the web-site;
  (ii) the address of the web-site;
  (iii) the place on the web-site where the notice may be accessed and how it may be accessed; and
  (iv) the place, date and time of the general meeting.

153. A notice published on a web-site in accordance with the preceding Article is deemed to be given at the time of the notification of such publication to the Member.

154. A Member present, either in person or by proxy, at any meeting of the Company or of the holders of any Class of shares in the Company shall be deemed to have received notice of the meeting, and, where requisite, of the purposes for which it was called.

155. Every person who becomes entitled to any share shall be bound by any notice in respect of that share which, before his name is entered in the Register, has been given to the person from whom he derives his title.

156. A notice sent to a Member (or other person entitled to receive notices under the Articles) by post to an address within the Islands is deemed to be given twenty four (24) hours after posting, if pre-paid.

157. A notice sent to a Member (or other person entitled to receive notice under the Articles) by post to an address outside the Islands is deemed to be given seventy two (72) hours after posting, if pre-paid as airmail. Proof that an envelope containing the notice was properly addressed, pre-paid and posted is conclusive evidence that the notice was given. A notice not sent by post but left at a Member's registered address is deemed to have been given on the day it was left.

158. Where a notice is sent by an electronic communication service of the notice shall be deemed to be given by properly addressing and sending such notice through the appropriate transmitting medium. A notice contained in an electronic communication sent in accordance with these Articles, other than a notice published on a website and which, in accordance with these Articles, is deemed to be given at the time of the notification, is deemed to be given at the expiration of twenty four (24) hours after the time it was sent.

159. A notice may be given by the Company to the persons entitled to a share in consequence of the death or bankruptcy of a Member by sending or delivering it, in any manner authorised by the Articles for the giving of notice to a Member, addressed to them by name, or by the title of representatives of the deceased, or trustee of the bankrupt

or by any like description, at the address, if any, supplied for that purpose by the persons claiming to be so entitled. Until such an address has been supplied, a notice may be given in any manner in which it might have been given if the death or bankruptcy had not occurred.

Winding Up

160. If the Company shall be wound up the liquidator shall apply the assets of the Company in such manner and order as he thinks fit in satisfaction of creditors' claims.
161. The assets available for distribution to the Members shall be distributed in the following manner and priority:
    (a) first, in the payment to the holders of the shares of each Class, Sub-Class or Series of a sum as nearly as possible equal to the nominal amount of the shares of that Class, Sub-Class or Series held by such holders respectively; and
    (b) second, in the payment to the holders of each Class, Sub-Class or Series of any remaining balance then attributable to the relevant Record, such payment being made in proportion to the number of shares of that Class, Sub-Class or Series held.
162. If the Company is wound up (whether the liquidation is voluntary, or under supervision by the Court) the liquidator may, with the sanction of a Special Resolution and any other sanction required by the Law, divide among the Members in specie the whole or any part of the assets of the Company and whether or not the assets shall consist of property of a single kind, and may for such purposes set such value as he deemed fair upon any one or more class or classes of property, and may determine how such division shall be carried out as between the Members or different classes of Members. The liquidator may, with the like sanction, vest the whole or any part of the assets in trustees upon such trusts for the benefit of Members as the liquidator, with the like authority, shall think fit, and the liquidation of the Company may be closed and the Company dissolved, but so that no Member shall be compelled to accept any shares in respect of which there is a liability.

Indemnity

163. Every Director (including for the purposes of this Article, any alternate Director appointed pursuant to the provisions of these Articles), managing Director, agent, Secretary, or other officer for the time being and from time to time of the Company and the personal representatives of the same shall be indemnified and secured harmless out

of the assets and funds of the Company against all actions, proceedings, costs, charges, expenses, losses, damages or liabilities incurred or sustained by him otherwise than by reason of his own Gross Negligence or wilful default in or about the conduct of the Company's business or affairs or in the execution or discharge of his duties, powers, authorities or discretions, including without prejudice to the generality of the foregoing, any costs, expenses, losses or liabilities incurred by him in defending (whether successfully or otherwise) any civil proceedings concerning the Company or its affairs in any court whether in the Islands or elsewhere.

164. The Administrator, the Investment Manager and any other agent which the Company has appointed shall be entitled to such indemnity from the Company under such terms and subject to such conditions and exceptions and with such entitlement to have recourse to the assets of the Company with a view to meeting and discharging the cost thereof as shall be specified in the relevant contract or instrument appointing such agent.

165. No such Director, alternate Director, managing Director, agent, Secretary, or other officer of the Company and the personal representatives of the same shall be liable (i) for the acts, receipts, neglects, defaults or omissions of any other such Director or officer or agent of the Company, (ii) by reason of his having joined in any receipt for money not received by him personally or in any other act to which he was not a direct party for conformity, (iii) for any loss on account of defect of title to any property of the Company, (iv) on account of the insufficiency of any security in or upon which any money of the Company shall be invested, (v) for any loss incurred through any bank, broker or other agent or any other party with whom any of the Company's property may be deposited or (vi) for any loss, damage or misfortune whatsoever which may happen in or arise from the execution or discharge of the duties, powers, authorities or discretions of his office or in relation thereto unless the same shall happen through his own Gross Negligence or wilful default.

166. The Directors may exercise all the powers of the Company to purchase and maintain insurance for the benefit of a person who is or was a Director, alternate Director, Secretary or auditor of the Company indemnifying him against any liability which may lawfully be insured against by the Company.

Disclosure

167. Any Director, officer of the Company or authorised agent shall, if lawfully required to do so under the laws of any jurisdiction to which the Company is subject or in compliance with the rules of any stock

exchange upon which the Company's shares are listed or in accordance with any contract entered into by the Company, or if, in the opinion of the Directors, such disclosure would assist or facilitate the operations of the Company be entitled to release or disclose any information in his possession regarding the affairs of the Company including, without limitation, any information contained in the Register relating to any Member.

Financial Year

168. Unless the Directors otherwise prescribe, the financial year of the Company shall end on 31st December in each year and, following the year of incorporation, shall begin on 1st January in each year.

Amendment of Memorandum and Articles

169. Subject to the Law and without prejudice to the provisions of these Articles as to alteration of capital, the Company may by Special Resolution, change its name or change the provisions of the Memorandum with respect to its objects, powers or any other matter specified therein.
170. Subject to the Law, and as provided in these Articles, the Company may at any time and from time to time by Special Resolution alter or amend these Articles in whole or in part.

Transfer by way of Continuation

171. The Company may by Special Resolution resolve to be registered by way of continuation in a jurisdiction outside the Islands or such other jurisdiction in which it is for the time being incorporated, registered or existing. In furtherance of a resolution adopted pursuant to this Article, the Directors may cause an application to be made to the Registrar of Companies to deregister the Company in the Islands or such other jurisdiction in which it is for the time being incorporated, registered or existing and may cause all such further steps as they consider appropriate to be taken to effect the transfer by way of continuation of the Company.

Appendix 2

Documents to launch a Cayman Islands hedge fund[1]

Certificate of Incorporation/Formation and Memorandum of Association and Articles of Association/By-laws
Required Cayman Islands Forms (eg, MF1, s.184 Declaration, Certificate of Mutual Fund Registration, appointment of first directors, SIBL Application)
Directors meetings minutes (incorporation and approvals of service providers, documents, bank accounts and launch)
Resolution(s) for Founders Shares and Share Transfer Forms (if required)
Offering Memorandum and *Private Placement Memorandum*
Verification Notes
Application, Redemption and Exchange Forms
Administration Agreement
Investment Management Agreement
Investment Advisory Agreement (if required)
Prime Brokerage Agreement(s)
Global Master Securities Lending Agreement
Distribution Agreement(s)
Executing Broker Agreement(s)
Registered Office Agreement(s)
ISDA, and CSA Schedule
Investment Agreement (invest onshore feeder fund assets in the master fund)
Feeder Fund Agreement (invest offshore feeder fund assets into master fund)
Operating Agreement (permits corporate director to manage onshore feeder fund)
Consents – auditor and administrator
Documents to open bank account(s) and prime broker accounts
US tax forms (eg, W-8BEN, W-8IMY, Form SS-4, Form 8832)
Legal opinion(s)
Specimen Signature Sheets
Powers of Attorney
Tax advice
CFTC NEA exemption CEA Rule 4.13(a)(3) or 4.13(a)(4) (if trading futures)

Schedule of Fees and Costs to Launch and For the First Year of Operations
Exchange listing documents and disclosures
Local Market Trading Agreements

1 Documents are for the onshore feeder fund, offshore feeder fund, master fund and/or the corporate director of onshore feeder fund. Documents in *italics* are used only in a master feeder structure.

Index

(page numbers in italic type refer to illustrations)